ABOUT THE EDITOR

Joseph Mersand, Ph.D., has devoted himself throughout his long career as a teacher to the theatre and its literature. He has written and edited books about the drama over a period of twenty years. Among these are *The American Drama, 1930–1940; The Play's the Thing* and *The American Drama Since 1930*. Dr. Mersand was chairman of the Editorial Committee of the National Council of Teachers of English, which authorized the publication of *Guide to Play Selection*, a standard work.

For ten years Dr. Mersand served as chairman of the English and Speech departments at Long Island City High School, in New York City. Highly regarded in his field, he has been an instructor at Cornell University, Queens College, Teachers College, Columbia University, Syracuse University and New York University. He is past president of the National Council of Teachers of English and is presently chairman of the English department at Jamaica High School, in New York City.

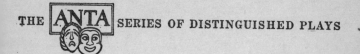

THE **ANTA** SERIES OF DISTINGUISHED PLAYS

Three Dramas of American Realism.

Idiot's Delight
by Robert E. Sherwood

Street Scene
by Elmer L. Rice

The Time of Your Life
by William Saroyan

Edited and with Introductions
by Joseph Mersand

WASHINGTON SQUARE PRESS
POCKET BOOKS • NEW YORK

THREE DRAMAS OF AMERICAN REALISM

WASHINGTON SQUARE PRESS edition published April, 1961

4th printing.........................April, 1973

L

Published by
POCKET BOOKS, a division of Simon & Schuster, Inc.,
630 Fifth Avenue, New York, N. Y.

WASHINGTON SQUARE PRESS editions are distributed
in the U.S. by Simon & Schuster, Inc., 630 Fifth Avenue,
New York, N.Y. 10020 and in Canada by Simon & Schuster of Canada, Ltd., Richmond Hill, Ontario, Canada.

CONTENTS

Any group that wishes to produce any of these plays will find production information for each play on page 313.

10563

IDIOT'S DELIGHT

INTRODUCTION

In a postscript to *Idiot's Delight*, Robert E. Sherwood wrote these prophetic words:

> If decent people will continue to be intoxicated by the synthetic spirit of patriotism, pumped into them by megalomaniac leaders, and will continue to have faith in the security provided by those lethal weapons sold to them by the armaments industry, then war *is* inevitable; and the world will soon resolve itself into the semblance of an anthill, governed by commissars who owe their power to the profundity of their contempt for the individual members of their species.[1]

Sherwood had touched on the futility of settling disputes by armed force in his first play, *The Road to Rome* (1927), and on the gradual degeneration of life in the face of brutalizing forces in *The Petrified Forest* (1935). The 1930's had seen many antiwar plays come to Broadway, tell their tragic message and quickly depart. Such plays as R. C. Sheriff's *Journey's End* (1929), Sidney Howard's *Paths of Glory* (1935), Paul Green's *Johnny Johnson* (1936) and Irwin Shaw's *Bury the Dead* (1936) were acclaimed in their day by liberal and thoughtful audiences.

What differentiates *Idiot's Delight* from these is the mixture of farce and earnest truth—a combination rare in the theatre. John Mason Brown in his review of the play felt that

---

[1] *Idiot's Delight*, pp. 189–190.

Sherwood managed to do his job so well as a result of his "ability to mix aphrodisiac with allegory, flesh with spirit, sunshine with sermons, comedy with tragedy and good showmanship with interesting thinking." [2]

The imminence of war was felt by countless novelists, dramatists and other creative artists throughout the 1930's, particularly after Hitler assumed power. Each day's headlines seemed more intolerable than those of the previous day. The almost daily crises in the Far East, in the Spanish Civil War, in the Italo-Ethiopian war and the ruthless onward march of Hitler's armies inspired many men of letters to issue warnings, to stir up feelings of defiance to fascism or to strike a note of defeatism.

In *Idiot's Delight* Sherwood shows us a group of individuals collected in an Italian hotel near the Swiss and Austrian borders. Among them is a German scientist about to conclude his studies on a cure for cancer, an English couple on their honeymoon, a French Communist, a munitions manufacturer with his supposedly Russian mistress and an American entertainer with a bevy of chorus girls back from a Balkan tour. How each of these reacts when war planes begin to bomb an Italian airport near the hotel is skillfully and entertainingly told. Yet the grim message is always there, and it is left to Irene, the pseudo-Russian, to give it:

> We don't do half enough justice to Him. Poor, lonely old soul. Sitting up in heaven, with nothing to do but play solitaire. Poor, dear God. Playing Idiot's Delight. The game that never means anything, and never ends.

"When all has been said and done," wrote Joseph Wood Krutch, in his *American Drama Since 1918*, "there is no doubt about the fact that despite all the comic interludes, the sense of the folly and horror of war has been conveyed almost as effectively as it has ever been conveyed on the stage." [3]

[2] *Two on the Aisle*, p. 167.
[3] P. 223.

4

"No other native dramatist has so successfully combined sane thinking with exciting writing, and no one has put honest melodrama to such good use as he." [4] Thus did Burns Mantle, in 1938, praise Robert E. Sherwood, who by that time had been awarded two Pulitzer Prizes for drama and who was to win a third in 1941 for *There Shall Be No Night*. Considering that his playwriting career had begun in 1927 and that he had written only ten plays by 1938, this was truly a remarkable record.

Prior to his debut as a dramatist, Sherwood had been known only in limited circles as the motion picture critic of the magazine *Vanity Fair* at the time when Frank Crowninshield was its editor and Dorothy Parker and Robert Benchley were writing dramatic criticism. Resigning out of sympathy with Dorothy Parker, who was fired because she refused to retract a caustic criticism, Sherwood became motion picture critic of *Life* (then a humor magazine), later associate editor and finally editor-in-chief. His career at Harvard as an editor of the *Lampoon*, the humor magazine, his disillusioning experiences in the first World War, his close association with that brilliant set of writers known as the Algonquin Round Table, whose names became almost household words—Dorothy Parker, Robert Benchley, Alexander Woollcott, Heywood Broun—these may cast some light on his comic preferences, his glittering diction and his hatred of war and the degenerating civilization that causes it.

If one word were to epitomize his dramatic gifts, "versatility" might be the most appropriate. One should keep in mind the amazing shifts in literary styles that have occurred since his first play, *The Road to Rome* (1927). It came at a time when history was being debunked, when such books as John Erskine's *Private Life of Helen of Troy, Galahad* and *Penelope's Man* were best sellers. Great historical personages were

---
[4] *Contemporary American Playwrights*, p. 23.

treated by novelists, biographers and historians as human beings subject to the same weaknesses and foibles that most people are heir to.

In *The Road to Rome*, Sherwood explains Hannibal's failure to sack Rome as being a personal favor to Amytes, lovely wife of the weak-willed Fabius, who has been immortalized, because of his delaying tactics, in the term *Fabianism*. Graced by two superb performers, Jane Cowl as Amytes and Philip Merivale as Hannibal, the play introduced a brilliant new writing personality to Broadway.

Not all of Sherwood's plays were unqualified successes. *The Love Nest* (1927) was a dramatization of a Ring Lardner story about a movie director's wife who, under the influence of liquor, told the world all that should not have been told of her husband. It failed. *The Queen's Husband* (1928) was suggested by the American tour of Queen Marie of Romania. The husband, played by Roland Young, took advantage of his spouse's absence to assert himself in a manner that made the play more entertaining than *The Love Nest* but inferior to *The Road to Rome*.

Sherwood lived in England for a few years, during which time he wrote *Waterloo Bridge* (1930). This is a melodramatic study of an American chorus girl stranded in London during World War I, who manages to retain enough goodness to impress an idealistic, young American doughboy. Sherwood was obviously using his knowledge of wartime characters and experiences, but he did not make a truly significant contribution to the theme of war until he wrote *Idiot's Delight* (1936).

This Is New York (1930) was one of the melodramatic, frothy bits that folded its tents almost as soon as it came to rest. This ended the groping period in Sherwood's career. His next few plays were all hits and three of them carried off the highest honors of the year.

When *Reunion in Vienna* was produced with fabulous success in 1931, Sherwood was called the American Molnar, so expertly had he captured the form and spirit of the Hungarian master's light comedies. Thanks to the delightful performances of Alfred Lunt and Lynn Fontanne, *Reunion in Vienna* was heralded as one of the gayest comedies in years. The reunion takes place between Prince Maximilian Rudolph, who since the peace has been driving a taxi in Nice, and Elena, who was once his favorite mistress. Although she is happily married to a famous psychoanalyst, she cannot resist the impulsive and emotional royal lover, and they have one more tryst. Sherwood proved in this play that he had recaptured his comic gifts so startlingly displayed in *The Road to Rome.*

For the next four years he devoted his talents to writing for the screen, but then the yearning for a living stage became too strong. In 1935 *The Petrified Forest* revealed an entirely new Sherwood, one no longer gay and flippant, but one deeply concerned with the gradual decay of the civilization around him. Since this play was subsequently made into a motion picture, it was the first of his works to make Sherwood familiar to the many American drama-lovers who do not live in New York.

In this play Sherwood collected various representatives of our civilization, including a gangster and his mob, a sensitive artist who cannot endure the raw disintegration of society represented by the gangster and a talented young daughter of a gas-station owner, who is spiritually dying on the desert. The hero signs over his life-insurance policy to the gifted girl and begs the escaping bandit to "rub him out." In *The Petrified Forest* Sherwood achieved new heights of dramatic dialogue, emotional richness and characterization.

Professor Allardyce Nicoll, of the Yale School of Drama, commented upon the similarity in motif between *The Petrified Forest* and other great English plays based on sacrifices made by the principal characters. Though Professor Nicoll may have indirectly deprecated Sherwood's lack of originality, he at the same time indicated that he was writing in a great and permanent tradition and not, as heretofore, in the momentarily clever manner of a commentator in a humor magazine.

Of one thing we may be certain when we read a preface by Sherwood to one of his plays. It will be truly illuminating and will often explain the genesis, motives and methods of composition. For the student of dramatic literature such prefaces are of incalculable value in forming standards of judgment, in developing insight into the mystery of a play's origin and development and in appreciating the author's intentions.

Sherwood's next play, *Idiot's Delight*, won the Pulitzer Prize for 1936 and is one of the most effective antiwar messages in dramatic form. It revealed not only the Sherwood of brilliant dialogue, gay situations tinged slightly by the intimacies of the liaison, but also the Sherwood who was troubled by the march of brute force and the inevitable collapse of civilization.

There have been many antiwar plays in modern American drama, like *Peace on Earth, Ten Million Ghosts, For Services Rendered, The Drums Begin*, but most theatre-goers will hardly recognize these titles. *Idiot's Delight* not only states an important message, perhaps the most important that any artist can state in our times, but it is at the same time a compelling drama. Many varied personalities are accurately delineated, the story unfolds with unerring deftness and the climax, punctuated by the explosion of bombs bursting, is unforgettable. In 1939 it was made into a motion picture, which has been shown recently on television.

Tovarich (1936), adapted from the French comedy of Jacques Deval, is hardly one of Sherwood's major contributions. *Abe Lincoln in Illinois* (1938) is his most important play and was awarded the Pulitzer Prize. Sherwood's task in this biographical drama is a more exhausting one than that of Drinkwater in *Abraham Lincoln* or E. P. Conkle in *Prologue to Glory*, to mention but two other modern Lincoln dramas. Sherwood covers a period of thirty years of Lincoln's remarkable growth from the awkward young man of twenty-two to the President-elect about to take the train to Washington.

Few plays about American heroes have been successful. Even Maxwell Anderson could do little with the character of

Washington in his *Valley Forge*. Plays about Nathan Hale, Benedict Arnold, Aaron Burr, John Brown and Peter Stuyvesant have failed to hold audiences. Sherwood's *Abe Lincoln in Illinois* established a record run for plays of this type. Modestly refusing too much credit for fashioning one of the most stirring biographical dramas of modern times, Sherwood declared in a newspaper interview that Carl Sandburg's *The Prairie Years* awakened his interest in the strange emotionalism of Lincoln as a young man.

> Up to then I'd thought that he was a statue, even while he was living. I thought he certainly was the embodiment of all that was noble and courageous and heroic.[5]

After reading considerable material on Lincoln's life—speeches, letters and memoirs of Lincoln's contemporaries—Sherwood found that "this wasn't a job of playwriting. It was a job of editing. After I got my material together, it was just a job of carpentering."[6] It may have been just a job of carpentering for Sherwood, but many a dramatist has banged his fingers trying to do the same job. Enough articles have been written on *Abe Lincoln in Illinois* to make a good-sized volume. It is safe to say that it is the most human and believable portrait of the Great Emancipator in American drama.

Sherwood was one of the five dramatists who, in 1938, formed the Playwrights' Company, an organization devoted to the artistic production of the plays of its members. His was one of the most successful plays presented by the organization. Others include Maxwell Anderson's *Knickerbocker Holiday* and *Key Largo*, S. N. Behrman's *No Time for Comedy* and Elmer Rice's *American Landscape*.

Sherwood spent the war years working with the Office of War Information. His last two plays were inspired by World War II. *There Shall Be No Night* (1940) is a bitter indictment of the U.S.S.R. for its attack on Finland in 1939. In *The*

---

[5] Edd Johnson, "Sherwood Tells Why He Wrote *Lincoln*," *New York World-Telegram*, October 29, 1938, p. 6.
[6] *Ibid.*

Rugged Path (1945), which starred Spencer Tracy, he depicted the evolution of a liberal American reporter into a fighting soldier, who finally gives his life in the Philippine campaign.

Sherwood's final, and possibly one of his most enduring works, is not in the field of drama at all, though it is sufficiently dramatic. This is his best-selling book, *Roosevelt and Hopkins*, which won him a Pulitzer Prize in biography in 1949. Based on his own intimate knowledge of the inner workings of the Roosevelt Administration, this book is a fascinating account of the relationship of the wartime President and one of his most controversial unofficial aides. It showed Sherwood in a new light, as a masterful writer of detailed modern history with a sure touch in describing many of the highlights of the Washington scene and an uncanny flair for presenting pen portraits of some of the most colorful figures of the time.

Sherwood died in 1955 leaving a substantial heritage of work, principally in the drama, which should earn him a permanent position in American letters. He demonstrated a gift for brilliant comic dialogue, a sure grasp of dramatic technique, an ability to write plays that have social and ethical overtones but are still effective works of art, a mastery of biography in dramatic—and historical—form and an open-mindedness that permitted him to use varied subjects and styles of writing.

FURTHER READING

Brown, John Mason. *Two on the Aisle*. New York: W. W. Norton, 1938, pp. 166–168.

Flexner, Eleanor. *American Playwrights, 1918–1938*. New York: Simon and Schuster, 1938, pp. 272, 273, 279–281.

Gagey, Edmond M. *Revolution in American Drama*. New York: Columbia, 1947, pp. 131–132.

Gassner, John. *Masters of the Drama*. 3rd ed. New York: Dover, 1954, pp. 674–676.

Krutch, Joseph Wood. *The American Drama Since 1918*. New York: Random House, 1938, pp. 221–225.

Mantle, Burns. *Contemporary American Playwrights*. New York: Dodd, Mead, 1938, pp. 20–24.

Morehouse, Ward. *Matinee Tomorrow*. McGraw-Hill, 1949, pp. 253–254, 269.

O'Hara, Frank Hurburt. *Today in American Drama*. Chicago: University of Chicago, 1939, pp. 258–259.

Sherwood, Robert E. "The Dwelling Place of Wonder," *Theatre Arts Anthology*. New York: Theatre Arts Books, 1950, pp. 1–4.

Shipley, Joseph T. *Guide to Great Plays*. Washington: Public Affairs, 1956, pp. 726–727.

Williamson, Audrey. *Theatre of Two Decades*. New York: Macmillan, 1951, pp. 161, 169–171.

IDIOT'S DELIGHT

ROBERT E. SHERWOOD

ACT I

SCENE: *The modernistic cocktail lounge of the Hotel Monte Gabriele. The hotel is a small one, which would like to consider itself a first-class resort. Its Italian management (this was formerly Austrian territory) has refurnished it, added this cocktail lounge and a few modern bedrooms with baths, in the hope that some day Monte Gabriele may become a rival for St. Moritz. So far, this is still a hope. Although the weather is fine, the supply of winter-sports enthusiasts at Monte Gabriele is negligible, and the hotel is relying for its trade upon those itinerants who, because of the current political situation, are desirous of leaving Italy. Near at hand are a railway line into Switzerland, highways into Switzerland and Austria, and an Italian Army airport. At the rear* is a large doorway, leading to the lobby. At the right front is a staircase. A few steps up is a landing, above which are three large windows with a fine view of the Alpine scenery to the north and west. There is a Venetian blind on each window. They are rolled up at the moment. From the landing the stairs continue up to a gallery which leads to bedrooms off to the left. In the front is a swinging door marked above with the word "BAR." Behind that is another door over which is marked "SALONE." This door is never used in the action. At rear center is a long, modernistic built-in leather seat. In front of the seat are two small, round modernistic tables. They are spaced about four feet apart. There is another similar seat, but smaller, in front of the bar door. It, too, has a small table in front of it. Another table at the right with chair behind it. Another table at the rear left corner behind the piano with a chair behind the table. Also a table in corner of where center seat goes up vertically. A slightly larger, round table, but of the same design and color, stands at the front, below piano. It has an armchair left of it, a side chair behind it and a side chair right of it. There are hand-bells and ashtrays and matches on each table. At left behind entrance to bar is a platform, on which is a modernistic piano. There is a piano bench behind piano. Left of piano, on platform, are two chairs, one for the saxophonist and the other for the drummer, who also has his drum, etc., left of piano. When first curtain rises a dismal little four-piece orchestra is playing.

PITTALUGA is the owner and manager of the hotel. He is a fussy, worried Italian in the conventional morning coat and striped pants. Stretched out on seat looking dolefully out window, is DONALD NAVADEL, a rather precious, youngish American, suitably costumed for winter sports by Saks Fifth Avenue. Experienced in the resort business, he was imported this year to organize sporting and social life at Monte Gabriele with a view to making it a Mecca for American tourists. He is not pleased with the way things have turned out. DUMPTSY stands at the rear between seat and piano plat-

form. He is a humble, gentle little bellboy, aged about forty, born in this district when it was part of Austria, but now a subject of the Fascist Empire. He has been cleaning ash- trays. He listens to music. (The name is pronounced "DOOM- PTSY.") The employees of the hotel and the Italian officers converse with each other in Italian. There are also a few words of German here and there.

DUMPTSY: Come si chiama questa musica che sonate?

ORCHESTRA LEADER: "Giugno in Gennaio."

DUMPTSY: Oh, com'è bello! Mi piace! (*Turns to* DON.) It's good.

DON (*seated on rear seat; his patience is exhausted*): Will you please for God's sake stop playing that same damned tiresome thing?

DUMPTSY: You don't like it, Mr. Navadel? (*Speaks English with a slight German accent.*)

DON: I'm so sick of it I could scream!

DUMPTSY: I like it. To me it's good.

DON: Go on and clean the ashtrays.

DUMPTSY: But they're not dirty, sir. Because there's nobody using them.

DON: There's no need to remind me of *that!* Do as you're told!

DUMPTSY: If you please, sir. (*Picks up ashtray, blows on it, whistles tune, exits through arch.*)

DON (*to* LEADER): You've played enough. Get out!

PALETA: Is not yet three o'clock.

DON: Never mind what time it is. (*Orchestra stops playing.*) There's nobody here to listen to you. So you can just save the wear and tear on your harpsichord and go grab your- selves a smoke.

PALETA: Very good, Mr. Navadel. (*To other musicians.*) È inutile suonare più. Non ascolta. No, andiamo e fumar una sigarette. (*They put away instruments and music and start to go out as* PITTALUGA, *bristling, enters from arch.*)

PITTALUGA (*to* PALETA, *the pianist*): Eh, professori? Perchè avete fermato di suonari? Non sono ancora le tre.

PALETA: Domanda il Signor Navadel. (*Exits through arch, followed by musicians.*)

PITTALUGA (*comes to* DON): You told my orchestra it would stop? (*He speaks English with marked Italian accent.*)

DON (*untroubled*): I did.

PITTALUGA: My orders to them are they play in here until three o'clock. Why do you take it to yourself to countermand my orders?

DON: Because their performance was just a little too macabre to be bearable.

PITTALUGA (*furious*): So! You have made yourself the manager of this hotel, have you? You give orders to the musicians. Next you will be giving orders to me—and to the guests themselves, I have no doubt. . . . (*Crosses to table and rearranges ashtray and bell on table.*)

DON: The guests! (*Laughs dryly, sits up.*) That's really very funny. Consult your room chart, my dear Signor Pittaluga, and let me know how many guests there are that I can give orders to. The number when last I counted was three.

PITTALUGA (*crosses to* DON): And you stop being insolent, you—animale fetente. I pay you my money, when I am plunging myself into bankruptcy. . . .

DON: Yes, yes—we know all about that. You pay me your money. And you have a perfect right to know that I'm fed to the teeth with this little pension that you euphemistically call a high-grade resort hotel. Indeed, I'm fed to the teeth with you personally.

PITTALUGA (*in a much friendlier tone*): Ah! So you wish to leave us! I'm very sorry, my dear Donald. We shall miss you.

DON: My contract expires on March the first. I shall bear it until then. (*Lies down, fully stretched out on seat.*)

PITTALUGA: You insult me by saying you are fed with me, but you go on taking my money?

DON (*yawning*): Yeah!

PITTALUGA (*sits left of* DON *on rear seat*): Mascalzone di prima sfera prepotente, farabutto, canaglia . . .

16

Don: And it's not going to do you any good to call me names in your native tongue. I've had a conspicuously successful career in the resort hotel business, all the way from Santa Barbara to St. Moritz. And you lured me away from a superb job . . . with your glowing descriptions of this place, crowds of sport-lovers, desperately chic—(Pittaluga *rises, crosses to* Don, *faces him*)—flocking here from London, Paris, New York. . . .

Pittaluga: Did *I* know what was going to happen? Am *I* the king of Europe?

Don: You are the proprietor of this obscure tavern, and you're responsible for the fact that it's a deadly, boring dump!

Pittaluga: Yes! And I engaged you because I thought you had friends—rich friends . . . and they would come here after you instead of St. Moritz, and Muerren, and Chamonix. And where are your friends? What am I paying you for? To countermand my orders and tell me you are fed . . . (*Wails from warning sirens are heard offstage.*) Cosa succede?

Don (*sits up quickly*): That's from down on the flying fields.

Pittaluga: It is the warning for the air raids. (Don *rises, crosses to window, followed by* Pittaluga. Auguste, *the barman, is heard in bar offstage.*)

Auguste (*offstage*): Was ist los? (*Comes in from bar, stands in front of piano.*) Che cosa?

Pittaluga (*left of* Don, *looking through window*): Segnali d'incursione. La guerra è incominciata e il nemico viene. (*Airplane motors heard offstage.*)

Don (*looking through window*): Look! The planes are taking off. They're the little ones—the combat planes. (Captain Locicero *enters from arch. He is the officer in charge of the frontier station. He is tired, quiet, nice. He comes to the table downstage.* Dumptsy *follows* Captain *on through arch.*)

Auguste: Signor Capitano!

Captain: Buona sera! (Auguste *helps him take off his cape and* Captain *gives him his hat.*)

Dumptsy: Cosa succede, Signor Capitano? È la guerra?

Captain: No—no—datemi un cognac e soda. (*Takes off gloves and puts them and riding crop on table.* Auguste *gives* Captain's *cape and hat to* Dumptsy *and exits into bar.* Dumptsy *puts cape and hat on seat, and exits through arch.* Captain *sits at table, takes a cigarette case from pocket of his tunic as* Pittaluga *crosses to* Captain. Don *follows to right of* Pittaluga.)

Auguste (*as he goes out*): Si, signore.

Pittaluga: Cosa significano quei terribili segnali? È il nemico che arriva, forse?

Don: What's happened, Captain? Is there an air raid? Has war started?

Captain (*speaks English with a Continental accent, but it would be difficult to say of what country he is a native; smiling*): Who knows? But there is no air raid. They're only testing the sirens, to see how fast the combat (*hand-bell is heard offstage*) planes can go into action. You understand —it's like lifeboat drill on a ship. (*Lights cigarette.* Dumptsy *enters through arch.*)

Dumptsy: Scusi, padrone. Due inglesi arrivato. (*Exits hurriedly.*)

Pittaluga: Vengo subito. Scusi, Signor Capitano. (*Exits hurriedly.*)

Captain: Have a drink, Mr. Navadel?

Don (*puts on skiing jacket*): Forgive me, Captain—but two guests are actually arriving. I must go out and be affable. (*Exits through arch.* Dr. Waldersee *appears on gallery above with a book in his hand, and pauses on stairs as* Auguste *enters from bar and serves* Captain *with brandy and soda, and exits into bar.* Doctor *is an elderly, stout, crotchety, sad German.*)

Captain: Good afternoon, Doctor. Have a drink?

Doctor: Thank you very much—no. What is all that airplanes? (*Speaks English with a German accent.*)

Captain: This is a crucial spot, Dr. Waldersee. We must be prepared for visits from the enemy.

DOCTOR: Enemy, eh? And who is that?

CAPTAIN: I don't quite know, yet. The map of Europe supplies us with a wide choice of opponents. I suppose, in due time, our government will announce its selection—and we shall know just whom we are to shoot at.

DOCTOR (*starts coming downstairs*): Nonsense! Obscene nonsense.

CAPTAIN: Yes—yes. But the taste for obscenity is incurable, isn't it? (*Takes sip of his brandy and soda.*)

DOCTOR (*stops on middle landing*): When will you let me go into Switzerland?

CAPTAIN: Again I am powerless to answer you. My orders are that no one for the time being shall cross the frontiers, either into Switzerland or Austria.

DOCTOR: And when will this "time being" end?

CAPTAIN: When Rome makes its decision between friend and foe.

DOCTOR: I am a German subject. I am not your foe.

CAPTAIN: I am sure of that, Dr. Waldersee. The two great Fascist states stand together, against the world.

DOCTOR (*passionately*): More than that, I am a scientist. I am a servant of the whole damn stupid human race. (*Comes down rest of stairs.*) If you delay me any longer here, my experiments will be ruined. (*Puts book on table, crosses to* CAPTAIN.) Can't you appreciate that? I must get my rats at once to the laboratory in Zurich, or all my months and years of research will have gone for nothing. (DON *enters arch, followed by* MR. *and* MRS. CHERRY, *a pleasant young English couple in the first flush of their honeymoon.*)

DON: And this is our cocktail lounge. Here is the American bar. We have a thé dansant here every afternoon at four-thirty and supper dancing in the evening.

CHERRY (*left of* MRS. CHERRY, *holding her hand*): Oh, it's charming!

DON: Your rooms are up there, opening off that gallery. All this part of the hotel is quite new. (*Crosses to window.*) I think you'll concede that the view from here is absolutely unparalleled. From here we can look into four countries. (DUMPTSY *crosses from left to right at back with* CHERRY's *suitcases.* CAPTAIN *takes out notebook and pencil from breast pocket and jots down some notes.* DOCTOR *reads his book.*) Here in the foreground, of course, is Italy. This was formerly Austrian territory, transferred by the treaty of Versailles. It's called Monte Gabriele in honor of d'Annunzio, Italian poet and patriot. Over there is Austria—and over there is Switzerland. (*The* CHERRYS *go up two steps and look through window, backs to audience.*) And far off, you can just see the tip of a mountain peak which is in the Bavarian Tyrol. Rather gorgeous, isn't it?

CHERRY: Yes.

MRS. CHERRY: Darling—*look* at that sky!

CHERRY: I say! it is good.

DON: Do you go in for winter sports, Mrs. Cherry?

MRS. CHERRY: Oh, yes—I—my husband and I are very keen on them. (PITTALUGA *and* DUMPTSY *appear in arch. They speak in Italian through following dialogue on stage.* QUILLERY *crosses from left to right at back, behind* PITTALUGA *and* DUMPTSY. *He is wearing hat and overcoat.*)

PITTALUGA: Dumptsy!

DUMPTSY: Si, padrone?

PITTALUGA: Il bagalio è portato su?

DUMPTSY: Già sopra. Portato su. Portato su.

PITTALUGA: Sta bene va fare, va fare. (*Crosses to stairs.*)

(PITTALUGA *and* DUMPTSY *speak at the same time as* DON *and* CHERRY.)

DON: Splendid! We have everything here.

CHERRY: I've usually gone to Kitzbühel.

DON: It's lovely there, too.

CHERRY: But I hear it has become much too crowded there now. I—my wife and I hoped it would be quieter here.

DON: Well—at the moment—it is rather quiet here.

PITTALUGA (*at foot of stairs; to* CHERRY): Your luggage has been sent up, signore. Would you care to look at your rooms now?

CHERRY: Yes, thank you.

PITTALUGA: If you will have the goodness to step this way. (*Goes upstairs.*)

CHERRY (*pauses at window on way up with* MRS. CHERRY): What's that big bare patch down there?

DON (*casually*): Oh, that's the airport. (PITTALUGA *coughs discreetly.*) We have a great deal of flying here.

PITTALUGA: Right this way, please.

CHERRY: Oh—I see. (*They continue on up, preceded by* PITTALUGA.)

DON: And you will come down for the thé dansant?

MRS. CHERRY: We should love to.

DON: Splendid!

PITTALUGA (*stops at left of doorway and they pass him*): Right straight ahead, please. No, no per piacere! Non quella la stanza un apartamento nuziale! (*They exit through gallery.*)

DON (*standing on first step*): Honeymooners.

CAPTAIN (*puts notebook and pencil in breast pocket*): Yes— poor creatures.

DON: They wanted quiet.

DOCTOR: When will you know when I can go into Switzerland?

CAPTAIN: The instant that word comes through from Rome, Dr. Waldersee. (*Hand-bell is heard, offstage.*) You must understand that I am only an obscure frontier official. And here in Italy, as in your own Germany, authority is centralized.

DOCTOR (*rises, crosses to* CAPTAIN): But you can send a telegram to Rome, explaining the urgency of my position.

DUMPTSY (*appears in arch and comes forward greatly excited*): Mr. Navadel!

DON: Yes?

DUMPTSY: More guests from the bus, Mr. Navadel. Seven of them! (*Exits.*)

DON: Seven! *Good* God! (*Hurriedly exits.*)

DOCTOR: Ach, man hat keine Ruhe hier.

21

CAPTAIN: I assure you, Dr. Waldersee, I shall do all in my power.

DOCTOR: They must be made to understand that time is of vital importance.

CAPTAIN: Yes, yes. Of course.

DOCTOR: I have no equipment to examine them properly—no assistant for the constant observation that is essential if my experiments are to succeed. . . .

CAPTAIN (*a trifle wearily*): I'm so sorry. . . .

DOCTOR: Ja! You say you are so sorry. But what do you *do?* You have no comprehension of what is at stake. You are a soldier and indifferent to death. You say you are so sorry, but it is nothing to you that hundreds of thousands, *millions,* are dying from a disease that is within my power to cure!

CAPTAIN: Again, I assure you, Dr. Waldersee—

DON (*heard offstage in arch*): Our Mr. Pittaluga will be down in a moment. In the meantime, perhaps you and—the others . . . (*enters through arch, followed by* HARRY VAN, *a lean, thoughtful, lonely American vaudeville manager, promoter, press agent, book agent, crooner, hoofer, barker or shill. He has undertaken all sorts of jobs in his time, all of them capitalizing his powers of salesmanship, and none of them entirely honest. He wears a snappy, belted polo coat and a brown felt hat with brim turned down on all sides and carries a briefcase under his arm*) would care to wait in here. This is the cocktail lounge. We have a thé dansant here every afternoon at four-thirty and supper dancing in the evening. . . .

HARRY (*takes hat off*): Do you run this hotel?

DON: No. I'm the social manager.

HARRY: The what?

DON: The social manager.

HARRY: You're an American, aren't you?

DON: I am. Santa Barbara's my home, and Donald Navadel is my name.

HARRY: Glad to know you. My name's Harry Van. (*They shake hands.*)

DON: Glad to know you, Mr. Van. Are you—staying with us long?

DOCTOR (*rises; to* CAPTAIN): I will myself send a telegram to Rome, to the German Embassy. (*Exits.*)

CAPTAIN: They might well be able to expedite matters.

HARRY (*speaks to* DON *through two foregoing speeches*): Well, I don't know. Maybe you can help me out?

DON: I'm here to be of service, in any way I can. (DUMPTSY *crosses from left to right at back with* HARRY'S *Gladstone bag.*)

HARRY: I've got to get over that border. When I came in on the train from Fiume, they told me the border is closed, and maybe the train is stuck here for tonight or maybe longer. When I asked them why, they either didn't know or they refused to divulge their secret to me. What seems to be the trouble?

DON: Perhaps Captain Locicero can help you. He's the commander of Italian Headquarters here. This is Mr. Van, Captain.

CAPTAIN (*rising*): Mr. Van, my compliments. (*They shake hands over table.*)

HARRY: And mine to you, Captain. I'm trying to get to Geneva.

CAPTAIN: You have an American passport?

HARRY: I have. Several of them. (*Reaches in his pocket, takes out seven passports. He fans them like a deck of cards and hands them to* CAPTAIN.)

CAPTAIN: You have your family with you?

HARRY: Well—it isn't exactly a family. Come on in here, girls!

SHIRLEY (*offstage*): O.K., Harry. Come on in, kids. Harry wants us. (SIX CHORUS GIRLS *come in. They are wearing winter coats, hats, furs and galoshes and carry their hand luggage, umbrellas, etc. They are named and enter in following order:* SHIRLEY, EDNA, BEULAH, BEBE, FRANCINE *and* ELAINE. *Of these,* SHIRLEY *is the principal, a frank,*

23

knowing dancer. BEULAH *is a bubble dancer,* BEBE *is a hard, dumb little number who shimmies. The other three don't much matter.* DON *doesn't know quite how to take the surprising troupe, but* CAPTAIN *is impressed, favorably.*)

HARRY: Captain, allow me to introduce the girls. We call them "Les Blondes." We've been playing the Balkan circuit— Budapest, Bucharest, Sofia, Belgrade, Zagreb— (*Turns to* DON.) Back home, that would be the equivalent to "Pan Time."

CAPTAIN (*bowing*): How do you do?

GIRLS: How do you do? Pleased to meet you. . . .

HARRY: The situation in brief is this, Captain. We've got some very attractive bookings at a night spot in Geneva.

CAPTAIN: Um—h'm?

HARRY: Undoubtedly the League of Nations feels that they need us. Ha ha. It's important that we get there at once. So, I'd be grateful for prompt action.

CAPTAIN (*looking at first passport*): Miss Shirley—Lawlin.

HARRY: Laughlin. This is Shirley. Step up, honey. (SHIRLEY *steps forward and crosses to* CAPTAIN.)

CAPTAIN (*pleased with* SHIRLEY): How do you do?

SHIRLEY: How do you do?

CAPTAIN: This photograph hardly does you justice.

SHIRLEY: I know. It's terrible, isn't it!

HARRY (*interrupting* SHIRLEY's *obvious flirtation by snapping his fingers*): Who's next, Captain?

CAPTAIN: Miss Beulah Tremoyne.

HARRY: Come on, Beulah. (*She rises—comes forward in a wide sweep.*) Beulah is our bubble dancer. She's the product of the esthetic school, and therefore more of a dreamer.

CAPTAIN (*laughs*): Ho, ho, ho! Exquisite!

BEULAH (*about to sit on chair*): Thank you *ever* so much.

HARRY: That'll be all, Beulah. Who's next, Captain?

CAPTAIN (*reading off names from passports*): Miss Elaine Messiger!

HARRY: Elaine! (ELAINE *takes off hat, shakes her hair.*)

CAPTAIN: Miss Francine Merle!

HARRY: La Flame!

CAPTAIN: Miss Edna Creesh!

EDNA: Hiya!

HARRY (*to* EDNA, *under his breath*): Turn off the engine.

CAPTAIN: And Miss Bebe Gould!

HARRY: You'll find Bebe a very lovely little girl.

BEBE (*remonstratively*): Ha-rry!

HARRY: Come on, honey! (BEBE *comes forward.*) Bebe is our shimmy artiste, but incorrigibly unsophisticated! (BEBE *saucily tosses her head at* HARRY *and goes to center seat.*)

CAPTAIN: Very beautiful. Very, very beautiful!

SHIRLEY: Thank you!

CAPTAIN: Mr. Van, I congratulate you.

HARRY (*crosses to* CAPTAIN): And now can we—

CAPTAIN: And I wish that I, too, were going to Geneva. (*Hands passports back to* HARRY.)

HARRY: Then it's O.K. for us to pass?

CAPTAIN: But won't you young ladies sit down?

SHIRLEY: Thanks, Captain.

EDNA: We'd love to. ⎫ (*Spoken together.*)

FRANCINE: I'll say. (*They all sit.*) ⎭

HARRY: Listen, Captain, I don't want to seem oblivious to your courtesy, but the fact is we can't afford to hang around here any longer. That train may pull out and leave us.

CAPTAIN: I give you my word that train will not move tonight, and maybe not tomorrow night, and maybe never. (*Bows deeply.*) It is a matter of the deepest personal regret to me, Mr. Van, but—

HARRY: Listen, pal. Just stop being polite for a minute, will you? And tell me how do we get to Geneva.

CAPTAIN (*crosses to seat, picks up cape and hat*): That is not for me to say. I am as powerless as you are, Mr. Van. I, too, am a pawn. But, speaking for myself, I shall not be sorry if you and your very beautiful companions—are forced to remain here indefinitely. (*Salutes girls, smiles and exits.*)

SHIRLEY: Well!

HARRY (*leans on piano*): Did you hear that? He says he's a pawn.

BEBE: He's a wop.

BEULAH: But he's cute!

SHIRLEY: Well, personally, I'd just as soon stay here. I'm sick of the slats on those stinking day coaches.

HARRY: Say, listen, after the way we've been betrayed in the Balkans, we can't afford to stay any place. (*To* DON.) What's the matter, anyhow? (*Throws hat and briefcase on top of piano.*) Why can't decent people go about their own legitimate business?

DON: Evidently you're not fully aware of the international situation.

HARRY: I'm fully aware that the international situation is always regrettable. . . . But what's wrong now?

DON: Haven't you been reading the newspapers?

HARRY: In Bulgaria and Yugoslavia? (*Turns to girls, who laugh.*) No!

EDNA: Get *him!*

DON (*amused, laughs*): It may be difficult to understand, Mr. Van, but we happen to be on the brink of a frightful calamity.

HARRY: What?

DON: We're on the verge of war.

HARRY: Yeah, I heard rumors—you mean like that business in Spain?

DON: No, much more serious than that. All of them. World War.

HARRY: But they just had one. (PITTALUGA *appears on gallery, surveys crowd and starts coming down steps.*) Oh, no. I don't believe it. I don't believe—

PITTALUGA: Do you wish rooms, signore?

HARRY: Yeah, what've you got?

PITTALUGA: We can give you grande de luxe accommodations, rooms with baths.

HARRY: What's your scale of prices?

PITTALUGA: From fifty lira up.

DON: That's about five dollars a day.

HARRY: What?

DON: Meals included.

HARRY: I take it there's the usual professional discount.

DON: Oh, yes.

PITTALUGA (*to* DON): Che significa?

DON: Mr. Van and the young ladies are artists.

PITTALUGA: Ebbene?

DON: In America we always give special rates to artists.

PITTALUGA: Non posso, non posso. (*The* CHERRYS *appear on balcony above.*)

DON: I'm sure Signor Pittaluga will take care of you nicely, Mr. Van. He will show you attractive rooms on the *other* side of the hotel. They're delightful.

HARRY: No doubt. But I want to see the accommodations. (*Rises.*)

PITTALUGA: Step this way, please.

HARRY (*picks up hat and briefcase from piano*): Now, listen, I want two girls to a room, and a single room for me adjoining. (*All rise except* BEULAH, *who is busy putting on shoes.*) Come on, Beulah, put your shoes on. (*To* DON.) You see, Buddy, I promised their mothers I'd always be within earshot. (*Goes out with* DON, *preceded by* EDNA, FRANCINE, ELAINE *and* BEBE, SHIRLEY *with* BEULAH *last.* PITTALUGA *follows* HARRY *out.*)

BEULAH (*as they go*): I think this place is *attractive!*

SHIRLEY (*as they exit through arch*): Aw, nuts!

HARRY: Nuts to you.

MRS. CHERRY (*on top of stairs*): Well, that's an extraordinary gathering!

CHERRY: There's something I've never been able to understand—the tendency of Americans to travel en masse.

MRS. CHERRY (*looking at room*): This is a curious place, isn't it?

CHERRY: Yes, very!

MRS. CHERRY: It's a little bit dismal—don't you think so, Jimmy?

CHERRY: It's the Fascist idea of being desperately modern—dynamic symmetry! (*They pause to admire each other. He takes her in his arms.*) Darling!

MRS. CHERRY: What?

CHERRY: Nothing. I just said, "Darling!" My sweet. I love you.

MRS. CHERRY: That's right. (*He kisses her.*)

CHERRY: I think we're going to like it here, aren't we, darling?

MRS. CHERRY: Yes.

CHERRY: Even in spite of the dynamic symmetry?

MRS. CHERRY (*turns toward view through window*): You'll find a lot to paint.

CHERRY: No doubt. But I'm not going to waste any time painting.

MRS. CHERRY: Why not, Jimmy? You've got to work—

CHERRY: Don't ask "why not" in that laboriously girlish tone! You know damn well why not!

MRS. CHERRY (*laughing*): Now really, darling. We're old enough to be sensible!

CHERRY: God forbid that we should spoil everything by being sensible! This is a time for pure and beautiful foolishness. So don't irritate me by any further mention of work. (DOCTOR *enters.*)

MRS. CHERRY: Very well, darling. (CHERRY *kisses her again.* DOCTOR *crosses to seat and regards their love-making with scant enthusiasm. They look down and see him. They aren't embarrassed.*)

CHERRY: How do you do?

DOCTOR: Don't let me interrupt you. (*Rings hand-bell on table.*)

CHERRY: It's quite all right. We were just starting out for a walk. (*Takes* MRS. CHERRY *by arm and they start coming downstairs.* DUMPTSY *enters.* QUILLERY *enters with a French magazine in his hand, sits on chair at left of table, and reads.* QUILLERY *is a small, dark, brooding French extreme-left Radical Socialist.*)

DOCTOR (*to* DUMPTSY): Mineral water.

DUMPTSY: Jawohl, Herr Doktor.

DOCTOR: No ice—warm!

DUMPTSY: Gewiss, Herr Doktor. (*Comes forward to table, picks up* CAPTAIN'S *glass, exits into bar.*)

MRS. CHERRY (*to* DOCTOR): Isn't the air marvelous up here?

DOCTOR: Ja, ja. (*A group of four Italian Flying Corps OFFICERS enters, talking gaily in Italian.*)

CHERRY: Yes . . . we think so. Come on, darling. (*They wait until* OFFICERS *have passed through arch, then exit through arch.*)

FIRST OFFICER: Sono americane, eh?

SECOND OFFICER: Forse sarranno stelle cinematografiche di Hollywood.

FIRST OFFICER: Ma sono tutte ragazze belle!

THIRD OFFICER: Sono belle, ma proprio da far strabiliare.

(*All spoken together.*)

FOURTH OFFICER: E forse ora non ci rincrescerà che hanno cancellato la nostra licenza. (*They exit into bar.*)

HARRY (*enters through arch; he is chewing gum; to* DOCTOR): Good afternoon.

DOCTOR: Good afternoon.

HARRY: Have a drink?

DOCTOR: I am about to have one.

HARRY: Mind if I join you? (*Sits next to* DOCTOR *on center seat, takes out a small, silver snuff box, toys with it.*)

DOCTOR: This is a public room. (DUMPTSY *enters from bar, crosses and serves* DOCTOR *with glass of mineral water.*)

HARRY: It's a funny situation, isn't it?

DOCTOR (*rises*): To what situation do you refer?

HARRY: All this stopping of trains . . . and orders from Rome and we on the threshold of a calamity.

DOCTOR: To me it is not funny. (*Pays* DUMPTSY *with coins. Takes glass and starts for steps.*)

HARRY: Scotch.

DUMPTSY: With soda, sir?

HARRY: Yes.

DUMPTSY: Yes, sir.

QUILLERY (*speaks with a French accent*): I will have beer.

DUMPTSY: We have native or imported, sir. (DOCTOR *goes upstairs*.)

QUILLERY: Native will do.

DUMPTSY: Yes, sir. (*Goes into bar*.)

DOCTOR (*on top of stairs*): I repeat—to me it is *not* funny! (*He bows*.) You will excuse me.

HARRY: Certainly. . . . See you later, pal. (DOCTOR *exits. To* QUILLERY.) Friendly old bastard!

QUILLERY: Quite! But you were right. The situation *is* funny. There is always something essentially laughable about the thought of a lunatic asylum. Though, perhaps it is less humorous, when you are inside.

HARRY: I guess so. I guess it isn't easy for Germans to see the funny side of things these days. Do you mind if I join you?

QUILLERY: I beg of you to do so, my comrade.

HARRY: I don't want to thrust myself forward—but, you see, I travel with a group of blondes, and it's always a relief to find somebody to talk to. Have you seen the young ladies? (*Sits opposite* QUILLERY.)

QUILLERY: Oh, yes.

HARRY: Very alluring, aren't they?

QUILLERY: Very alluring. (DUMPTSY *comes in with drinks, goes into bar again.* HARRY *holds up snuff box, which he shows to* QUILLERY.)

HARRY: You know, that's a genuine antique snuff box, period of Louis Quinze.

QUILLERY: Very interesting.

HARRY: Yeah, a museum piece. (*Spits his chewing gum into snuff box, puts box into his pocket*.) You know, you've got to hoard your gum in Europe. I've been a long way with that gorgeous array of beautiful girls. I took 'em from New York to Monte Carlo. To say we were a sensation in Monte Carlo would be to state a simple incontrovertible fact. But then I made the mistake of accepting an offer from the manager of the Club Arizona in Budapest. I found that conditions in the Southeast are not so good.

QUILLERY: I traveled with you on the train from Zagreb.

HARRY: Zagreb—oh, boy! What were you doing there?

QUILLERY: I was attending a labor congress.

HARRY: Yeah—I heard about that. The night-club people thought that the congress would bring in business. They were wrong. But—excuse me—(*rises*)—my name is Harry Van.

QUILLERY (*rises*): Quillery is my name.

HARRY: Glad to know you, Mr.—? (*They shake hands over table.*)

QUILLERY: Quillery.

HARRY: Quillery. (*Sits.*) I'm an American. What's your nationality?

QUILLERY: I have no nationality. (*Sits.*) I drink to your good health.

HARRY: Well—I drink to your lack of nationality, of which I approve. (*They drink.* SIGNOR *and* SIGNORA ROSSI *enter. They have been skiing and are dressed in skiing clothes. He is a consumptive.*)

SIGNOR ROSSI: Una bella giornata, Nina. Una bella giornata! Beviamo un po'.

SIGNORA ROSSI: Dopo tutto quell' esercizio ti farebbe del male. Meglio riposarti per un'oretta.

SIGNOR ROSSI: Ma, se mi sento proprio bene. Andiamo. Mi reposerò più tardi. (*They exit into bar where they are greeted in Italian by officers.*)

HARRY: I always get an awful kick hearing Italian. It's beautiful. Do you speak it?

QUILLERY: Only a little. I was born a Frenchman.

HARRY: I see. You got over it.

QUILLERY: No. I loved my home. Perhaps if I had raised pigs —like my father, or his father before him, back to the time when Caesar's Roman legions came—perhaps, if I had done that, I would be a Frenchman, as they were. But I went to work in a factory—and machinery is international.

HARRY: I suppose pigs are exclusively French?

QUILLERY: Not all of them, but my father's pigs were! (HARRY *laughs.*) The factory where I worked made artificial limbs.

An industry that has been prosperous the last twenty years. But sometimes—in the evening—after my work—I would go out to the farm and help my father. And then, for a little while, I would become again a Frenchman.

HARRY (*takes out cigarette case*): That's a nice thought, pal. (*Offers* QUILLERY *cigarette*.) Will you have a cigarette?

QUILLERY: No, thank you.

HARRY: I don't blame you. These Yugoslav cigarettes are not made of the same high-grade manure to which I became accustomed in Bulgaria.

QUILLERY: You know, my comrade—you seem to have a rather long view of things.

HARRY: So long it grows tiresome. (*Lights cigarette*.)

QUILLERY: The long view is not easy to sustain in this short-sighted world.

HARRY: You're right there, pal.

QUILLERY: Let me give you an instance. There we were—gathered at Zagreb, representatives of all the workers of Europe. All brothers, collaborating harmoniously for a united front! And now—we are returning to our homes to prevent our people from plunging into mass murder—mass suicide!

HARRY: Oh, you're going back to France to stop the war?

QUILLERY: Yes.

HARRY: Do you think you'll succeed?

QUILLERY: Unquestionably! This is not 1914, remember! (*A ferocious-looking* MAJOR *of the Italian Flying Corps enters and crosses to bar*.) Since then, some new voices have been heard in the world—loud voices—I need only mention one of them—Lenin! Nicolai Lenin.

MAJOR (*bangs bar door open and shouts*): Attenti! (OFFICERS *in bar put their glasses down and stand at attention*. MAJOR *exits into bar*.)

HARRY: Yeah! But what are you going to do about people like that?

QUILLERY: Expose them! That's all we have to do. Expose

32

them—for what they are—atavistic children! Occupying their undeveloped minds playing with outmoded toys.

HARRY: Have you ever *seen* any of those toys?

QUILLERY: Mais oui! France is full of them. But there is a force more potent than all the bombing planes, the submarines, the tanks. It is the mature intelligence of the workers of the world! There is one antidote for war—revolution! And the cause of revolution gains steadily in strength. Even here in Italy, despite all this repressive power of Fascism, sanity has survived, and it becomes more and more articulate. . . .

HARRY: Well—you've got a fine point there, pal. And I hope you stick to it.

QUILLERY: I'm afraid you think it is all futile idealism!

HARRY: No—I don't. And what if I did? I am an idealist myself.

QUILLERY: You too believe in the revolution?

HARRY: Well, not exactly in *the* revolution. I'm just in favor of any revolution. Anything to wake people up, and give them some convictions. Have you ever taken cocaine?

QUILLERY: Why—I believe I have—at my dentist's.

HARRY: No—I mean, for pleasure. You know—a vice.

QUILLERY: No! I've never indulged in that folly.

HARRY: Well, I did once—during a stage of my career when luck was bad and confusion prevailed.

QUILLERY: Ah! You needed delusions of grandeur.

HARRY: That's just what they were.

QUILLERY: It must have been an interesting experience.

HARRY: It was illuminating. It taught me precisely what's the trouble with the world today. We've become a race of drug addicts—hopped up with false fears—false enthusiasms. . . . (*Three* OFFICERS *enter from bar, talking excitedly, stand behind* HARRY *and* QUILLERY.)

SECOND OFFICER: Ma, è stato fatto la dichiarazione di guerra attuale?

FIRST OFFICER: Portano le bombe esplosive?

THIRD OFFICER: Se la guerra ha veramente cominciata, allora vuol dire che noi . . .

MAJOR (*enters from bar, followed by* FOURTH OFFICER): Silencio! Solo il vostro commandante conosce gli ordini. Andiamo!

FOURTH OFFICER: Aspetta mi, Signor Maggiori, la guerra è cominciata fra Il Italia e La Francia? (*All above speeches are said together, as* MAJOR *enters from bar. All five hurriedly exit. Airplane motors are heard offstage.*)

QUILLERY (*jumps up*): Mother of God! Did you hear what they were saying?

HARRY (*rises*): I heard, but I couldn't understand.

QUILLERY: It was about war. I know only a little Italian—but I thought they were saying that war was already declared. I *must* go and demand that they let me cross the border! At once!

HARRY: Yeah, you've got no time to lose.

QUILLERY: Wait—I haven't paid—(*He is fumbling for money.*)

HARRY: That's all right, pal. The drink's on me. (*Waves him off.*) Go on, go on!

QUILLERY: Thank you, my comrade. (*Goes out quickly.* HARRY *crosses to window and looks.* DUMPTSY *enters from bar with tray, picks up empty beer glass.*)

DUMPTSY: Fine view, isn't it, sir?

HARRY: I've seen worse.

DUMPTSY: Nothing quite like it, sir. From here, we look into four nations. Where you see that little village, at the far end of the valley—that is Austria. Isn't that beautiful over there?

HARRY (*turns and looks at* DUMPTSY): Are you Italian?

DUMPTSY: Well, yes, sir. That is to say, I didn't used to be. (*Airplane motors begin to dim out.*)

HARRY: What did you used to be?

DUMPTSY: Austrian. All this part was Austria, until after the big war, when they decided these mountains must go to Italy, and I went with them. Ja, in one day I became a foreigner. So now, my children learn only Italian in school, and when I and my wife talk our own language they can't understand us. (DUMPTSY *gets* HARRY's *drink and brings it over to him.*) They changed the name of this mountain. Monte Gabriele—that's what it is now. They named it after an Italian who dropped bombs on Vienna. Even my old father, they got him, too. He's dead. But the writing on the gravestone was all in German, so they rubbed it out and translated it. So now he's Italian, too. (HARRY *takes Scotch from* DUMPTSY's *tray.*) But they didn't get my sister. She married a Swiss. She lives over there, in Schleins.

HARRY: She's lucky.

DUMPTSY: Ja . . . those Swiss are smart.

HARRY: Yeah, I wonder how the hell they ever got over there?

DUMPTSY (*laughs dryly*): But it doesn't make much difference who your masters are. When you get used to them, they're all the same. (HARRY *drains his glass. Porter's bell rings offstage.* PITTALUGA *appears in arch.*)

PITTALUGA: Dumptsy! Dumptsy!

DUMPTSY: Si, padrone.

PITTALUGA: Una grande signora arriva. Prende i suoi bagaglio.

DUMPTSY: Si, signore. Vengo subito. (*Puts tray with beer glass on it, on table in nook, and exits.*)

PITTALUGA (*in arch, claps hands*): Affretta! Sciocco! Anna, per Dio! (ANNA, *the maid, enters.*) Va sopra prepara la stanza.

ANNA: Si, si, subito.

PITTALUGA: Fa, presto, presto! (ANNA *hurriedly runs up steps, exits.*) PITTALUGA *stands at left of arch, showing* IRENE *in.*)

IRENE (*heard offstage*): Tu viens, Achille.

WEBER (*offstage*): In a minute, my dear. (*He speaks English with a slight Continental accent.*)

DON (*enters*): This is our cocktail lounge, madame. (IRENE *enters. She is somewhere between thirty and forty, beautiful, heavily and smartly furred in the Russian manner. Her hair is blond and quite straight. She is a model of worldly wisdom, chic and carefully applied graciousness. She sur-*

veys the room with polite appreciation, glancing briefly at HARRY. IRENE *is pronounced "Ear-ray-na." She speaks with a Russian accent.*) Your suite is up there, madame. All this part of the hotel is new.

IRENE (*stands a moment in arch, then comes forward*): How very nice. (PITTALUGA *exits.*)

DON: We have our best view from this side of the hotel. (*Goes to window.* IRENE *follows slowly.*) From here we can look into four countries—Italy, Austria, Switzerland and Bavaria.

IRENE: Magnificent!

DON: Yes—we're very proud of it.

IRENE (*goes up two steps to platform*): All those countries. And they all look so very much alike, don't they?

DON: Yes—they do really—from this distance.

IRENE: All covered up with the beautiful snow. (*Goes up to next landing.*) I think the whole world should be covered with snow. It would be much more clean, wouldn't it?

DON: By all means!

IRENE: Like in my Russia. White Russia. (IRENE *turns and looks through window.*) Oh, how exciting! A flying field. Look! They're bringing out the big bombers.

DON: You are interested in aviation, madame?

IRENE: Just ordinary flying? Oh, no, it bores me. But there is no experience so thrilling as a parachute jump.

DON (*below her on stairs*): I've never had that thrill, I'm ashamed to say.

IRENE: No? Once I had to jump when I was flying over the jungle.

DON: Really? Where?

IRENE: Indochina. It was indescribable. Drifting down, sinking into that great green sea of trees.

DON: And you weren't afraid?

IRENE: Afraid? Oh, no, no. I have fallen so many times. (HARRY *viciously rings hand-bell on table in front of him.* DUMPTSY *enters through arch, picks up tray with beer glass.*)

IRENE (*her gaze wandering about the room*):
But your place is really quite charming.

DON: You're very kind, madame.

IRENE: I must tell all my friends in Paris about
it.

HARRY: Scotch!   (*Spoken*

DUMPTSY (*removes glass of Scotch from table*   *together.*)
at which HARRY *sits*): Yes, sir.

HARRY: And I want some ice in it. If you
haven't got any ice, scoop up some snow.

DUMPTSY: *Yes, sir.* (*Exits into bar.*)

IRENE (*looking at left wall*): I don't like that design—it sug-
gests a—a kind of horror.

DON (*not knowing quite how to interpret that*): You are a
student of decoration, madame? (*Goes up steps toward
her.*)

IRENE: Only an amateur, my friend. (*Air-raid siren is heard
offstage.*) An amateur, I'm afraid, in everything. What is
that?

DON: It's just a sort of warning, madame. They've been testing it.

IRENE: A warning? Against what?

DON: I think they installed it for use in case of war.

IRENE: War? There will be no war. (PITTALUGA *and* ACHILLE
enter. ACHILLE WEBER *is a thin, keen Frenchman wearing
a neat little mustache and excellent clothes. Carries a leather
portfolio under his arm. The name is pronounced "Vay-
bair."*)

PITTALUGA: Par ici, Monsieur Weber. Votre
suite est par ici—   (*Spoken
                                                 together.*)
IRENE: They are all too much prepared.

DON: I'm sure of it, madame.

IRENE: Achille, Achille, there will be no war, will there?

WEBER: No, no, Irene, there will be no war.

IRENE (*to* DON): There you are. See—they are all too much
afraid of each other.

DON: Of course, madame. (ACHILLE *goes up steps, followed by* PITTALUGA.)

IRENE: Achille, I'm mad about this place. Je raffole de cette place. (*Starts upstairs.*)

WEBER: Yes, my dear.

IRENE: We must tell the Maharajah of Rajpipla about this. How dear little Pippi will love it. A droite—à gauche?

PITTALUGA: A gauche, madame, à gauche. (*She exits upstairs into gallery, followed by* WEBER *and* PITTALUGA.)

HARRY (*his back to audience, looking up after* IRENE): Who is that?

DON (*right of* HARRY, *his back to audience*): That was Achille Weber. One of the biggest men in France. I used to see a great deal of him at St. Moritz.

HARRY: Who is the dame? Is that his wife?

DON (*bristling*): Are you implying that she's not?

HARRY: No, no. I'm not implying anything. (*Goes to piano.*) I'm just being kind of—baffled. (*Sits on piano bench. Sound of airplane motors from far off.* DUMPTSY *enters from bar and serves* HARRY *with Scotch at piano.*)

DON: Evidently! (*Exits.*)

DUMPTSY (*crosses to window*): Do you see them—those airplanes—flying up from the field down there?

HARRY (*glances toward window, without interest*): Yes—I see them. (*Drinks Scotch in one gulp.*)

DUMPTSY: Those are the big ones. They're full of bombs, to drop on people. Look! They're going north. Maybe Berlin. Maybe Paris. (HARRY *strikes chord of* "Kak Stranna.")

HARRY: Did you ever jump with a parachute?

DUMPTSY: Why, no—sir. (*He looks questioningly at* HARRY.)

HARRY: Well, I did—a couple of times. And it's nothing. But —I didn't land in any jungle. I landed in the Fair Grounds. (*Sound of airplanes begins to die out.*)

DUMPTSY (*seriously*): That's interesting, sir. (*Crosses to center.* SIGNOR *and* SIGNORA ROSSI *enter from bar. She is supporting him as they cross in front of* HARRY.)

SIGNORA ROSSI: Non t'ho detto che devevi prender cura? Te l'ho detto.

SIGNOR ROSSI (*in hoarse whisper*): Scusatemi, Nina.

SIGNORA ROSSI: Te l'ho detto che accadrebbe così, ora vedi, ti piglia un accesso di tosse. (*They exit through arch.*)

DUMPTSY (*crosses to* HARRY *at piano*): That's Signor Rossi— he has tuberculosis.

HARRY: He's getting cured up here? (DOCTOR *appears on gallery, smoking cigar, book under his arm. He starts coming downstairs.*)

DUMPTSY: Pittaluga will ask him to leave when he finds out. This used to be a sanatorium in the old days. But the Fascisti, they don't like to admit that anyone can be sick! (*Moves toward bar as* HARRY *starts playing "Kak Stranna."*)

DOCTOR (*on first landing*): Dumptsy!

DUMPTSY (*stops*): Ja, Herr Doktor?

DOCTOR: Mineral water.

DUMPTSY: Gewiss, Herr Doktor. (*Exits into bar.* DOCTOR *comes downstairs, looks at* HARRY *with some surprise.*)

DOCTOR: What is that you're playing?

HARRY: A Russian song! Entitled "Kak Stranna," meaning "how strange." One of those morose ballads about how once we met, for one immortal moment, like ships that pass in the night. Or, maybe like a couple of trucks sideswiping each other. And now we meet again! How strange! Kak Stranna! A sentimental trifle. (DUMPTSY *enters from bar, serves* DOCTOR *with mineral water,* DOCTOR *pays him with coins, and* DUMPTSY *crosses to table, picks up magazine left by* QUILLERY, *stands at bar door listening to music.*)

DOCTOR: You're a musician?

HARRY: Certainly. (*Stops playing "Kak Stranna" and shifts into "When My Baby Smiles at Me."*) I used to play the piano in picture theatres—when that was the only kind of sound they had—except the peanuts. (HARRY *sings "My Baby—My Baby" to accompaniment of piano.*)

DOCTOR: Do you know any Bach?

HARRY: Bach? (*Stops playing.*) Certainly. (*Plays Two-Part*

Invention in D minor, by Bach, which he plays pretty badly.)

DOCTOR: You have good appreciation, but not much skill.

HARRY (*stops the Bach*): What do you mean, not much skill? Listen to this. (*He goes into a trick arrangement of "The Waters of the Minnetonka."*) "The Waters of the Minnetonka"—Cadman. (*Goes on playing.*) Suitable for scenics—Niagara Falls by moonlight. Or—(*he shifts into an Indian motif of same piece*)—if you play it this way—it goes great with the scene where the Indian chief turns out to be a Yale man. (*Shifts into "Boola Boola," then plays arpeggios.*)

DOCTOR: Will you have a drink?

HARRY: Oh! So you want me to stop playing?

DOCTOR: No, no! I like your music very much.

HARRY: Then in that case, I'd be delighted to have a drink with you. . . . Another Scotch, Dumptsy. (*Stops playing.*)

DUMPTSY: Yes, sir. (*Exits into bar.*)

DOCTOR: I'm afraid I was rude to you.

HARRY: That's all right, pal. I've been rude to lots of people, and I never regretted it.

DOCTOR: The fact is I am very gravely distressed.

HARRY: I can see that, and I sympathize with you.

DOCTOR (*fiercely*): You cannot sympathize with me, because you do not know!

HARRY: Perhaps not—except in a general way.

DOCTOR: You are familiar with the writings of Thomas Mann. (*It is a challenge, rather than a question.*)

HARRY: I'm afraid not, pal.

DOCTOR (*opens book and reads*): "Backsliding"—he said—"spiritual backsliding to that dark and tortured age—that, believe me, is disease! A degradation of mankind—a degradation painful and offensive to conceive." True words, eh?

HARRY: Absolutely! (DUMPTSY *enters from bar, places Scotch on piano and exits into bar.*)

DOCTOR: Have you had any experience with the disease of cancer?

HARRY: Certainly. I used to sell a remedy for it.

DOCTOR (*exploding*): There *is* no remedy for it, so far!

HARRY: Well—this was a kind of remedy for everything.

DOCTOR: I am within *that* of finding the cure for cancer! You probably have not heard of Fibiger, no?

HARRY: I may have. I'm not sure. (*Lights cigarette.*)

DOCTOR: He was a Dane—experimented with rats. He did good work, but he died before it was completed. I carry it on. I have been working with Oriental rats, in Bologna. But because of this war scare, I must go to neutral territory. You see, nothing must be allowed to interfere with my experiments. Nothing!

HARRY: No. No.

DOCTOR: The laboratory of the University of Zurich has been placed at my disposal—and in Switzerland, I can work, undisturbed. I have twenty-eight rats with me, all in various carefully tabulated stages of the disease. It is the disease of civilization—and I can cure it. And now they say I must not cross the border.

HARRY (*laughs*): You know, Doctor, it *is* funny.

DOCTOR: *What's* funny? To you, everything is funny!

HARRY: No—I mean you and me being in the same fix. Both trying to get across that line—you with rats—me with girls. Of course, I realize that civilization at large won't suffer much if *we* get stuck in the war zone. Whereas with you, there's a lot at stake—

DOCTOR: It is for me to win one of the greatest victories of all time. And the victory belongs to Germany.

HARRY: Sure it does!

DOCTOR (*continues*): Unfortunately, just now the situation in Germany is not good for research. They are infected with the same virus as here. Chauvinistic nationalism!

HARRY: Is that so?

DOCTOR: Ja, they expect all bacteriologists to work on germs to put in bombs to drop from airplanes, to fill people with death, when we've given our lives to *save* people. Lieber Gott! Why don't they let me do what is good? Good for the whole world? Forgive me, I become excited.

41

HARRY: No, I know exactly how you feel. You know, back in 1918, I was a shill for a carnival show, and I was doing fine. The boss thought very highly of me. He offered to give me a piece of the show, and I had a chance to get somewhere. And then what do you suppose happened? Along comes the United States Government and they drafted me! You're in the Army now! They slapped me into a uniform and for three months before the Armistice, I was parading up and down guarding the Ashokan Reservoir. They were afraid your people might poison it. I've always figured that little interruption ruined my career. But I've remained an optimist, Doctor.

DOCTOR: *You* can afford to.

HARRY: No, I remained an optimist because I'm essentially a student of human nature. Now you dissect rats and corpses and similar unpleasant things. Well—it's been my job in life to dissect suckers! I've probed into the souls of some of the God damnedest specimens. And what have I found? Now, don't sneer at me, Doctor—but above everything else I've found Faith. Faith in peace on earth, good will to men— Faith that Muma—Muma the three-legged girl—really has got three legs. All my life I've been selling phony goods to people of meager intelligence and great faith. I suppose you'd think that would make me contemptuous of the human race? But—on the contrary—it has given *me* Faith. It's made me sure that no matter how much the meek may be bulldozed or gypped they will eventually inherit the earth. (SHIRLEY *and* BEBE *enter.*)

SHIRLEY: Harry!

HARRY: What is it, honey?

SHIRLEY (*crosses to* HARRY, *hands him printed notice*): Say, Harry, did you see this?

HARRY: Allow me to introduce Miss Shirley Laughlin and Miss Bebe Gould.

SHIRLEY and BEBE: How do you do?

DOCTOR (*grunts*): How do you do? (HARRY *looks at notice.*)

SHIRLEY (*sits left of* HARRY): They got one of those things posted in each of our rooms.

HARRY (*showing it to* DOCTOR): Look—"What to do in case of air raids"—in all languages.

DOCTOR: Ja—I saw that.

SHIRLEY: Give it back to me. I'm going to send it home to Mama.

HARRY (*handing it to her*): Souvenir of Europe.

SHIRLEY: It'll scare the hell out of her.

BEBE: Say, what's the matter with these people? Are they all screwy?

HARRY: You hit it right on the nose, dear! (*Turns to* DOCTOR.) Oh, Doctor, these are very wonderful, very profound little girls. The mothers of tomorrow. (BEULAH *enters.*)

SHIRLEY: Oh—shut up!

BEULAH: Say—Harry . . .

HARRY: Yeah, what do you want?

BEULAH: Is it all right if I go out with Mr. Navadel and learn how to do this skiing? (WEBER *comes out on gallery and starts downstairs, takes cigar out of his case.*)

HARRY: What? And risk breaking those pretty legs? Emphatically—no!

BEULAH: But it's healthy. (*Comes forward.*)

HARRY: But not for me, dear. Those gams of yours are my bread and butter. (BEULAH *sits in rear corner.* FRANCINE *enters. She and* BEBE *sit on seat.* CAPTAIN *enters, apparently alarmed about something.* FRANCINE *and* BEBE *stare at him.*) Sit down, girls, and amuse yourself—with your own thoughts.

CAPTAIN: Monsieur Weber, I have been trying to get through to headquarters.

WEBER: And when can we leave?

CAPTAIN: Not before tomorrow, I regret to say. (IRENE *appears on gallery.*)

WEBER: Signor Lanza in Venice assured me there would be no delay.

CAPTAIN: There would be none, if only I could get into communication with the proper authorities. But—the wires are crowded. The whole nation is in a state of uproar.

WEBER: Already? It's absurd lack of organization. (PIANIST *and* DRUMMER *come in and go on platform.* VIOLINIST *and* SAXOPHONIST *follow.* IRENE *comes downstairs.*)

CAPTAIN: There is good excuse for the excitement now, Monsieur Weber. The report has just come to us that a state of war exists between Italy and France.

HARRY: What?

CAPTAIN: There is a rumor of war between Italy and France!

HARRY: Rumors—rumors—everything's rumors! When are we going to *know?*

CAPTAIN: You'll know soon enough.

DOCTOR: And what of Germany?

CAPTAIN: Germany has mobilized. (IRENE, *at bottom of steps, pauses to listen.*) But I don't know if any decision has been reached. Nor do I know of the situation anywhere else. But —God help us—it will soon be serious enough for everyone on this earth.

IRENE: I thought you said there would be no war, Achille. Has there been some mistake somewhere?

WEBER: There is only one way to account for it, my dear. . . . Spontaneous combustion of the dictatorial age.

IRENE: How thrilling it must be in Paris at this moment! Just like 1914. All the lovely soldiers singing—marching—marching— (DUMPTSY *enters from bar and stands behind* WEBER, *awaiting orders.*)

HARRY: What's the matter with the music? Us young folks want to dance. (ELAINE *and* EDNA *enter on last of* IRENE'S *speech.*)

IRENE: We must get across that border. We must get to Paris at once, Achille.

ELAINE: Harry, can I have a drink now? ⎤
HARRY: Yeah, sure, sit down anywhere. ⎟ (*Spoken together.*)
WEBER: Will you have a drink, Irene? ⎟
IRENE: No. (*Musicians start playing.*) ⎦

BEBE (*calling to* EDNA): Edna?

WEBER: Will you, Captain Locicero?

CAPTAIN: Thank you. Brandy and soda, Dumptsy. (*Sits on chair right of table.*)

DUMPTSY: Si, signore.

WEBER: For me, Cinzano.

DUMPTSY: Cinzano? Oui, monsieur. (*Exits into bar.*)

DOCTOR: It's all incredible.

HARRY (*rises*): Yes, Doctor, but I still remain an optimist. (*Looks searchingly at* IRENE.) Let doubt prevail throughout this night—with dawn will come again, the light of truth. (*Takes* SHIRLEY *and begins to dance with her, always keeping his eyes on* IRENE. DON *has entered arch, and goes over to* BEULAH, *begins to dance with her.* CAPTAIN *turns to watch dancing and catches sight of* SHIRLEY'S *posterior sticking way out and facing audience.* CAPTAIN *roars with laughter.*)

ACT II

SCENE 1

SCENE: *The same. About seven-thirty, evening of same day. Venetian blinds on the three windows are down. The* CHERRYS *are seated. Both are dressed for dinner. He is smoking a cigarette, as curtain rises.* AUGUSTE *serves them cocktails.*

CHERRY: Thank you. (*Puts coins on* AUGUSTE's *tray.*) Has any more news come through?

AUGUSTE: No, signore. They permit the radio to say nothing.

CHERRY: I suppose nothing really will happen.

AUGUSTE: Let us pray that is so, signore. (*Crosses left and exits into bar.*)

CHERRY (*leans over affectionately toward* MRS. CHERRY): My sweet . . . you're really very lovely.

MRS. CHERRY: Yes. (CHERRY *picks up glass and hands it to her, then picks up his glass.*)

CHERRY: Here's to us, darling.

MRS. CHERRY: And to hell with all the rest.

CHERRY: And to hell with all the rest. (*They drink solemnly.*)

MRS. CHERRY: Jimmy—

CHERRY: What is it, darling? (*Puts his drink down.*)

MRS. CHERRY: Were you just saying that—or do you believe it?

CHERRY: That you're lovely? I can give you the most solemn assurance. . . .

MRS. CHERRY: No—that nothing is going to happen?

CHERRY: Oh.

46

MRS. CHERRY: Do you believe that?

CHERRY: I know this much: they can't start any real war without England. And no matter how stupid and blundering our government may be, our people won't stand for it.

MRS. CHERRY: But people can be such complete fools. (*Puts drink down.*)

CHERRY: I know it, darling. Why can't they be like us?

MRS. CHERRY: You mean—nice?

CHERRY: Yes—nice.

MRS. CHERRY: And intelligent.

CHERRY: And happy.

MRS. CHERRY: We're very conceited, aren't we?

CHERRY: Of course. And for good and sufficient reason.

MRS. CHERRY: Yes, I'm glad we're such superior people, darling. It's so comforting. (HARRY *enters and goes to piano.*)

CHERRY: Oh, hello. (HARRY, *not wishing to intrude on them, starts out.*) Oh, don't run away. Play something, won't you?

MRS. CHERRY: Won't you have a drink with us?

HARRY (*puts out his cigarette in ashtray on piano*): No thanks, Mrs. Cherry—if you don't mind. (*Sits at piano.*) I'm afraid I put down too many Scotches this afternoon. As a result of which I've had to treat myself to a bicarbonate of soda. (HARRY *starts playing.*)

CHERRY (*sotto voce*): I intend to get completely blotto. (*Drinks.*)

MRS. CHERRY: Oh, I love that!

HARRY: Thanks, Mrs. Cherry—always grateful for applause from the discriminating. (*Finishes the strain and stops.*)

CHERRY: Do play some more.

HARRY: No. The mood ain't right.

MRS. CHERRY: I can't tell you what a relief it is to have you here in this hotel.

HARRY: It's very nice of you, Mrs. Cherry. But I don't deserve your handsome tribute. Frequently I can be an asset at any gathering—contributing amusing anecdotes and bits of homely philosophy. But here and now, I'm not at my best.

47

CHERRY: You're the only one who seems to have retained any degree of sanity.

MRS. CHERRY: You and your young ladies.

HARRY: The girls are lucky. They don't know anything. (*Lights another cigarette with his lighter.*) And I guess the trouble with me is I don't give a damn.

MRS. CHERRY: We've been trying hard not to know anything —or not to give a damn. But it isn't easy.

HARRY: You haven't been married very long, have you? I hope you don't mind my asking. . . .

CHERRY: We were married the day before yesterday.

HARRY: Let me offer my congratulations.

CHERRY: Thank you very much.

HARRY: It's my purely intuitive hunch that you two ought to get along fine.

CHERRY: That's our intention, Mr. Van.

MRS. CHERRY: Yes. And we'll do it, what's more. You see— we have one supreme thing in common: We're both independent.

CHERRY: We're like you Americans in that respect.

HARRY: You flatter us.

MRS. CHERRY: Jimmy's been out in Australia, doing colossal murals for some government building. He won't show me the photographs of them, but I'm sure they're simply awful.

CHERRY: They're allegorical.

HARRY: At that I'll bet they're pretty good. (CHERRY *laughs.*) What do you do, Mrs. Cherry?

MRS. CHERRY: I work in the gift department at Fortnum's—

HARRY: You mean behind a counter?

MRS. CHERRY: Yes—wearing a smock, and disgracing my family.

HARRY: Well, what d'ye know!

MRS. CHERRY: Both our families hoped we'd be married in some nice little church, and settle down in a nice little cottage, in a nice little state of decay. But when I heard Jimmy was on the way home I just dropped everything and rushed out here to meet him, and we were married in Florence.

CHERRY: We hadn't seen each other for nearly a year—so, you can imagine, it was all rather exciting.

HARRY: Yeah, I can imagine.

MRS. CHERRY: Florence is the most perfect place in the world to be married in.

HARRY: I guess that's true of any place.

CHERRY: You see, we both happen to love Italy. And—well—we're both rather on the romantic side.

HARRY: You stay on that side, no matter what happens.

MRS. CHERRY (*quickly*): I say, what do you think is going to happen?

HARRY: I haven't the slightest idea.

CHERRY: We've looked forward so much to being here with no one bothering us, and plenty of winter sports. You see, we're both keen on skiing. (*He pronounces it "she-ing," the English way.*) And now—we may have to go dashing back to England at any moment.

MRS. CHERRY: It's rotten luck, isn't it?

HARRY: Yes, Mrs. Cherry. It is rotten. (QUILLERY *enters from bar reading Italian newspaper.*) Any news?

QUILLERY (*glaring*): News? Not in this patriotic journal! "Unconfirmed rumors"—from Vienna, London, Berlin, Moscow, Tokyo. And a lot of confirmed lies (*he slaps paper down on table*) from Fascist headquarters in Rome.

CHERRY: I don't suppose one can get the truth anywhere—not even in the *Times*.

MRS. CHERRY: Perhaps it's just as well.

QUILLERY: If you want to know what is really happening, ask *him*—up there!

CHERRY: Who?

QUILLERY: Weber! The great Monsieur Achille Weber, of the Comité des Forges! He can tell you all the war news. Because he *made* it. You don't know who he is? Or what he is doing here in Italy?

CHERRY: No.

QUILLERY: He is organizing the arms industry. Munitions. To kill French babies and English babies. France and Italy are at war. (DOCTOR *enters on balcony, comes to middle landing, listens.*) England joins France. Germany joins Italy. And that will drag in the Soviet Union and the Japanese Empire and the United States. In every part of the world the good desire of men for peace and decency is undermined by the dynamite of jingoism. And it needs only one spark, set off by one egomaniac, to blow it all up in one final explosion. Then love becomes hatred, courage becomes terror, hope becomes despair. But—it will all be very nice for Achille Weber. Because he is a master of the one *real* League of Nations—the League of Schneider-Creusot, of Krupp, Skoda, Vickers and Du Pont. The League of Death! (DOCTOR *slowly comes down rest of steps. Outburst.*) And the workers of the world are expected to pay him for it, with their sweat, and their life's blood.

DOCTOR: Marxian nonsense!

QUILLERY: Ah! Who speaks?

DOCTOR: I speak.

QUILLERY: Yes! The eminent Dr. Hugo Waldersee. A wearer of the sacred swastika. Down with the Communists! Off with their heads! So the world may be safe for the Nazi murderers.

DOCTOR: So that Germany may be safe from its oppressors! It is the same with all of you—Englishmen, Frenchmen and the Marxists—you manage to forget that Germany, too, has a right to live! (*Rings hand-bell on table.*)

QUILLERY: If you love your Germany so much, why aren't you there now—with your rats?

DOCTOR: I am not concerned with politics. (AUGUSTE *enters from bar.*) I am a scientist. (*To* AUGUSTE.) Mineral water! (AUGUSTE *bows, exits into bar.* DOCTOR *sits.*)

QUILLERY: A scientist—that's it, Herr Doktor! A servant of humanity! And you know, if you were in your dear Fatherland, the Nazis would make you abandon your cure for

cancer. It might benefit too many people outside Germany—
maybe even some Jews. (DOCTOR *lights cigar.*) They
would force you to devote yourself to breeding malignant
bacteria—millions of little germs, each one taught to give
the Nazi salute . . . (*gives Nazi salute*) and then go out
and poison the enemy. (AUGUSTE *enters from bar, serves*
DOCTOR *with mineral water.* DOCTOR *puts some coins on
his tray, and exits into bar.*) You—a fighter against disease
and death—you become a Judas goat in a slaughterhouse.

CHERRY: I say, Quillery, old chap—do we have to have so
much blood and sweat just before dinner?

QUILLERY (*turning on him*): Just before dinner! And now
we hear the voice of England! The great, well-fed, pious
hypocrite! The grabber—the exploiter—the immaculate
butcher! It was *you* who forced this war, because miserable
little Italy dared to drag its black shirt across your trail
of Empire. But what do *you* care if civilization goes to
pieces—(DON *crosses from left to right at back, stops to listen in arch*)—so long as you have your dinner, and your
dinner jacket!

CHERRY (*rising*): I'm sorry, Quillery, old chap—but I think
we'd better conclude this discussion out on the terrace.

MRS. CHERRY: Don't be a damned fool, Jimmy. You'll prove
nothing by thrashing him.

QUILLERY: It's the Anglo-Saxon method of proving everything! Very well—I am at your disposal.

DON: No! Please, Mr. Cherry. (*He turns to* QUILLERY.) I
must ask you to leave if you can't conduct yourself as a
gentleman.

QUILLERY: Don't say any more. Evidently I cannot conduct
myself properly. I apologize, Mr. Cherry.

CHERRY: That's quite all right, old man. (*Offers hand and*
QUILLERY *shakes it.* DON *goes to arch.*) Have a drink.

QUILLERY: No, thank you. My apologies, Herr Doktor.

DOCTOR: There is no need for apologizing.

QUILLERY: If I let my speech run away with me, it is because
I have a hatred for certain things. And you should hate

them, too. They are the things that make us blind—and ignorant, and dirty. (*Turns and goes out quickly through arch. He is followed by* DON.)

MRS. CHERRY: He's so right about everything.

CHERRY: Yes, I know, poor chap. Will you have another cocktail, darling?

MRS. CHERRY: No, I don't think so. Will you, Doctor? (DOCTOR *shakes head. Rises.*) Well, let's dine. (DOCTOR *drinks his water, then lets his eyeglasses hang on left ear as he rubs his eyes.*)

CHERRY: It will be a bit difficult to summon up much relish. (*They go out, hand in hand.*)

HARRY (*still seated at piano*): I find these two very appealing, don't you, Doctor? Did you know they were only married the day before yesterday? Yeah, got themselves sealed in Florence—because they love Italy. They came up here hoping to spend their honeymoon on skis. . . . Kind of pathetic, isn't it?

DOCTOR (*after a short pause*): What are you saying? (*Adjusts eyeglasses.*)

HARRY: Nothing. I was only making conversation.

DOCTOR: That Communist! (DON *appears in arch.*) Making me a criminal because I am a German!

DON: I'm dreadfully sorry, Dr. Waldersee. We should never have allowed that insufferable little cad to come in here.

DOCTOR (*rises*): Oh—it's no matter. I have heard too many hymns of hate before this. To be a German is to be used to insults and injuries. (*Exits.* DON *starts to go out.*)

HARRY: Say, Don.

DON: Yes?

HARRY: Did you find out who that dame is?

DON: What "dame"?

HARRY: That Russian number—you know, the one with Weber.

DON: I have not inquired as to her identity.

HARRY: Did he register her as his wife?

DON: They registered separately! And if it's not too much

to ask, might I suggest that you mind your own damned business?

HARRY: Yeah, you might suggest just that. And I would still be troubled by one of the most tantalizing of questions —"Where have I seen that face before?" Usually, it turns out to be somebody in the second row, one night-yawning!

DON: Yeah, I'm sure that such is the case right now. (*Starts out.*)

HARRY: Say, Don.

DON (*impatiently*): Well, what is it?

HARRY: I take it your job around here is that of a professional greeter?

DON: You're at liberty to call it that, if you choose.

HARRY: I mean a sort of a YMCA secretary—I mean one that sees to it that everybody gets together and has a good time.

DON: Well?

HARRY: Well—do you think you're making a good job of it right now?

DON: Have you any suggestions for the improvement of the performance of my duties?

HARRY: Yes, Don—I have.

DON (*simply furious*): I'd very much like to know just exactly who the hell you think you are to be offering criticism of my work. . . .

HARRY: Please, don't scream at me. I'm only trying to be helpful. I'm making you an offer.

DON: Well, what is it?

HARRY (*looks to the right*): I see you've got a color wheel here.

DON (*turns right and looks*): Yes, yes. We use it during the supper dance. Now if you don't mind . . .

HARRY: Well—yeah—how would it be if the girls and me put on part of our act tonight? For purposes of wholesome merriment—and to relieve the general tension?

DON: What kind of an act is it?

HARRY: Don't say "What kind of an act is it" in that tone.

The act is good enough for this place. Those girls have played before the King of Romania, and if my suspicions are correct—well, we won't pursue that subject. All that need concern you is that we can adapt ourselves to our audience, and tonight we'll omit the bubble dance and Bebe's shimmy with the detachable gardenias, unless there's a special request for it.

DON: Do you expect to be paid for this?

HARRY: Certainly not. I'm making this offer out of the goodness of my heart. Of course, if you want to make a little generous adjustment on our hotel bill . . . (IRENE *appears on gallery and starts to come down. She is wearing a dinner dress. Stops on lowest platform, peers through slats of Venetian blinds.*)

DON: And you'll give me your guarantee that there'll be no vulgarity?

HARRY (*looks up, sees* IRENE; DON *also turns and sees her*): One more crack like that and the offer is withdrawn. . . .

DON (*changes his tone entirely*): Oh, I think it's a splendid idea, Mr. Van. I'm sure we'll all greatly appreciate your little performance. Good evening, madame.

IRENE (*with the utmost graciousness*): Good evening, Mr. Navadel. It *is* a lovely view. It is like a landscape on the moon.

DON: Yes—yes. That's exactly what it's like.

HARRY: Of course you realize we'll have to rehearse with the orchestra.

DON: Oh, yes—our staff will be completely at your disposal, Mr. Van. (HARRY *goes to arch.*)

IRENE: What became of those planes that flew off this afternoon? I haven't heard them come back yet. (*Takes out long Russian cigarette from her purse.*)

DON: I expect they've gone to some base farther from the frontier. I certainly hope so. They used to make the most appalling racket. (*Lights cigarette for her.*)

HARRY: About eleven o'clock? (*Exits.* WEBER *appears on*

54

*gallery smoking a cigar. He is not in evening dress. Comes
downstairs and also peers through blinds.*)

DON: Yes, Mr. Van. Eleven o'clock will do nicely. Could I
bring you a cocktail, madame?

IRENE: Vodka, if you please.

DON: Vodka? Why, certainly, I shall have it sent right in.
(*Exits into bar.*)

WEBER: A perfectly cloudless night. They are very lucky.

IRENE: Did you get your call?

WEBER: Yes. I talked with Lanza.

IRENE: The news was I suppose as usual—very good.

WEBER (*sits right of* IRENE): It is extremely serious! You
saw those bombers that left here this afternoon?

IRENE: Yes.

WEBER: They were headed for Paris. Italy is evidently in a
great hurry to deliver the first blow.

IRENE: How soon may we leave here?

WEBER: None too soon, I can assure you. The French High
Command will know that the bombers came from this
field. There will be reprisals—

IRENE: Huh!

WEBER: —probably within the next twenty-four hours.

IRENE: That will be exciting to see.

WEBER: An air raid?

IRENE: What—here?—with the bombs bursting in the snow?
Sending up great geysers of diamonds?

WEBER: Or perhaps great geysers of us.

IRENE: I suppose many people in Paris are now being killed.

WEBER: I am afraid so. Unless the Italians bungle it.

IRENE: Perhaps your sister—Madame d'Hilaire—and her
darling little children—ils sont toutes mortes. C'est vraiment
terrible!

WEBER: No, no, Irene. Don't talk French. Your French is
worse than your Russian.

IRENE: Not so bad as my Cockney. (*Drops Russian accent
and goes into Cockney dialect.*) You should have heard

55

my Cockney. (*Begins to sing in Cockney dialect.*) "If those lips could only speak—"

WEBER (*admonishing her*): Irene!

IRENE: "And those eyes could only see—" "And those beautiful golden tresses—"

WEBER: Someone will hear you. Stop, stop it, Irene.

IRENE: I have stopped.

WEBER: I prefer you Russian—as you were when I first met you. Two years ago now, isn't it, Irene?

IRENE: Four years ago, Achille. Thank you very much.

WEBER: Yes! I greatly prefer you Russian.

IRENE (*in plain English—without any dialect*): I know. Russian makes me more mysterious. A Russian accent gives me a romantic past. They think perhaps I'm a daughter of the Czar—or a spy or something. At any rate they have to watch me. Oh, Achille, I don't want you to be ashamed of me. And I know when I talk English however well, sooner or later some Cockneyism pops out. And then everybody knows me for what I am—a London guttersnipe—with a piquant dash of Armenian. Just—nobody.

WEBER: My dear, you could never be nobody.

IRENE: Everybody can be nobody by merely removing their masks. But I know you prefer people with their masks on. So I shall continue with my Russian. (*Resumes Russian accent.*) It is the easiest for me. I have been doing it for so long, now. (DUMPTSY *enters from bar with glass of vodka, book of waiter's checks and small pencil on tray. Serves vodka.*)

WEBER: I shall telegraph to Joseph to have the house ready. (*He signs check on* DUMPTSY's *tray.*) It will be rather cold in Biarritz now—but far healthier than in Paris. Am I right?

IRENE: Oh, Achille.

WEBER: You are going to dinner now?

IRENE: Yes.

WEBER: I shall join you later. (*He goes out.* DUMPTSY *picks up the* CHERRYS' *glasses.*)

DUMPTSY: We will have a great treat tonight, madame.

IRENE: Really?

DUMPTSY: That American impresario, that Mr. Harry Van—he will give us an entertainment with his dancing girls.

IRENE: Is he employed here regularly? (*Drinks vodka in one neat gulp.*)

DUMPTSY: Oh, no, madame. He is just passing, like you. This is a special treat. It will be very fine.

IRENE: Let us hope so.

DUMPTSY: Madame is Russian, if I may say so.

IRENE (*pleased*): What makes you think that I am Russian, hm? Is it because I am drinking vodka?

DUMPTSY: Oh, no, madame. Many people try to drink vodka. But only true Russians can do it gracefully. You see—I was a prisoner with your people in the war.

IRENE: So?

DUMPTSY: I liked them.

IRENE: You're very charming. What is your name?

DUMPTSY: I am called Dumptsy, madame.

IRENE: Dumptsy! You are going again to the war, Dumptsy?

DUMPTSY: If they tell me to, madame.

IRENE: You will like being a soldier?

DUMPTSY: Yes—if I'm taken prisoner soon enough.

IRENE: I see. Tell me—who do you think will win?

DUMPTSY: I cannot think, madame. It is all very doubtful. But one thing I can tell you, madame. Whoever wins, it will be the same as last time—Austria will lose. (*The* CHERRYS *come in.*)

IRENE: Austria will lose, and they will all lose. (*She greets* CHERRYS *pleasantly.*) Good evening.

CHERRY: Good evening, madame. (*Draws chair forward to left.* MRS. CHERRY *sits on it.*)

IRENE (*to* DUMPTSY): Bring me some more vodka. Perhaps Mr. and Mrs. Cherry will have some, too.

CHERRY: To tell you the truth, madame—

MRS. CHERRY: I'd love to. I've never tasted vodka.

IRENE: Ah—then it is high time. Bring in the bottle.

DUMPTSY: Yes, madame. (*Exits into bar.*)

IRENE: Come and sit down over here. You know, vodka is the perfect stimulant to the appetite. It is so much better than that hybrid atrocity, the American cocktail!

CHERRY: To tell you the truth, madame—we've already dined.

IRENE: Then it is just as good as a liqueur.

MRS. CHERRY: We didn't really dine at all. We merely looked at the minestrone and the Parmesan cheese—we felt too depressed to eat anything.

IRENE: I know. It is the altitude. (DUMPTSY *enters from bar with bottle of vodka and three more glasses already poured, places them on table, picks up newspaper which* QUILLERY *left on table, exits into bar.*) After the first exhilaration there comes a depressive reaction, especially for you, who are accustomed to the heavy Pickwickian atmosphere of England.

CHERRY: Oh—you know England, madame?

IRENE (*fondly*): Of course I know England! My governess was a sweet old ogre from your north country—and when I was a very little girl I used to visit often at Sandringham.

CHERRY (*impressed*): Sandringham? ⎱ (*Speak together.*)
MRS. CHERRY: The palace? ⎰

IRENE: Yes. That was before your time, my dear. In the days of King Edward and the beautiful Alexandra. (*Sighs a little for those days.*) I used to have such fun playing with my cousin David. Of course, I was much smaller than he. And when he tried to teach me to play cricket, and I could not swing the bat properly, he would say, "Oh, you Russians, you will never be civilized!" (CHERRY *laughs.*) When I went home to Petersburg, I told my uncle, the Tsar, what David had said, and he was so amused! But come now— you must drink your vodka. (*They rise, lift their glasses.*) A toast! To his most gracious majesty, the King! (*They clink glasses.*) God bless him! (*All three drink,* MRS. CHERRY *coughs.* IRENE, *to* MRS. CHERRY.) No—no! Drink it right down. Comme ça! (*She swallows it in a gulp as do the* CHERRYS.) Poor child! The second glass will go more easily. (*Refills glasses from bottle as they sit.*) I used to laugh so at your funny British Tommies in Archangel. How they all hated vodka, until one of them thought of mixing it with beer.

MRS. CHERRY: How loathsome!

IRENE: It was! But I shall be forever grateful to them—those Tommies. They saved my life when I escaped from the Soviets. For days and nights—I don't know how many—I was driving through the snow—snow—snow—snow—it was, in a little sleigh, with the body of my father beside me, and the wolves running along like an escort of dragoons. You know—you always think of wolves as howling constantly, don't you?

CHERRY: Why, yes—I suppose one does.

IRENE: Well, they don't. No, these wolves don't howl! They are horribly, confidently silent. I think silence is so much more terrifying, don't you?

CHERRY: Yes! You must have been terribly afraid.

IRENE: No, I was not afraid—not for myself. No, it was the thought of my father . . .

MRS. CHERRY: Please! I know you don't want to talk about it any more.

IRENE: Oh, no—it is so long ago now. But I shall never forget the moment when I came through that haze of delirium, and saw the faces of your Tommies! Those simple, friendly faces. And the snow—and the wolves—and the terrible cold —p-s-s-t! they was all gone—and I was looking at Kew Gardens on a Sunday afternoon, (WEBER *comes in*) with the sea of golden daffodils—"fluttering and dancing in the breezes."

WEBER: Shall we go in to dinner now, Irene? (CHERRY *rises.*)

IRENE: What is that poem— Yes, yes, all right, Achille. (WEBER *exits.* IRENE *and* MRS. CHERRY *rise, pick up glasses.*) Now, remember— (*They lift their glasses.*) Go! (*All three drink. To* MRS. CHERRY.) You feel better now?

MRS. CHERRY: Yes, madame.

IRENE: And now you must make another try to eat something.

CHERRY (*picks up* IRENE's *purse off table*): Thank you so much, madame.

IRENE: And later on, we must all be here for that Mr.—? What's his name?

CHERRY: Van?

IRENE: Van's entertainment—and we must all applaud vigorously. (*Crosses a few steps toward* CHERRY, *who gives her back her purse.*)

MRS. CHERRY: We shall, madame.

CHERRY: He's such a nice chap, isn't he?

IRENE: Oh yes—and a real artist, too.

CHERRY: Oh—you've seen him? (*The three start to go out.*)

IRENE: Oh, yes—I've seen him somewhere. In some café chantant, somewhere. I forget just where it was. You know when you are traveling . . . you don't know if it is Wednesday or Rome or what—

ACT II

SCENE 2

SCENE: *The same. About eleven o'clock.* WEBER *is sitting, sipping brandy.* CAPTAIN *is standing, hat in hand.*

CAPTAIN: Monsieur Weber, the situation is puzzling and alarming!

WEBER: You have received no *definite* news?

CAPTAIN: I have been listening to the radio. Utter bedlam! Of course, every government has imposed the strictest censorship—but they can't silence the intimation of chaos. It is very frightening—like one of those films where ghostly hands suddenly reach in and switch off all the lights.

WEBER: Any suggestion of air raids?

CAPTAIN: None—but there is ominous quiet from Paris. Think of it—Paris—utterly silent! Only one station there is sending messages, and they are in code.

WEBER: Probably instructions to the frontier.

CAPTAIN: I heard a man in Prague saying something that sounded interesting, but him I could not understand. Then I turned to London, hopefully, and listened to a gentleman describing the disastrous effects of ivy upon that traditional institution, the oak tree.

WEBER: Well—we shall soon know. . . . There'll be no trouble about crossing the frontier tomorrow?

CAPTAIN: Oh, no, Monsieur Weber. Except that I am still a little worried about madame's passport. (*A faint sound of airplanes heard approaching.*)

61

WEBER: That will be all right. (*Takes out leather cigar case.*) Have a cigar, Captain?

CAPTAIN: No, thank you.

IRENE (*appears at top of stairs smoking a long, Russian cigarette; comes forward*): Do you hear the sound of airplanes, Captain? (*All stop to listen intently.* CAPTAIN *dashes to window, looks upward through Venetian blind.*)

CAPTAIN: It is our bombers. One—two—three. Seven of them. Seven out of eighteen. You will excuse me? (*Salutes, dashes out.*)

WEBER: Seven out of eighteen! Not bad, for Italians.

IRENE (*standing on platform, two steps up; speaks clear English*): I'm so happy for you, Achille.

WEBER: What was that, my dear?

IRENE: I said—I'm so happy for you.

WEBER: Happy? Why? (*He smiles.*)

IRENE: All this great, wonderful death and destruction. And you promoted it!

WEBER: Don't give me too much credit, Irene. (*Sound of airplanes begins to die out.*)

IRENE: But I *know* what you've done.

WEBER: Yes, my dear. You know a great deal. But don't forget to do honor to Him—up there—who put fear into man. I am but the humble instrument of His divine will.

IRENE (*looking upward sympathetically*): Yes—that's quite true. We don't do half enough justice to Him. Poor, lonely old soul. Sitting up in heaven, with nothing to do but play solitaire. Poor, dear God. Playing Idiot's Delight. The game that never means anything, and never ends.

WEBER: What an engaging fancy you have, my dear.

IRENE: Yes.

WEBER: It is the quality in you that fascinates me most. Limitless imagination! It is what has made you such an admirable, brilliant liar. Am I right? (*Cuts end of cigar with cutter.*)

IRENE: Of course you are right. Had I been bound by any

stuffy respect for the truth, I should never have escaped from the Soviets.

WEBER: I'm sure of it.

IRENE: Did I ever tell you of my escape from the Soviets?

WEBER: You have told me about it at least eleven times. And each time it was different. (*Lights cigar.*)

IRENE: Oh, well, that is because I have made several escapes. I am always making escapes, Achille. When I am worrying about you, and your career, I have to run away from the terror of my own thoughts. So I amuse myself by studying the faces of the people I see. Just the ordinary, little people. (*She is speaking in a tone that is sweetly sadistic.*) That young English couple, for instance. I was watching them during dinner, sitting close together, holding hands, and rubbing their knees together under the table. And I saw him in his nice, smart, British uniform, shooting a little pistol at a tank. And the tank rolled over him. And his fine strong body, that was so full of the capacity for ecstasy, was a mass of mashed flesh and bones—a smear of purple blood—like a stepped-on snail. But before that moment of death, he consoled himself by thinking: "Thank God *she* is safe! She is bearing the child I gave her, and he will live to see a better world." But I know where she is. She is lying in a cellar that has been wrecked by an air raid, and the embryo from her womb is splattered against the face of a— dead bishop? That is the kind of thought with which I amuse myself, Achille. And it makes me very proud to think I am so close to you—who made all this possible.

WEBER: Do you talk in this whimsical vein to many people?

IRENE: No. I betray my thoughts to nobody but you. You know I am shut off from the world. I am a contented prisoner in your ivory tower.

WEBER: I'm beginning to wonder about that.

IRENE: Why? You think I could interest myself in somebody else?

WEBER: No—my dear. I am merely wondering whether the

time has come for you to turn commonplace, like all the others?

IRENE: The others?

WEBER: All those who have shared my life. My former wife now boasts that she abandoned me because part of my income is derived from the sale of poison gas. Revolvers and rifles and bullets she did not mind—because they are used by sportsmen. Battleships, too, are permissible; they look so splendid in the news films. But she could not stomach poison gas. (*Drops ashes in ashtray on table.*) So now she is married to an anemic duke, and the large fortune that she obtained from me enables the duke to indulge his principal passion, which is the slaughtering of wild animals, like rabbits, and pigeons and rather small deer. My wife is presumably happy with him. I am glad you are not a fool as she was, Irene.

IRENE: No. I don't care for battleships. And I shall not marry an anemic duke.

WEBER: But—there is something a little reminiscent in the gaudy picture you paint of a wrecked cellar. I gather that this young couple has touched a tender spot, eh?

IRENE: Oh, Achille!

WEBER: Apply your intelligence!

IRENE: I do!

WEBER (*quietly, but with rapier-like thrusts*): Ask yourself: Why shouldn't they die? And who are the greater criminals —those who sell the instruments of death, or those who buy them, and use them? You know there is no logical reply to that.

IRENE: No.

WEBER: But all these little people like your new friends—they all consider me an arch-villain because I furnish them with what they want—the illusion of power. Big guns—to protect them from the consequences of their own obvious inferiority! That is what they vote for in their pious governments, what they cheer for on their national holidays—what they glorify in their anthems, and their monuments, and their waving flags! They shout bravely about something they call "national honor"! And what does it amount to? Mistrust of the motives of everyone else! Dog in the manger defense of what they've got, and greed for the other fellow's possessions! Honor! Honor among thieves! I assure you, Irene— that for such *little* people the deadliest weapons are the most merciful. (CHERRY *is heard singing offstage "I went down to St. James infirmary."*) I hoped I would never have to explain such obvious things to you. And now I must go up— and see about— (MR. *and* MRS. CHERRY *enter. They are in high spirits now.* AUGUSTE *enters from bar.*)

IRENE (*puts out cigarette; resumes Russian accent*): Ah! Mr. and Mrs. Cherry!

CHERRY: Hello, there!

IRENE: You have dined well?

MRS. CHERRY: Superbly!

CHERRY: We ate everything—up to and including the zabaglione.

IRENE: You may thank the vodka for that. Vodka never fails in an emergency. (*Lights another cigarette.*)

CHERRY: We do so, and we thank you, madame.

IRENE: May I introduce Monsieur Weber, Mr. and Mrs. Cherry. (*"How do you do's" from the* CHERRYS *and* WEBER. DON *enters in dinner jacket.*)

DON: Bonsoir, madame, Monsieur Weber. We're going to have a little cabaret show for you now, madame. (*Goes to arch, looks offstage.* MUSICIANS *enter through arch and go onto platform, take their places.*)

WEBER: I don't think I shall wait for it, my dear.

IRENE: But you must—please, Achille. Mr. Van is a real artist. You will be so amused.

WEBER (*sits opposite her at table*): Very well, Irene. (CHERRY *orders two demitasses from* AUGUSTE. AUGUSTE *comes to* WEBER, *who gives his order for one brandy.* AUGUSTE *bows, exits into bar.*)

DON (*comes to table, his tone blandly confidential*): I can't vouch for the quality of the entertainment. But it may be unintentionally amusing.

IRENE: We shall love it.

CHERRY: I think it's a splendid idea, Mr. Navadel.

DON: Oh, thank you. We try to contrive some novelty for our guests each evening. Won't you sit down? (*The* ROSSIS *enter in evening clothes.* SIGNOR ROSSI *is left of* SIGNORA ROSSI *and she is holding him by the arm.* AUGUSTE *enters from bar with two demitasses and a liqueur glass on tray.*)

CHERRY (*takes out cigarette case, offers it to* MRS. CHERRY): Have a cigar, darling? (*Laughs, takes a cigarette for himself. Following conversations go on simultaneously as* CHERRY *speaks to* IRENE, DON *speaks to the* ROSSIS, DUMPTSY *speaks with* DOCTOR.)

CHERRY (*to* IRENE): Do you have any zabaglione in Russia?

IRENE: No, that is purely an Italian dish. Do you like it?

CHERRY: Yes, very much.

MRS. CHERRY: I don't. (AUGUSTE *serves* CHERRYS *with coffee and serves* WEBER *with liqueur.*)

DON (*as he shows* ROSSIS *to seat in front of bar*): Signor Rossi —signora—prego—vieni qui—

ROSSI: Ah, Signor Navadel! Buona sera. Grazie, grazie per l'invitazione.

DON: Buona appetita—sta sera?

ROSSI: Si, si, mangia bene sta sera.

DON: Buona.

SIGNORA ROSSI: Vedremo teatro di Stati Uniti?

DON: Si, come piccolo teatro americano.

ROSSI (*to* DON): Successo, signore, successo! (*To* SIGNORA ROSSI.) Sedetevi, carina. (*They sit.* DOCTOR *appears in arch and* DUMPTSY *with two chairs nested together bumps into him.*)

DUMPTSY: Entschuldigen Sie, Herr Doktor.

DOCTOR: Schon wieder was los?

DUMPTSY: Heut' was ganz spezielles—der Mr. Van und seine Tanzmädeln, Gott! Haben sie flinke Beine. Pst! Pst! Es wird Ihnen glänzend gefallen, Herr Doktor.

DOCTOR: Jawohl! (DUMPTSY *places chairs around table in front of steps and* PITTALUGA *comes forward to superintend.* HARRY *enters wearing a dinner jacket.* DON *stands at right of piano.*)

HARRY (*in arch*): All set, Don?

DON: Quite ready whenever you are.

HARRY: Are the lights O.K.?

DON: Yes, everything is ready.

HARRY: Give me a spot and a little fanfare. You know a little —tra—tra—tra.

DON (*turns to leader*): A fanfare, please. (MUSICIANS *play a fanfare. The spot goes on and lights go off.* ANNA, *the maid, comes out on balcony and watches the show.*)

HARRY (*makes entrance, on which there is considerable applause; puts straw hat and swagger stick on top of piano*): Before we begin, folks, I just want to explain that we haven't had much chance to rehearse with my good friend, Signor Palota, and his talented little band here. (*Applauds.* PALOTA *rises and bows. All on stage applaud. He indicates orchestra, and applauds. Everyone on stage applauds, too.*) So—we must crave your indulgence and beg you to give us a break if the rhythm isn't all strictly kosher.

DON (*laughs heartily*): Ho—ho—ho.

HARRY: Thank you very much. (*Shakes* DON's *hand.*) All we ask of you, kind friends, is "The Christian pearl of Charity," to quote our great American poet, John Greenleaf Whittier. (*Applauds. Everyone on stage applauds.*) Oakie-doakie, signore, take it away.

ROSSI (*to* HARRY): Successo, signore! (PITTALUGA *exits. Music starts playing, and* HARRY *begins singing. After first verse sung by* HARRY, *lights go on as* GIRLS *in costume appear three by three in arch.* GIRLS *go into a dancing routine as* HARRY *crosses in front of them and to piano, keeps time to music by hitting top of piano. During the number* PITTALUGA *enters, followed by* CAPTAIN, FIRST OFFICER, MAJOR *and* THIRD OFFICER.)

PITTALUGA: Stiamo dando un trattenimento di gala, Capitano!

CAPTAIN: Ah, che—belle ragazze!

PITTALUGA: Potrebbe divertirvi e i vostri compagni, guardare —questo spettacolo.

CAPTAIN: Ma proprio— !

HARRY (*crosses through line of girls to center, holds up hand and stops music*): Customers, customers— (*To* CAPTAIN, *who has come to center with* OFFICERS *following.*) What's up, Captain?

CAPTAIN: Some of my friends have come here to admire your art.

HARRY (*to* CAPTAIN): Tell the boys to sit down. (*To violinist.*) Give the boys a little tra—tra. (CAPTAIN *and* OFFICERS *cross to table, followed by* PITTALUGA. DUMPTSY *exits into bar. Orchestra strikes up the Fascist song "Giovinezza" and the* CAPTAIN *and* OFFICERS *at table raise their arms in Fascist salute. The* ROSSIS *also rise and give salute.* CHERRY *and* DON *rise and stand at attention. . . .* GIRLS *try to imitate the* OFFICERS' *salute by waving their arms. After song the music segues into the dance,* GIRLS *resume their dancing and* OFFICERS *sit at table.* CAPTAIN *stands on platform of stairs, two steps up.* PITTALUGA, *after showing* OFFICERS *to their places, exits, and returns immediately with two more chairs nested together, which he brings down to their table, then to arch and greets* SECOND *and* FOURTH OFFICERS, *who drift in. The dance over,* DUMPTSY *enters from bar with demitasse and sugar and creamer on tray—crosses in front of* GIRLS *and serves* DOCTOR. *There is applause from everyone on stage and music segues into "Swanee River."*

HARRY (*crosses through girls and begins to sing*):

> They used to sing the Swanee River
> > And Old Black Joe.
> They used to do the soft-shoe essence
> > But that was long, long ago.
> They left their mammies—Mammy!
> > Down in Dixie
> And they began to roam.

Now they're a lot of Harlem nuttin's
Far from the old folks at home.
(HARRY *and* GIRLS *go into a soft-shoe dance to the tune of*
"*Swanee River.*")
Now they're a lot of Harlem nuttin's
Far from the old folks at home.
(*As drummer accentuates last note,* HARRY *does a bump. They
go into a dance routine at the end of which* GIRLS *pick*
HARRY *up and take him off into bar.* HARRY *throws kisses
to his audience as* GIRLS *are taking him off. As he passes*
ROSSI *he shakes hands with him. Much applause on stage
and particularly from* OFFICERS, *who rise and shout "Brava"
—"Bravissima"—"Bis," and stamp their feet with enthusiasm.*
GIRLS *re-enter from bar, followed by* HARRY. *They bow and
exit, as* HARRY *gyrates like a cheer leader, bringing on more
applause. As* GIRLS *go to rear,* DUMPTSY, *followed by*
AUGUSTE, *exits into bar. During applause* OFFICERS *ad lib,
and indicate to* CAPTAIN *that they would like him to ask*
HARRY *to let the* GIRLS *sit down with them.*)

CAPTAIN (*crosses to* HARRY): My friends wish to know re-
spectfully if the young ladies would care to join them in a
little drink?

HARRY: Why, certainly!

CAPTAIN (*crosses to* OFFICERS): Sarrano con noi subito.

HARRY: Come on in, girls. (GIRLS *enter from arch, led by*
ELAINE.)

ELAINE: Say, Harry, what do we do now?

HARRY (*indicates* OFFICERS): Join the Army! (ELAINE, FRAN-
CINE *and* BEBE *cross to* MAJOR *and* OFFICERS. CAPTAIN *goes
up two steps, stands on platform.* BEBE *decides* DOCTOR *is
fair game and sits on his lap.* DOCTOR *rises indignantly,*
HARRY *apologizes to him, at same time pushes* BEBE *to
right. During this,* SECOND OFFICER *is trying to converse
with* SHIRLEY *and* FOURTH OFFICER *is similarly engaged
with* BEULAH *and* EDNA. *When* HARRY *goes to piano with*
SHIRLEY *and* EDNA, FOURTH OFFICER *takes* BEULAH *into
bar.*) And now, while I give some of the girls a little rest—

I'll slay you with a little specialty of my own. (*During above speech* DRUMMER *and* VIOLINIST *softly play a hoochy-koochy melody. All on stage applaud.*) Your strict attention is not obligatory! (HARRY *sits at piano.* SHIRLEY *is left of him at piano,* EDNA *right of him.*) My next number will be a little song entitled "Where have you been all my life—and why didn't you stay there?" (*Looks significantly at* IRENE *and starts to play the vamp of "Pardon My Southern Accent."*)

SHIRLEY, EDNA: Yeah, man! Swing it, honey! (HARRY, SHIRLEY *and* EDNA *begin singing in swing time.*)

> Pardon My Southern Accent
> Pardon My Southern Drawl.
> It May Sound Funny
> Ah, But Honey, I Love Y'all.*

(HARRY *and* EDNA *go into their specialty, each singing a verse alone.*)

EDNA: How'm I doin', Harry?

HARRY (*singing*): Not—so good!

ALL THREE (*sing*): What do—whada ya do! Wha do—whada ya do. (SHIRLEY *and* EDNA *gesture with their hands.* HARRY *and* SHIRLEY *each sing a verse.*)

ALL THREE (*singing*): Wha do—whada ya do. Wha do—whada ya do.

HARRY (*sings alone*):

> This little girl speaks German.
> She counts up to sixteen—

SHIRLEY: Eins—zwei—drei—vier—fünf—and—sex—

HARRY: Oh, Shirley, keep it clean. (*All three start singing chorus of "Pardon My Southern Accent."* DUMPTSY *enters from bar with two buckets filled with champagne bottles, followed by* AUGUSTE, *bearing six glasses on tray. As they enter,* WEBER *rises, excuses himself to* IRENE, *goes up two steps and talks with* CAPTAIN. DUMPTSY *and* AUGUSTE *serve* OFFICERS *and* GIRLS. DUMPTSY *crosses in front of group,*

*exits into bar, returns at once with bucket of champagne
and tray with three glasses, serves* ROSSIS *and* FOURTH OF-
FICER *and exits into bar.* QUILLERY, *much excited, enters,
looks wild-eyed at the gay crowd.*)

QUILLERY: Do you know what has happened?

DON: I told you we didn't want you here. ⎱ (*Spoken*

PITTALUGA: We're having an entertainment ⎰ *together.*)
here.

QUILLERY: An entertainment! Yes!

HARRY: If you'll just sit down, pal . . .

QUILLERY: An entertainment—while Paris is in ruins!

CHERRY: What? What is that you're saying?

QUILLERY: They've bombed Paris! The Fascisti have bombed
Paris!

DON: What? But it can't be possible— (HARRY ⎱ (*Spoken*
keeps on playing.) ⎰ *together.*)

CHERRY: But how do you know this?

QUILLERY: It is on the wireless—everywhere. I talked to one
of their mechanics, who was on the flight, and saw, with his
own eyes—

HARRY: Please sit down, pal. We're trying to give a little entertainment—

QUILLERY: But tonight—while you sit here laughing and drinking—(HARRY *stops playing piano*)—Italian planes dropped
twenty thousand kilos of bombs on Paris!

CHERRY: Good God!

QUILLERY: God knows how many people are killed! God
knows how much of life and beauty is forever destroyed!
(*Turns toward* OFFICERS.) And you sit here, drinking with
them—the murderers! (*Breaks away from* DON, PITTALUGA
and CHERRY *who are holding him and swiftly crosses to*
OFFICERS. HARRY *rises.* AUGUSTE *hurriedly crosses to piano.*)
They did it. It was their planes from that field down there!
(CHERRY *swiftly crosses to left of* QUILLERY *as* HARRY
rushes to CAPTAIN, *who comes down from platform threateningly.*)

HARRY: Hey, Captain, speak to your men before anything starts!

SHIRLEY (*as* HARRY *goes to right*): Keep out of this, Harry! (CAPTAIN *motions* OFFICERS, *who are muttering, to be still.* DON *and* PITTALUGA *also cross to right.*)

QUILLERY (*to* OFFICERS): I say, God damn you! Assassins!

MAJOR, FIRST, THIRD OFFICERS and SECOND OFFICER (*jump to their feet*): Assassini!

CAPTAIN (*turns right and commands*): Vi accomodiate! Io mi occupero di lui! Io sono il capo qui!

HARRY (*as he and* CHERRY *and* DON *drag* QUILLERY *across stage*): Shut up! (MRS. CHERRY *has risen during melee, as have the* ROSSIS. PITTALUGA *stands right of* MRS. CHERRY.)

QUILLERY: You see, you see, we stand together. France—England—America! ALLIES!

HARRY: Shut up, will you?

QUILLERY: They don't dare fight against the power of England and France! The free democracies against the Fascist tyranny! (FOURTH OFFICER *and* BEULAH *enter from bar.*)

HARRY: Stop fluctuating, will you?

QUILLERY: England and France are fighting for the hopes of mankind!

HARRY: Sure, and a minute ago, England was a butcher in a dress suit. Now we're allies!

QUILLERY: We stand together.

CHERRY: Yes, I know, but—

QUILLERY: We stand together forever. (*Turns to* OFFICERS.) I say, God damn them. God damn the villains that sent them on their errand of death!

CAPTAIN (*takes few steps toward* QUILLERY, *slapping his right boot with his riding crop*): If you don't close your mouth, Frenchman, we shall be forced to arrest you.

QUILLERY: Go on, Fascisti! Commit national suicide. That's the last gesture left to you toy soldiers. (FRANCINE *rises, goes to* MAJOR.)

FRANCINE (*sotto voce*): What's the matter—what's happened?

MAJOR (*gently pushes her aside*): No, no! (*Signals to* FIRST *and* THIRD OFFICERS *to keep her quiet.*)

(*Spoken through other dialogue going on.*)

HARRY: It's all right, Captain. Mr. Quillery is for peace. He's going back to France to stop the war.

QUILLERY (*turns on* HARRY): You're not authorized to speak for me. I am competent to say what I feel. And what I say is, (*breaks through* HARRY *and* CHERRY, *who still hold his arms*) down with the Fascisti! Abbasso gli Fascisti!

CAPTAIN (*ordinarily gentle, now hot with rage*): Attenti!

QUILLERY: Vive la France! (HARRY *claps his left hand over* QUILLERY'S *mouth.*)

CAPTAIN: Vi dichiaro sotto arresto! (*To* SECOND OFFICER.) Molinari, Vieni con me porco francese! (SECOND OFFICER *grabs* QUILLERY *from* HARRY *and* CAPTAIN *grabs* QUILLERY *from his end. They exit followed by* MAJOR. FIRST, THIRD *and* FOURTH OFFICERS *follow to arch.* ROSSI *collapses from excitement on seat.*)

BEULAH: Did he hurt you, Harry?

CHERRY (*to* HARRY): You'd better carry on with your turn, old boy. (WEBER *exits in gallery as* QUILLERY *is taken out.*)

HARRY: No, pal, the act is cold. (*Claps his hands to orchestra.*) Give us some music, signore. Let dancing become general! (*Orchestra starts playing.*)

SHIRLEY: Come on, get hot! (*Begins singing the number.* HARRY *picks up his straw hat and swagger stick and starts to do a dance routine, notices* IRENE *sitting alone, puts hat and stick on piano and crosses to her.* OFFICERS *in arch, when they see that* QUILLERY *is disposed of, come forward.* FIRST OFFICER *dances with* BEBE. THIRD OFFICER *crosses, dances with* FRANCINE. FOURTH OFFICER *dances with* BEULAH. DON *dances with* EDNA. CHERRY *dances with his wife.* DOCTOR *sits where he was.* AUGUSTE *exits hurriedly into bar and returns almost immediately with glass of water, which he gives to* SIGNORA ROSSI, *who in turn tries to revive*

Rossi *as* Pittaluga *comes to them. All above happens simultaneously.*)

HARRY (*to* IRENE): Would you care to dance?

IRENE: Why—why, thank you. (*She rises and they dance. The color wheels on both sides of stage now go into action as rest of lights go out.*)

ELAINE (*at front of stage*): Hey, Shirley! I'm all alone.

SHIRLEY: O.K. (*She starts to cross right as curtain falls.*)

ACT II

SCENE 3

SCENE: *Later that night. Everyone seems to have gone to bed.* IRENE *and* HARRY *are alone. She is telling the story of her life. He is listening with fascination and doubt.*

IRENE: I was young and strong but—my father was old. The hardships of that terrible journey had broken his body. But his spirit was strong—the spirit that is Russia. He lay there, in that little boat, and he looked up at me. Never can I forget this face, so thin, so white, so beautiful in the starlight. And he said to me, "Irene—little daughter—" and then—he died. For four days, I was alone, with his body, in that little boat sailing through the storms of the Black Sea. I had no food—no water—I was in agony from the bayonet wounds of the Bolsheviki. I knew I must die. But then—an American cruiser rescued me. May God bless those good men! I've talked too much about myself. What about you, my friend?

HARRY: Oh—I'm not very interesting. I'm just what I seem to be. (*Looks at her significantly.*)

IRENE: I do not believe it. C'est impossible!

HARRY: Oh, c'est possible! The facts of my case are eloquent. I'm a potential genius—reduced to piloting six blondes through the Balkans.

IRENE: But there is something you hide from the world—even, I suspect, from yourself. How did you acquire your superior education?

HARRY: I worked my way through college selling encyclopedias.

IRENE: I knew it! I knew you had culture! What college was it?

HARRY: Oh—just any college. You know my sales talk was so good I finally fell for it myself and I bought the whole God damned encyclopedia. And I read it all.

IRENE: How did you?

HARRY: Oh, traveling around, in day coaches, depot hotels, Foxtime dressing rooms. It was worth the money.

IRENE: And how much of all this have you retained?

HARRY (*significantly*): I—never forget anything.

IRENE: Oh, dear, how unfortunate for you! Tell me, does your encyclopedia help you in your dealings with those young ladies?

HARRY: Yes, Mrs. Weber. . . . I get considerable benefit from reading about the great courtesans, and getting to understand their technique. . . .

IRENE: Forgive me for interrupting—but that is not my name.

HARRY: Oh—pardon me, I thought . . .

IRENE: I know—I know what you thought. Monsieur Weber and I are associated in a sort of a—business way.

HARRY: I see.

IRENE: He does me the honor to consult me in matters of policy.

HARRY: That's quite an honor! Business is pretty good, isn't it?!

IRENE: I gather you are one of those noble souls who do not entirely approve of the munitions industry?

HARRY: No—I'm not noble. Your friend is just another salesman. I make it a point never to criticize anybody else's racket.

IRENE: Monsieur Weber is a very distinguished man. He has rendered very distinguished services to all the governments of the world. For that he has been decorated with the Legion of Honor, the Order of the White Eagle, the Order of St. James of the Sword, the Military Order of Christ—

HARRY: The Military Order of Christ? I never heard of that one.

IRENE: No? Haven't you? Oh, well, it is from Portugal. There are many others.

HARRY: Have you ever been in America?

IRENE: Oh, yes—I have seen it *all*—New York, Washington, Palm Beach!

HARRY: No, I said America. Have you ever been in the West?

IRENE: Certainly. I flew across your continent. There are many White Russians in California.

HARRY: Did you ever happen to make any parachute landings in places like Iowa, or Kansas, or Nebraska?

IRENE: I have seen enough of your countrymen to know that you are typical.

HARRY (*coyly*): Oh, no—oh, no!

IRENE: Oh, yes you are. You are just like all of them—an ingenuous, sentimental idealist. You believe in the goodness of human nature, don't you?

HARRY: Well, what if I do? I've known millions of people, intimately—and I never found more than one out of a hundred that I didn't like, once you got to know them.

IRENE: That is very charming—but it is naïve.

HARRY: Maybe so. But experience prevents my working up much enthusiasm over anyone who considers the human race just so many clay pigeons, even if he does belong to the Military Order of Christ.

IRENE: If you came from an older culture, you would realize that men like Monsieur Weber are necessary to civilization.

HARRY: Is that so?

IRENE: I mean the sort of civilization that we have got.

HARRY: Oh!

IRENE: People consider him an arch-villain because it is his duty to stir up a little trouble here and there to stimulate the sale of his products. Do you understand me, my friend?

HARRY: I shouldn't wonder.

IRENE: He is a true man of the world. He is above petty nationalism; he can be a Frenchman in France—a German in Germany—a Greek—a Turk—whenever the occasion needs it.

HARRY: Yeah, that little Quillery, he was an internationalist too. He believed in the brotherhood, but the minute he got a whiff of gunpowder he began to spout hate and revenge. And now I suppose those nice, polite wops will have to shut him up with a firing squad.

IRENE (*takes cigarette from her case*): It is a painful necessity.

HARRY: Well, it just demonstrates the sort of little trouble your friend stirs up. (*He takes out his lighter and lights her cigarette.*)

IRENE: Do you know you can be extremely rude?

HARRY: Well, I'm very sorry if I've hurt your feelings about Mr. Weber, but he happens to represent the one percent that I *don't* like.

IRENE: I was not referring to that. Why do you stare at me so?

HARRY: Was I staring?

IRENE: Steadily. Ever since we arrived here this afternoon. Why do you do it?

HARRY: I was thinking I could notice a funny resemblance to somebody I used to know.

IRENE: You should know better than to tell a woman that she resembles somebody else. We none of us like to think our appearance is commonplace.

HARRY: The one you look like wasn't commonplace.

IRENE: Oh! She was someone near and dear to you?

HARRY: It was somebody who occupies a unique shrine in the temple of my memory.

IRENE: What a glowing tribute. The temple of your memory— Oh, dear! Well, now I am keeping you from your duties.

HARRY: What duties?

IRENE: Shouldn't you be worrying about those young ladies?

HARRY: They're all right; they've gone to bed.

IRENE: But there are several Italian officers about. Aren't you the chaperon?

HARRY: I leave the girls to their own resources, of which they have plenty. (*Stares hard at her.*) Were you always a blonde?

IRENE: Yes—as far back as I can remember.

HARRY: You don't mind my asking?

IRENE: No, not at all. And now, may I ask you something?

HARRY: Please do so.

IRENE: Why do you waste yourself in this degraded business? Touring about with those obvious little harlots?

HARRY: You mean you think I'm fitted for something that requires a little more mentality?

IRENE: Oh, yes.

HARRY: How do you know so much about me? (*All through this scene* HARRY *is studying her, trying to fit together the pieces of the jigsaw puzzle of his memory.*)

IRENE: For one thing, I saw your performance tonight.

HARRY: You thought it was punk?

IRENE: No. I thought it was unworthy.

HARRY: It was unfortunately interrupted. If you'd seen the little bit—

IRENE: I saw enough. You are a very bad dancer.

HARRY: The King of Romania thought I was pretty good.

IRENE: Just the same—my opinion remains unchanged.

HARRY: Well, I'll admit I've done better things. Would it surprise you to know that I was once with a mind-reading act? (*Stares hard at her.*)

IRENE: Really?

HARRY: Yeah.

IRENE: Now, look, you are staring at me like that again.

HARRY: Have you ever been in Omaha?

IRENE: Have I ever been where?

HARRY: In Omaha.

IRENE: Omaha? Where is that? Persia?

HARRY: No. Nebraska. That's one of our states.

IRENE: Really?

HARRY: I was there once with the greatest act of my career. I was the stooge for Zuleika, the Mind Reader. At least she called me her stooge. But I was the one that did all the brain work. (IRENE *laughs.*) But that didn't bother me none.

79

IRENE: And she read people's minds?

HARRY: I did it for her. I passed through the audience and fed her the cues. We were sensational, played the finest picture theatres in the key cities. Zuleika sat on the stage, blind-folded—usually blind drunk.

IRENE: Oh, dear. And was *she* the one that I resemble?

HARRY: No! There was another act on the same bill. A troupe of Russians . . .

IRENE: Russians?

HARRY: Singers, mandolin players, squat dancers. One of them was a redheaded dame. She was fascinated by our act, kept pestering me to teach her the code. She said she could do it better than Zuleika.

IRENE: Those poor Russians. There are so many of them all over the world. You know that some of them are completely counterfeit.

HARRY: Yeah, this dame was counterfeit, all right.

IRENE: She was?

HARRY: In fact she was the very finest liar I ever met. She kept after me so much that finally I asked her to come up to my room at the hotel one night, and we'd talk it over.

IRENE: I hope you didn't give her that code.

HARRY: No. After the week in Omaha the bill split. The Russians went to Sioux Falls, we went on Interstate Time. I played with Zuleika for another year until the drink finally got her and she couldn't retain. So the act busted up. I always hoped I'd meet up with that redhead again sometime. She might have been good. She had the voice for it, and a kind of overtone of mystery.

IRENE: It is a characteristic gypsy quality. And you never saw her again?

HARRY: No!

IRENE: No?

HARRY: No? No!

IRENE: Perhaps it is just as well. She could not have been so very clever—to be duped so easily into coming to your room.

HARRY: She wasn't being duped. She knew what she was doing. If there was any duping going on, she's the one that did it.

IRENE: She did make an impression!

HARRY (*looking straight at her*): I was crazy about her. She was womanhood at its most desirable—and most unreliable.

IRENE: And you such a connoisseur! (*She sighs.*) It is getting very late.

HARRY (*rises*): Do you know any Russian music? (*Crosses to piano.*)

IRENE: Oh, yes. When I was a little girl my father used to engage Chaliapin to come often to our house. Oh, those were the days! (*Rises.*) He taught me many songs.

HARRY: Chaliapin, eh? My! Your father spared no expense! (*Sits at piano.*)

IRENE (*crossing toward piano*): Why should he? That was in *old* Russia! (HARRY *starts playing "Kak Stranna.*") Ah, "Kak Stranna" . . . how strange.

HARRY: How very strange! (*Segues into another Russian song.*) Do you know this one?

IRENE (*follows music, singing in Russian*): "Zamiya tziganiya ikh noviy zheeznee ukhaju att vas—"

HARRY: How do you spell that name—Ear-ray-na?

IRENE: "Vi'monya zhaleyte, minya tziganiya—" What did you say?

HARRY: I say, how do you spell that name—Ear-ray-na?

IRENE: Ear-ray-na? I-R-E-N-E. (*As she gives him each letter, he punctuates it with a note on piano, going up scale, and when she finishes, he bangs piano and jumps up.*)

HARRY: That's it! Irene! (*He pronounces it I-reen.*)

IRENE: I-reen?

HARRY: I knew it! You're the one!

IRENE: What one?

HARRY: That redheaded liar! Irene! I knew I could never be mistaken. . . .

IRENE (*laughs*): Ear-ray-na is a very usual name in Russia.

HARRY: I don't care how usual it is. Everything fits together perfectly now. The name—the face—the voice—Chaliapin for a teacher! (IRENE *rocks with laughter, shakes her head negatively*.) Certainly it's you! And it's no good shaking your head or trying to look astounded! Because no matter how much you may lie, you can't deny the fact that you slept with me in the Governor Bryan Hotel in Omaha in the fall of 1925. (IRENE *laughs heartily again and ad libs remonstrating. Crosses right and picks up her purse from table, then crosses left again*.) Go ahead and laugh. That blond hair had me fooled for a while—but now I know it's just as phony as the bayonet wounds—parachute jumps into the jungle—

IRENE (*still laughing*): Oh—you amuse me.

HARRY: It's a pleasure to be entertaining. But you can't get away with it.

IRENE: You amuse me very much indeed.

HARRY: Yeah! Ah, ah!

IRENE: Here we are—on a mountain peak in Bedlam. Tonight, the Italians have bombed Paris. At this moment, the French may be bombing Rome, and the English bombing Germany —and the Soviets bombing Tokyo, and all you worry about is whether I am a girl you once met casually in Omaha. (*She crosses right, laughing heartily*.)

HARRY (*comes down off platform*): Did I say it was casual?

IRENE (*laughing*): Oh, you amuse me very much.

HARRY: I admit it's all very amusing. I've admitted a lot of things, tonight, haven't I? I admitted I was crazy about you, didn't I? Well, why don't you come across and give me a break?

IRENE: You! So troubled—so uncertain about everything.

HARRY: I'm not uncertain about it any more. (*Passionately*.) Oh—there was something about you that was—indelible . . . something I couldn't forget all these years. (WEBER *appears on gallery wearing dressing gown and smoking cigar*.)

WEBER: Forgive me for intruding, Irene. But I suggest that it is time for you to go to bed.

IRENE: Yes. Yes, Achille. At once! (WEBER *treats* HARRY *to a rather disparaging glance and exits*. IRENE *starts upstairs*.)

At once! I am coming. I am coming. Poor Achille! You know, he suffers with the most dreadful insomnia—oh, it is something on his mind. (*At top of stairs.*) He is like Macbeth. Good night, my friend—my funny friend.

HARRY: Good night.

IRENE: Thank you for making me laugh so much—tonight.

HARRY: You know, I could still teach you that code.

IRENE: Perhaps—we shall meet again—in—what was the name of that hotel?

HARRY: The Governor Bryan.

IRENE: Oh, yes! The Governor Bryan! (*Laughing, she exits off gallery.* DUMPTSY *enters from bar, coat off, sleeves rolled up, a large white apron on, and towel in his hand.*)

DUMPTSY: Ach, that was wonderful—that singing and dancing.

HARRY: Thanks, pal. Glad you enjoyed it. (*Picks up straw hat and swagger stick off piano.*)

DUMPTSY: Oh, yes, Mr. Van—that was good.

HARRY: Chaliapin! For God's sake! (*Puts his fist through crown of straw hat, goes to arch.*)

ACT III

SCENE: *The following afternoon. Venetian blinds are up and the waning sun is streaming through window. HARRY, seated at piano smoking a cigarette, is playing an improvised tune. SHIRLEY is darning a pair of black silk stockings which are used in the "number." BEBE stands on platform of first two steps, leaning against balustrade with a small mirror, and a pair of tweezers, plucking at her eyebrows. EDNA is writing letters in a portable writing portfolio. BEULAH is seated in armchair, with cards laid out on table telling ELAINE's fortune. ELAINE is seated right of table. FRANCINE stands behind BEULAH, watching cards.*

SHIRLEY: What's that number, Harry?

HARRY (*curtly*): I don't know.

SHIRLEY: It's pretty.

HARRY: You think so? (*Stops playing and puts his cigarette out in ashtray. Starts to play same number in furious jazz rhythm.*)

BEULAH: You are going to marry.

ELAINE: Again?

BEULAH: The cards indicate *distinctly* two marriages, and maybe a third.

ELAINE (*chewing furiously*): For God's sake!

SHIRLEY (*to HARRY*): We certainly need some new stockings.

HARRY: I'm conscious of that.

BEULAH: Now—let's see what the fates tell us next.

BEBE: Say, Harry—when do we lam it out of here?

HARRY: Ask Beulah. Maybe she can get it out of the cards.

BEULAH: What'd you say, honey?

ELAINE: Ah—don't pay any attention to him.

BEBE: I'll be glad to go. It's kind of spooky around here.

ELAINE: What else do they say about me?

BEULAH: Well, you're going to enter upon a period of very poor health.

ELAINE: When?

BEULAH: Along about your thirty-seventh year.

SHIRLEY: That means any day now.

HARRY (*stops playing*): Listen to me, girls! We can't be wasting our time with card tricks. We've got to do a little rehearsing.

SHIRLEY: Say, Harry—what are you mad about now?

HARRY: Who said I was mad about anything?

SHIRLEY: Well—every time you get yourself into a peeve, you take it out on us. You start hollering, "Come on, girls—we got to rehearse."

HARRY: I am not peeved. Merely a little disgusted. The act needs brushing up.

BEBE: Honestly, Harry—don't you think we know the routine by now?

HARRY: I'm not saying you don't know it. I'm saying your performance last night grieved me and irked me.

FRANCINE: Oh, for God's sake.

HARRY: You had your mind on those officers and not on your work. That kind of attitude went big in Romania, but now we're going to a town where artistry counts. Some day I'll take the bunch of you to see the Russian ballet, give you a rough idea of what dancing really is.

CAPTAIN (*enters*): Your pardon, Mr. Van.

GIRLS: Good afternoon, Captain.

HARRY: Rest, girls, rest. (*To* CAPTAIN.) Any news?

CAPTAIN: Good news, I hope. May I have your passports?

HARRY: Yes, certainly. (*Crosses toward his coat as* BEBE *gets*

passports out of pocket of his coat and gives them to
HARRY.)

CAPTAIN (*crosses to* HARRY): I hope to have definite word
for you very shortly.

HARRY: Oh, thanks. (HARRY *gives him passports.*)

CAPTAIN: Thank you. (*Salutes and starts to go to rear.*)

HARRY: What happened to Mr. Quillery?

CAPTAIN: Mr. Quillery was very injudicious. Very injudicious.
I am glad that you are so much more intelligent. (*Salutes
and goes out.*)

SHIRLEY: Oh, I don't think they could have done anything
cruel to him. They're awfully nice boys, those wops.

HARRY: Yeah, so I observed. . . . Now listen to me, girls.
Geneva's big time, and we've got to be good. You know
your audiences aren't going to be a lot of hunkies, who
don't care what you do as long as you don't wear practically
any pants. These people are big shots. They're mains—
they're used to the best, they're like prime ministers, maha-
rajas, arch-a-bishops. If we click with them, we're all set
for London and Paris. Maybe we'll even get enough money
to get home.

BEBE: Oh—don't speak of such a thing! Home!

HARRY: The trouble with you girls is, you're thinking too
much about your own specialties. You're trying to steal the
act, and you wreck it. Remember what the late Knute
Rockne said: "Somebody else can have the all-star, all-
American aggregations. All *I* ask is a team!" Now, you—
Beulah. You've got plenty of chance to score individually
in your bubble number. But when you come to the chorus
routine, you've got to submerge your genius to the mass.

BEULAH: What do I do wrong?

HARRY: What do you do wrong? Your Maxie Ford is lack-
luster. (*He demonstrates it.*)

SHIRLEY: Come here, Beulah—*I'll* show you.

HARRY: Just a minute, Miss Laughlin. Who's directing this
act, you or me?

SHIRLEY (*good-naturedly slaps his face*): You are, you old poop. But you just don't know the steps. $\left.\begin{array}{c}\end{array}\right\}$ (*Spoken together.*)

ELAINE: Don't let her get fresh, Harry.

BEBE: Slap her down!

SHIRLEY: Give us the music, Harry.

BEULAH: Please, Harry. Shirley just wants to be helpful.

HARRY (*goes to piano*): I feel I ought to resent this.

SHIRLEY: Don't be silly. Give us a pick-up. (HARRY *sits at piano, starts to play chorus "Putting on the Ritz."* FRANCINE *rises, crosses right and sits on chair left of table and lays out cards.* EDNA *rises and crosses right, stands behind* FRANCINE. BEBE *rises, crosses left and stands behind table.* SHIRLEY *and* BEULAH *are doing the number. During this, the following conversation goes on.*)

ELAINE (*still seated*): You know that wop was giving me a play last night?

FRANCINE: You mean the one with the bent nose?

BEBE: I thought he was terrible. But the boy I had is a count.

SHIRLEY (*finishing her demonstration to* BEULAH): Get it? (HARRY *keeps on playing.*)

ELAINE (*taking out a coin*): Well, look what he gave me.

EDNA: What is it?

BEBE: Let me see it.

ELAINE: I don't know what it is.

BEBE (*takes coin*): Looks like money. (*Goes to piano, followed by other* GIRLS *in group.*) What kind of money is this, Harry?

HARRY: What? (*Stops playing.*)

BEBE: What kind of money is this?

HARRY (*looks at it*): That's an old Roman coin.

SHIRLEY: How much is it worth?

HARRY: I haven't looked up the latest rate of exchange on dinars—but, dear, I'm afraid you've been betrayed. (BEBE *gives* ELAINE *the coin.*) Now listen to me, girls, pay attention. I said the act needed improving, and with that in mind . . . (*he rises*) I'm going to retire from all dance routines.

BEBE: What?

ELAINE: Why, Harry.

BEULAH: Why, Harry, we couldn't get along without you.

(Spoken together.)

SHIRLEY: Why, Harry, I hurt you, didn't I! I'm sorry. I didn't mean it.

HARRY: Never mind the regrets, Shirley.

SHIRLEY: Give me a kiss.

HARRY: Save your lipstick.

SHIRLEY: But why do you want to do that?

HARRY: I've decided I'm more of a thinker than a performer. From now on I shall devote myself purely to the creative side of the act, and of course, negotiate all contracts. (*He sits.*)

FRANCINE: What the hell is the matter with you? Have you gone screwy?

BEBE: When did you make up your mind to that, Harry?

(Spoken together.)

HARRY: I've been considering this for some time.

SHIRLEY: Say! What were you talking about to that Russian dame?

HARRY: We discussed world politics.

FRANCINE: Oh!

SHIRLEY (*her elbow on* HARRY's *right shoulder, chin on her hand*): Oh! And how are politics these days?

BEBE: Harry, did you get anywhere near first base?

HARRY: I find it very difficult to explain certain things to you girls. You're children of nature.

SHIRLEY: We're *what?*

BEULAH: He means we're natural.

SHIRLEY: Oh.

HARRY (*to* BEULAH): Oh, God! Never mind, sweetheart. (*To* SHIRLEY.) You'll do the number, Shirley.

SHIRLEY (*pleased*): Me?

BEBE: With that terrible voice?

HARRY (*to* BEBE): She handled it fine that time I had bronchitis in Belgrade. And with a little rehearsing . . . (*turns to*

SHIRLEY) you'll have the whole League of Nations rooting for you. Come on, now! (*Starts playing the verse of "Putting on the Ritz."*)

SHIRLEY (*starts singing*): "Have you seen the well-to-do—" (BEBE *holds her nose in contempt.*) Ah, scram! Take it again, Harry. (HARRY *begins verse again.* BEBE *gets off platform, crosses right; as she passes* SHIRLEY, SHIRLEY *tries to kick her in the behind.*) "Have you seen the well-to-do—"

HARRY: That's fine!

SHIRLEY:

> Up on Lenox Avenue?
> On that famous thoroughfare.

(DON *enters from arch, hat and overcoat on. Stops at right corner of piano.*)

> With their noses in the air.

BEULAH and FRANCINE: Hello, Don.

DON (*takes hat off*): Hello . . . Say, Harry, Captain Locicero has got the orders to let us through and the train leaves at five o'clock.

GIRLS: Hurray!

DON: What a relief to be out of this foul place! (*Goes up steps.*)

HARRY (*still playing*): You going, too, Don?

DON: Yes. There's nothing for me here. As a matter of fact, I'm sick of Europe as a whole. (*At top of stairs.*) I was in town this morning when they shot Quillery. (HARRY *stops playing.*)

BEBE (*looking up at* DON): Shot who?

SHIRLEY: That little guy that bawled out the wops.

BEULAH (*looking up at* DON): They *shot* him? Why did they have to do that?

DON: Well, he asked for it. But even so, it's pretty sickening to see one of your fellow human beings crumpled up in violent death. There'll be lots more like him, and right here, too. The French know about this air base, and pretty soon they'll be over with their bombs. So—it's California here I come! (*Starts to go.*)

HARRY: Yeah, and bump right into the Japs? You'd better stop off at Wichita.

DON: I'll see you on the train. (*Goes out.*)

HARRY: You girls go get yourselves ready.

ELAINE: O.K., Harry. (*She starts for arch, goes out.*)

FRANCINE (*rises, takes cards with her*): Hey! Let's see that coin again.

EDNA: Maybe you can pass it off in a slot machine. (*Exits.*) I just love to hear those wops talk. They make everything sound like opera.

FRANCINE: I'll say!

BEULAH (*rises, crosses to piano; to* HARRY): But I can't understand . . . why did they have to shoot the poor boy? (SHIRLEY *is getting her sewing box together.*)

HARRY: Well, it's hard to explain, Beulah. But it seems they're having an argument over here, and the only way they can settle it is by murdering a lot of people. *The* CHERRYS *appear on gallery, all dressed for traveling, as in Act I, and come forward.* CHERRY *is carrying* MRS. CHERRY's *coat on his arm.*)

SHIRLEY (*crosses to right of* BEULAH): Say—you don't need to tell me what that's like. I was in the Club Grotto in Detroit the night the Purple Gang shot it out with the G's. (*She and* BEULAH *start out.*) And was that terrible! Blood all over everything! You never saw such a mess. (*They exit.*)

HARRY (*to* CHERRY): Well, you heard what happened to Quillery?

CHERRY: Yes. It seems he died like a true patriot, shouting, "Vive la France."

HARRY: Been better if he died like a man—sticking to what he thought was right.

CHERRY: He was such a nice little chap.

MRS. CHERRY (*comes down two steps from platform, crosses to* CHERRY): The Italians are swine! (DON *enters on gallery with bag and portable Victrola, comes downstairs.*)

CHERRY: Oh, they had a perfect right to do it.

MRS. CHERRY: I know, darling, but to kill a man just for saying what he thinks!

CHERRY: Many people will be killed for less than that.

HARRY (*rises, comes down off platform*): I'll have to be saying good-by pretty soon. (*To* DON.) The train does leave at five? Doesn't it?

DON: Yeah. Five o'clock sharp. (*Exits.*)

HARRY: I hope all this unpleasantness hasn't spoiled your winter sports.

CHERRY: Oh, that's all washed up. We're going back, too—that is if they'll let us cross the border.

HARRY: So the honeymoon is over already?

MRS. CHERRY (*on verge of tears*): Yes—I suppose so.

CHERRY: England's coming into this. We've got to stand by France, of course. And so—

MRS. CHERRY: And so Jimmy will have to do his bit, manning the guns for civilization. Perhaps he'll join in the bombardment of Florence, where we were married!

CHERRY: You know—after the ceremony we went into the Baptistry and we prayed to the soul of Leonardo da Vinci that we might never fail in our devotion to that which was beautiful and true. I told you we were a bit on the romantic side. Well, we forgot what Leonardo said about war. Bestial frenzy, he called it. And bestial frenzy it is.

MRS. CHERRY: Yes, but we mustn't think about that now. We have to stand by France. We have to make the world a decent place for heroes to live in. (*Breaks, begins to sob.*) Oh, Christ!

CHERRY (*quickly rises, crosses to her*): We've got to make the best of it. Now, darling, please don't cry!

HARRY: Let her cry, let her sob her heart out—for all the good it will do her. You know what I often think? I often think we ought to get together and elect somebody else God. Yeah, me for instance. I'd bet I'd make a much better job of it!

MRS. CHERRY (*through tears*): You'd be fine, Mr. Van.

HARRY: I think I would at that. There'd be a lot of people

object to my methods. That Mr. Weber, for instance. Would I begin the administration by beating the can off-a him!

CHERRY: Let's start the campaign now! Vote for good old Harry Van, and his Three Angels! (CAPTAIN *enters with briefcase full of papers and passports.*)

CAPTAIN: Good afternoon, Mrs. Cherry. Gentlemen.

HARRY: Well, do we get across?

CAPTAIN: Here is your passport, Mr. Van—and the young ladies', with my compliments. They have been duly stamped. (*Hands them over, crosses to table.*)

HARRY: How about Mr. Weber and his—friend? Do they go, too?

CAPTAIN: I have their passports here. I advise you to make ready, Mr. Van. (*Puts hat and gloves on chair behind table. Looks at wristwatch.*) The train will leave in about forty-five minutes. (*He opens briefcase on table and sits.*)

HARRY: O.K., Captain. See you later, Mr. and Mrs. Cherry. (*Goes out.*)

CHERRY: O.K., Harry.

MRS. CHERRY (*curtly*): What about us?

CAPTAIN: Due to a slight technicality, you will be permitted to cross the frontier. Here are your passports.

CHERRY (*crosses to table, followed by* MRS. CHERRY, *and takes passports*): I can't tell you how grateful we are.

CAPTAIN: You needn't be grateful to me, Mr. Cherry. The fact that you are allowed to pass is due to the superb centralization of authority in my country. The telegram authorizing your release was filed at eleven forty-three today, just seventeen minutes before a state of war was declared between Great Britain and Italy. I must obey the order of Rome, even though I know it's out of date. Is your luggage ready?

CHERRY: Yes, it's all out in the hall. Well, good-by and good luck!

CAPTAIN (*rises*): And good luck to you—both of you.

CHERRY: I need hardly say how terribly sorry we are about all this. It's really a damned rotten shame.

CAPTAIN: It is. All of that. Good-by, my friend. (*Extends*

hand and CHERRY *shakes it, then extends hand to* MRS.
CHERRY.)

CHERRY: Good-by.

MRS. CHERRY: Don't you call *me* your friend, because I say
what Quillery said—damn you—damn your whole country of
mad dogs for having started this horror. (WEBER *appears
on gallery, his overcoat and hat on and carrying leather
portfolio.*)

CAPTAIN (*bows*): It is not my fault, Mrs. Cherry.

CHERRY: It's utterly unfair to talk that way, darling. The Captain is doing his miserable duty as decently as he possibly
can. Now, please, darling.

MRS. CHERRY: I know . . . I know. Forgive me.

CAPTAIN: Madame!

MRS. CHERRY (*extends hand to* CAPTAIN, *shakes hands*): I
should have remembered that it's everybody's fault. (*To*
CHERRY.) Oh, I'll be all right, Jimmy.

CHERRY: Come on, my sweet. (*They exit.*)

CAPTAIN (*to* WEBER): Frankly, my heart bleeds for them.
(*Sits.*)

WEBER: They're young. They'll live through it, and be happy.

CAPTAIN: Will they? I was their age, and in their situation,
twenty years ago, when I was sent to the Isonzo front. And
people said just that to me: "Never mind—you are young—
and youth will survive and come to triumph." And I believed it. That is why I couldn't say such deceiving words
to them now.

WEBER: The cultivation of hope never does any immediate
harm. Is everything ready?

CAPTAIN (*rises*): Quite, Monsieur Weber. Here it is. (*Hands
over* WEBER's *passport. Five of the* GIRLS *and* HARRY *cross
from right to left at back in arch. They have on coats and
hats and carry their luggage, etc.* HARRY *carries his briefcase.*)

SHIRLEY: I'm certainly glad to get out of this joint.

BEBE: So long, Captain.

ELAINE: Have you got the music, Harry?

HARRY: Yeah. I got it. Have you got your overshoes?

FRANCINE (*to* CAPTAIN): Toodle-doo, Captain.

EDNA: See you in church, Cap. (*They disappear in passageway.*)

WEBER: And Madame's?

CAPTAIN (*holds up* IRENE's *passport*): Madame's passport is quite unusual, Monsieur Weber. It has given us some worry.

WEBER: The League of Nations issues documents like that to those whose nationality is uncertain.

CAPTAIN: I understand—but the attitude of Italy toward the League of Nations is not at the moment cordial. So the authorities insist that I ask some questions—as a mere matter of formality.

WEBER: You may ask questions, Captain, but you can be sure of none of the answers. All that I know is that her father was an Armenian, who got into trouble with the Tsarist government in Russia. I believe he was a thrower of bombs.

CAPTAIN: Does Madame inherit any of his tendencies?

WEBER: I shouldn't wonder. But she has learned to control them.

CAPTAIN: Very well, Monsieur Weber. My instructions are to accord you every consideration. In view of the fact that Madame is traveling with you, I shall be glad to approve her visa. (*Sits.*)

WEBER: Madame is not traveling with me. She has her own passport.

CAPTAIN: But it is understood that you vouch for her, and that is enough to satisfy the authorities.

WEBER: Vouch for her? It is not necessary for anybody to vouch for Madame! She is quite capable of taking care of herself. If her passport is not entirely in order, it is no affair of mine.

CAPTAIN: Monsieur Weber, I must tell you that this is something which I do not like. This places me in a—most embarrassing position. I shall be forced to detain Madame.

WEBER: You are a soldier, Captain, and you should be used to embarrassing positions. Undoubtedly, you were em-

barrassed this morning when you had to shoot that confused pacifist, Quillery. But this is war, and distasteful
responsibilities descend upon you as well as on me.

HARRY (*yells offstage*): Beulah! (*Appears in arch.*)

BEULAH (*yells offstage*): Yes, Harry.

HARRY: They're waiting for you in the bus.

BEULAH: I'm coming. (*Crosses from right to left in arch, hat
and coat on.*)

HARRY: Tell them I'll be right out. (BEULAH, *carrying luggage, disappears in hall left.* HARRY *comes forward.*)

BEULAH: O.K., Harry. (DOCTOR *appears on gallery with coat,
hat, books done in a bundle and umbrella. He has his overshoes on. Comes downstairs.*)

WEBER: I shall attend to my luggage. Thank you, Captain.
(*Exits.*)

CAPTAIN: Don't mention it. (*To* HARRY.) The young ladies
are ready?

HARRY: Yes—they're ready. And some of your aviators are out
there trying to persuade them into staying here perma-
nently.

CAPTAIN (*smiling*): And I add my entreaties to theirs.

HARRY: We aren't going to have any more trouble, are we?

CAPTAIN: Oh, no, Mr. Van. Geneva is a lovely spot. All of
Switzerland is beautiful these days. I envy you going there,
in such charming company.

HARRY: Hi, Doctor. Got your rats all packed?

DOCTOR: Good afternoon. I am privileged to go now? (*Puts
down all his belongings.*)

CAPTAIN: Yes, Dr. Waldersee. Here is your passport.

DOCTOR: Thank you. (DOCTOR *crosses to chair at right of table
and sits and takes out eyeglass case, puts on eyeglasses and
examines passports carefully.*)

HARRY (*rises, comes to behind table*): I can tell you this,
Doctor—I certainly will be proud to have known you. When
I read in the papers that you've wiped out cancer and won
the Nobel Prize, and are one of the greatest heroes on earth,
I'll be able to say: "He was a personal friend of mine."

(*Nudges* CAPTAIN, *who chuckles.*) "He once admired my music."

DOCTOR (*solemnly, to* HARRY): Thank you very much. (*To* CAPTAIN.) This visa is good for crossing the Austrian border!

CAPTAIN: Certainly. But you are going to Zurich!

DOCTOR (*puts eyeglasses in case, then in vest pocket*): I have changed my plans. I'm going back into Germany. (*Rises.*) Germany is at war. Perhaps I am needed. (*Picks up overcoat.*)

HARRY: Needed for what?

DOCTOR: I shall offer my services for what they are worth.

HARRY (*crosses right, helps* DOCTOR *put on coat*): But what about the rats?

DOCTOR: Why should I save people who don't want to be saved—so they can go out and exterminate each other? Obscene maniacs! (*Starts to put on gloves.*) Then I'll be a maniac, too. I'll be more dangerous than most of them. I know all the tricks of death! As for my rats, maybe they'll be useful. Britain will put down the blockade again, and we shall be starving. Maybe I'll cut up my rats into filets and eat them. (*Gets hat, books and umbrella from center seat.*)

HARRY: Wait a minute, Doctor. You're doing this without thinking. . . .

DOCTOR: I'm thinking—probably the remedy you sold is better than mine. Hasten to apply it. We're all diseased.

HARRY: But you can't change around like this! Don't you remember all those things you told me? All that about backsliding?

DOCTOR: No, I have not forgotten the degradation of mankind —that is painful and offensive to conceive. (*In arch.*) I'm sorry to disappoint you about the Nobel Prize! (*Grunts, exits.*)

HARRY: Good-by, Doctor! (*Speaks to* CAPTAIN, *with uncharacteristic vehemence.*) Why can't somebody answer the question everybody asks? Why! I know some of the answers —but then they aren't good enough. Weber—and a lot like him—they can't take the blame for *all* of this. Who is it did this trick on a lot of decent people? And why do you let 'em get away with it? That's the thing I'd like to know!

CAPTAIN: We have avalanches up here, my friend. They are disastrous. They start with a little crack in the ice, so tiny that one can hardly see it—until—suddenly—it bursts wide open. And then it is too late!

HARRY: That's all very well. But it doesn't satisfy me—because this avalanche isn't made of ice. (IRENE *appears on gallery all dressed for traveling. She is putting on her gloves as she comes downstairs.*) It's made of flesh and blood—and—*brains!*

IRENE: Still worrying about the situation, Mr. Van? Good afternoon, Captain Locicero.

CAPTAIN (*rises*): Good afternoon, madame. (HARRY *rises, too.*)

IRENE: I have had the most superb rest here. It is so calm, so soothing. I can't bear to think that I have to go to Biarritz (WEBER *enters, comes forward to* HARRY) with the dull, dismal old sea pounding in my ears. We are ready now, Achille?

WEBER (*takes off hat*): The—captain has raised some objections. (*Looks at* CAPTAIN *significantly.*)

CAPTAIN: I regret, madame, that there must be some further delay.

IRENE: The train is not going, after all?

CAPTAIN: The train is going, madame. But this passport of yours presents problems which, under the circumstances—

IRENE: Monsieur Weber will settle them, whatever the problems are. Won't you, Achille?

WEBER: I have just been arguing with the captain. There is some difficulty about your nationality.

CAPTAIN (*looking at passport*): Your birthplace is uncertain, madame—believed to be in Armenia.

IRENE: Yes—a province of Russia—

CAPTAIN: You subsequently became a resident of England—

IRENE: When I was a very little girl.

CAPTAIN: Then you went to the United States—and then to France— (HARRY *sits again.*)

IRENE: Yes, yes—it is all there—plain for you to see— I have never had the slightest difficulty about my passport. It was issued by the League of Nations. (*Sits.*)

WEBER (*gives* CAPTAIN *the eye*): I'm afraid that the standing of the League of Nations is not very high in Italy at this moment.

CAPTAIN (*taking his cue from* WEBER): The fact is, madame, the very existence of the League is no longer recognized by our government. For that reason, we cannot permit you to cross the frontier at this time. (*Significantly, to* IRENE.) I'm sure you will appreciate the *delicacy* of my position. (*Hands her passport over table. Picks up hat and briefcase.*) Perhaps we shall be able to adjust the matter—tomorrow. (*Puts hat on, clicks heels and salutes.* HARRY *rises, takes* CAPTAIN *by sleeve and pantomimes he would like to know why* IRENE *can't get out. They exit.*)

WEBER (*sits*): I should of course wait over, Irene. But you know how dangerous it is for me to delay my return to France by so much as one day. I have been in touch with our agents. The Premier is demanding that production be doubled—trebled—at once.

IRENE: I understand, Achille.

WEBER: Here—(*takes out envelope from overcoat pocket*)—this will take care of all possible expenses. (*Gives it to her.*) You must return to Venice immediately and see Lanza. I have already sent him full instructions.

IRENE: Thank you for being so very tactful.

WEBER (*rises, puts chair in place close to table*): You are a superior person, Irene. I consider it a great privilege to have known you.

IRENE: Thank you, again.

WEBER: Good-by, my dear. (*He goes to kiss her.*)

IRENE (*Offers him her hand to shake, instead.*) Good-by, good-by, Achille. (WEBER *shakes her hand and starts to go out as* HARRY *re-enters.*)

WEBER: Coming, Mr. Van? (*Exits.*)

HARRY: Yeah, certainly. Tough luck, babe.

IRENE: It is no matter.

HARRY: But I seriously doubt you'll suffer any bayonet wounds. You know, the captain isn't as brutal as the Bolsheviks were.

IRENE: You mean to be encouraging.

HARRY (*notices her passport on table*): How did you get that passport from the League of Nations?

IRENE: I am under oath not to say anything about that. (*She starts to pick it up.*)

HARRY (*reaches for it*): Let me see it.

IRENE: No!

HARRY: I want to see it. Give it to me.

IRENE: Don't you dare touch it! (HARRY *snatches it from her.* SHIRLEY *appears in arch.*)

SHIRLEY: Hey, Harry! It's time for us to go! (HARRY *looks up at* SHIRLEY.)

HARRY: All right, all right. (*He is looking at passport.* SHIRLEY *goes.*)

IRENE: Go away with your friends.

HARRY (*reading*): "Irene Kasmadjians"—Kasmadjians. Is that a branch of the Romanoffs, babe?

IRENE: Don't call me *babe!* (*Takes passport from him, puts it in her handbag.*)

HARRY: My apologies, madame. I just call everybody babe.

IRENE: Perhaps that is why I don't like it.

HARRY: I can see that you're in a tough spot. And considering what we were to each other in the old Governor Bryan Hotel—

IRENE: Must you always be in that place?

HARRY: I want to help you, Irene. Isn't there something I can do?

IRENE: I thank you, from the bottom of my heart, I thank you for that offer. But it is useless. . . .

HARRY: Listen, you don't have to thank me. Just tell me—what can I do?

IRENE: You're very kind, and very gallant. But unfortunately, you're no match for Achille Weber.

HARRY: Is he responsible for them stopping you?

IRENE: Of course he is. I knew it the moment I saw that ashamed look on the face of Captain Locicero, when he refused to permit me—

HARRY: So Weber double-crossed you, did he? Well, what's that son of a bitch got against you?

IRENE: He's afraid of me. I know too much about him and his methods of promoting his own business.

HARRY: Everybody knows about his methods. Even little Quillery was talking about them last night—

IRENE: And what happened to Quillery? It is what happens to everyone who dares to criticize him.

HARRY: Why? Did you split with him?

IRENE: Yes. Last night I could stand it no longer. So I did the one thing I knew he never would forgive.

HARRY: Yeah?

IRENE: I told him what I really thought about his business!

HARRY (*jubilant*): Yeah? (SHIRLEY *and* BEBE *appear in arch.*)

IRENE: See how quickly he strikes back.

SHIRLEY: Harry! The bus is going to leave!

HARRY (*to* SHIRLEY): All right—all right!

BEBE (*shouts as they go*): But we gotta go right this minute.

IRENE: Go along, go along. You can't help me now. Nobody can.

SHIRLEY AND BEBE (*offstage; yelling*): Harry!

IRENE: You will miss your train.

HARRY: All right! (*Gets coat, hat and briefcase from seat.*)

IRENE: But if it will make you any happier in your travels with Les Blondes I will tell you: I did know you—slightly— in Omaha.

HARRY: Are you lying again?

IRENE: It was room 974.

HARRY: Well how the hell can I remember what room it was?

IRENE: Well, then—you'll never be sure, Mr. Van.

DON (*appears in arch*): Will you come on? We can't wait another instant! (*Goes out again.*)

HARRY (*starts for arch*): Yeah, I'm coming.

DON (*offstage*): Hurry up, you can put your coat on in the bus.

HARRY: I said I'm coming, God damn it. Can't you hear me? (*Goes out. IRENE, left alone, takes off her gloves, puts handbag on seat, takes off cloak, puts it on table, takes off hat, puts it on top of cloak, and with a sigh, sits extreme right end of seat. DUMPTSY enters wearing uniform of a private in the Italian Alpini Corps, a full pack on his back.*)

DUMPTSY: Oh, good afternoon, madame.

IRENE: Why, Dumptsy—what is that costume?

DUMPTSY: They called me up. Look! I'm an Italian soldier.

IRENE: You look splendid!

DUMPTSY: If you please, madame. But why did you not go on that bus, madame?

IRENE: I have decided to remain here and enjoy the winter sports.

DUMPTSY: Oh, I don't think this is a good place any more, madame. They say the war is very big—bigger than last time.

IRENE: I heard that too.

DUMPTSY: The French will be here to drop bombs on everybody.

IRENE: That will be very exciting for us if they do, won't it?

DUMPTSY: It is possible, madame. But . . . I came to say good-by to Auguste, the barman, and Anna, the maid. They're both cousins of mine. They'll laugh when they see me in these clothes. Can I get you anything, madame?

IRENE: Yes, Dumptsy. Bring me a (PITTALUGA *pushes light switch on back wall of hall of arch, lights up room*) bottle of champagne. . . . Bring two glasses. . . . We'll have a drink together.

DUMPTSY: If you please, madame. (*Goes into bar.* PITTALUGA *enters.*)

PITTALUGA: Your luggage is in the hall, madame. Will you wish it taken to the same suite?

IRENE: No—I didn't really care for those rooms. Have you something a little smaller?

PITTALUGA: We have smaller rooms on the other side of the hotel.

IRENE: I will have the smallest. It will be cozier. (DUMPTSY *returns with champagne and two white champagne glasses on tray.*)

PITTALUGA: You wish to go to it now?

IRENE: No. Have my luggage sent up. I'll see it later. (PIT-TALUGA *bows, exits.*)

DUMPTSY (*puts tray on table*): I was right, madame. Auguste laughed very much.

IRENE: What will become of your wife and children, Dumptsy?

DUMPTSY: Oh—I suppose the Fascisti will feed them. They promised to feed all the families with a man out fighting for their country. (*He has filled her glass and gives it to her.*)

IRENE: So? Pour yourself one.

DUMPTSY: Thank you so much, madame. I was not sure I heard correctly. (*Pours for himself.*)

IRENE (*holds up glass*): To you, Dumptsy—and to Austria.

DUMPTSY: And to you, madame, if you please. (*Clinks her glass.*)

IRENE: Thank you. (*They drink.*)

DUMPTSY (*smacks lips*): This is good. And may you soon be restored to your home in Petersburg.

IRENE: My home—huh! (*Holds up her glass.*) No fear . . .

DUMPTSY: No, madame— (*They clink their glasses and drink.*) And now I must go find Anna, if you please.

IRENE (*rises*): One moment. Here. (*Digs into handbag, hands him note of money.*) For you—

DUMPTSY: Thank you so much, madame.

IRENE: Good-by, Dumptsy, and may God bless you. (*Offers her hand.*)

DUMPTSY: Kiss die hand, madame. (*Leans over, kisses her hand.* MAJOR *and* CAPTAIN *come in talking.*)

MAJOR: Non c'è molto tempo, Signor Capitano.

CAPTAIN: E allora, Signor Maggiori. Beviamo primo e dopo andiamo al campo d'avione. (DUMPTSY *salutes strenuously and exits.* MAJOR *crosses into bar.* CAPTAIN *is following him.*)

IRENE: Some champagne, Captain?

CAPTAIN: No, thank you very much, madame.

IRENE: You need not be so anxious to avoid me. I know perfectly well it was not your fault.

CAPTAIN (*takes off hat*): You are very understanding, madame.

IRENE: That is true. I am the most understanding woman in this world. I understand so damned much that I am alone on this cold mountain peak, and I have no one to turn to . . . and nowhere to go. . . .

CAPTAIN: If I can be of service to you, madame, in any way . . .

IRENE: I know, you'll be very kind and faultlessly polite.

CAPTAIN: I realize, madame, that politeness now means nothing. But under these tragic circumstances, what else can I do?

IRENE: What else can you do under these tragic circumstances? I will tell you what you can do. You are a man— you can refuse to fight—you can refuse to use those weapons they have sold you. (*Goes up to piano, champagne glass in hand, as* CAPTAIN *backs up toward her.*) But you were going into the bar. Don't let me detain you.

CAPTAIN: You will forgive me, madame?

IRENE: Fully, my dear Captain, fully.

CAPTAIN: Thank you, madame. Thank you very much. (*Salutes and goes into bar.* IRENE *sits at piano and plays with one finger a few notes of Russian song, then segues into Cockney song and sings.*)

IRENE:

If those lips could only speak.

And those eyes could only see,

And those beautiful golden tresses were here in reality

Could I only take your hand as I did when you took my name—

(HARRY *enters through arch with hat and overcoat on, carrying briefcase and Gladstone bag. Puts bag on floor below seat and briefcase on seat.* IRENE *rises.*) Did you have some trouble?

HARRY (*takes off coat and hat and puts them on briefcase*): No. Whose champagne is that?

IRENE: Mine. Will you have some?

HARRY: Thanks. (*Starts to pour it in* DUMPTSY'S *glass.*)

IRENE: Dumptsy used that glass.

HARRY (*his back to her*): That's all right. (*Fills glass.*)

IRENE: Did you miss your train?

HARRY: No. The train went. I got the girls on board. Mr. and Mrs. Cherry promised to look after them. They'll be O.K. (*Drinks.*)

IRENE: And you have come back here to me?

HARRY: It seems perfectly obvious I came back.

IRENE: Then you meant it when you said you wanted to help me.

HARRY (*turns to her*): You said I'd never be sure. Well, I came back to tell you that I *am* sure. I got thinking back, in that bus, and I came to the conclusion that it *was* room 974—or close to it, anyhow. And somehow or other, I couldn't help feeling a little flattered—and a little touched— to think that of all the sordid hotel rooms you must have been in, you should have remembered that one. (*Drinks.*)

IRENE: Bayard is not dead!

HARRY: Who?

IRENE: The Chevalier Bayard!

HARRY: Oh?

IRENE: Somewhere in that funny, music hall soul of yours is the spirit of Leander and Abelard and Galahad. You give up everything—you risk your life—you have walked unafraid into the valley of the shadow—to aid and comfort a damsel in distress. Isn't that the truth?

HARRY: Yeah—that's the truth—simply and plainly put. Now, listen to me, babe, when are you going to break down and tell me who the hell are you?

IRENE: Does it matter so very much who I am?

HARRY: No, no. I like you like you are.

IRENE: Give me some more champagne. (HARRY *crosses to her and pours some more in her glass, then empties bottle in his, and drinks.* IRENE *drops her Russian accent.*) I am not a Romanoff—far from it. I just like to see the light in people's eyes when I tell them I am a Russian princess. They are all such snobs. I am not going to tell the truth to them, why should I? Their whole life is a lie. But I can tell the truth to you, because you are an honest man.

HARRY (*draws himself up proudly*): Oh, I am, am I? (*Crosses to bar, bottle in hand.* IRENE *drains her glass.*) Another bottle of champagne! (*Opens bar door.*)

CAPTAIN (*in bar*): Mr. Van?

HARRY: Hi, Captain! (*Puts empty bottle of champagne on bar.*)

CAPTAIN (*in bar*): What happened? Did you miss the train?

HARRY: No. I didn't miss the train—just a God damned fool! (*Closes bar door.* IRENE *has come down from platform holding her empty glass, stands at right end of bend of piano.* HARRY *crosses to her. She kisses him.*)

IRENE: I love you, Harry.

HARRY: You do, eh?

IRENE: Yes, ever since that night in the Governor Bryan Hotel I have loved you. You have a heart that I can trust. And whatever I say to you I know it will never be misunderstood.

105

HARRY: Yeah! I had you tagged from the start.

IRENE: And you adore me too, don't you, darling?

HARRY: No, I told you once, no.

IRENE (*puts arms around his neck*): No, you mustn't admit it.

HARRY: And quit pawing me, will you? And we don't want any misunderstanding, do we?

IRENE: Oh, dear, no!

HARRY: If you're going to hook up with me, it's only for professional reasons—see?

IRENE: I see.

HARRY: And I'm the manager.

IRENE: Oh, yes.

HARRY: I'll fix it with the captain to get across the border tomorrow or the next day. We'll join the girls in Geneva— that's as good a place as any to rehearse the Code.

IRENE: The Code! No, you must tell it to me at once.

HARRY: At once! It's a very deep, complicated, scientific problem.

IRENE: I shall be able to do that very easily.

HARRY: Say, listen, if you're unusually smart and apply yourself, you'll get a fairly good idea of it after six months of study and rehearsal. (AUGUSTE *enters from bar with bottle of champagne, refills* IRENE's *glass, gives* HARRY *the bottle and exits into bar.*)

IRENE: A mind reader! You're right. I shall be able to do that very well!

HARRY: And another thing, if you're going to qualify for this act with me, you'll have to lay off liquor. I mean, after we finish this one. (*Pours some in his glass.*) It's a well-known fact that booze and science don't mix. (*Drains his glass.*)

IRENE (*as one in a trance, lapses into Russian accent*): I don't think I shall use my own name—

HARRY: No?

IRENE: No. I shall call myself—Namoura . . . Namoura the

Great—assisted by Harry Van. (*Drains her glass.* HARRY, *nonplused at her colossal nerve, is speechless.*) I shall wear black velvet—cut very plain—you know, with my skin, ivory white. I must have something to hold. One white flower, hah? No—a little white prayer book— (*Warning air-raid siren is heard offstage. She throws her glass down on floor.* HARRY *puts champagne bottle on table, goes to left of* IRENE. CAPTAIN, MAJOR *and* AUGUSTE *rush out of bar.* CAPTAIN *rushes across in front of* HARRY *and* IRENE *to window.* MAJOR *exits.* AUGUSTE *rushes for window.* PITTALUGA *enters at same time, and comes forward.*)

CAPTAIN (*as he comes rushing out*): Signor Maggiori andate alla caserma e date l'allarme del gas!

MAJOR: Venga lei anche!

HARRY: What's up, Captain?

PITTALUGA (*to* AUGUSTE): Auguste! Chiude le persiane. . . . Fa presto, presto! (*Rushes out.* AUGUSTE *begins to let Venetian blinds down. Airplanes' motors overhead are now heard coming nearer.*)

CAPTAIN (*looks up through window and turns to* IRENE *and* HARRY): French airplanes. It is reprisal for last night. They are coming to destroy our base here. They have no right to attack this hotel. But—there may easily be an accident. I advise the cellar. (*Quickly crosses behind them to arch.*)

IRENE: Oh, no, no, no.

CAPTAIN: I entreat you, madame, not to be reckless. I have enough on my conscience now, without adding to it your innocent life!

IRENE: Don't worry, Captain!

CAPTAIN: God be with you, madame! (*Rushes out.*)

IRENE: We're in the war, Harry. (AUGUSTE *has put down three Venetian blinds and rushes across behind* HARRY *and* IRENE, *exits.*)

HARRY: Yeah. What are we going to do? Go out and say "boo"?

IRENE: Sing to them!

HARRY: My voice don't feel appropriate. Too bad we can't get Chaliapin. (SIGNOR *and* SIGNORA ROSSI *rush across at back from right to left, followed by* PITTALUGA.)

PITTALUGA (*in arch*): Everyone goes into the cellar. Quick! It is dangerous here!

IRENE: Ridiculous!

HARRY: Thanks very much, signore.

PITTALUGA: You have been warned! (*Rushes out.*)

IRENE: Here we are, on the top of the world—and he wants us to go in the cellar! Do you want to go in the cellar?

HARRY: Do you?

IRENE: No. If a bomb comes, it is worse in the cellar.

HARRY: All right, babe, I'll stick by you. (*Bomb bursts quite near, and room is plunged into darkness. Weird flares of light off windows at right.*)

IRENE (*rushes to windows*): Come and watch it, Harry, come and watch it. (*She peers through slats of blind.*) Oh, it is superb! (HARRY *has crossed to her at window.*) It is positively Wagnerian!

HARRY: It looks to me exactly like "Hell's Angels." (*Another bomb explosion, followed by a flare and a burst of machine-gun fire.* HARRY *grabs* IRENE *by hand and rushes across stage to piano. Lights his cigarette lighter to give light to darkened room, puts it on keyboard of piano.* HARRY *sits at piano and begins playing "The Ride of the Valkyries."* IRENE *stands right of him on platform.*) I used to play the piano in picture theatres!

IRENE: I hate those films.

HARRY: I don't. I love 'em. I love every one of them. (*From the time the first bomb has burst there is a constant roar of plane motors and distant cannonading.*)

IRENE: Do you realize—the whole world has gone to war? The *whole world!*

HARRY: Yeah. I realize it. But don't ask me why. Because I've stopped trying to figure it out.

IRENE: I know why. It is just to kill us—you and me. (*Bomb bursts very close,* HARRY *stops playing.*) Because we are the little people and for us the deadliest weapons are the most merciful. . . . (*Another bomb bursts close by.* HARRY *starts playing "Onward, Christian Soldiers." Both begin singing.*)

BOTH:

> Onward, Christian Soldiers,
> Marching as to war—

STREET SCENE

INTRODUCTION

Certain writers have become associated with particular areas, rural and urban, which always influence their books: Thomas Hardy with Wessex, Arnold Bennett with the English Pottery District, Ben Hecht with Chicago, Mary E. W. Freeman with New England, Arthur Schnitzler with prewar Vienna. Elmer Rice is the interpreter of New York. His novel *Imperial City* (1937) is the most complete picture of the metropolis ever attempted, and there have been many attempts.

Of the numerous plays about New York, Rice's *Street Scene* is probably the most convincing. However, Rice has not confined himself to writing about Manhattan. *Between Two Worlds* (1934) takes place on an Atlantic liner on its way to Europe. *Judgment Day* (1934) is laid in an unnamed European country, though it is obviously a dramatization of the trial of Dimitrov for the burning of the German Reichstag. *The Left Bank* (1931) has Paris as its setting. Yet critics will agree that he has been most successful when he has described New York and its inhabitants, in *Street Scene* (1929), in *Counsellor-at-Law* (1931) and in his various other plays about the law.

Rice's study of law may explain his qualities as a playwright. From almost his first play to the most recent, he has exhibited a passionate hatred for injustice, which at times worked to the detriment of his dramaturgy. He has always been admired for his marvelously accurate observation of little, though vital, details. New

Yorkers experienced many pleasures in *Street Scene* and in *Counsellor-at-Law* that were denied to a visitor, because they could more easily recognize characters by the appropriateness of their speech, their dress and their mannerisms.

Elmer Rice's plays abound in many small cameos of portraiture. *Street Scene* has more than forty characters, most of whom are sharply delineated and clearly differentiated. *Counsellor-at-Law* and *We, the People* also have large casts that require full-length roles, not merely walk-on parts.

Equally apparent throughout his plays is his awareness and dislike of the materialistic aspects of contemporary American civilization. In one of his early plays, *The Subway,* which was not produced until *Street Scene* had become a hit, he describes the wearying effects of daily office routine upon a sensitive young girl. *The Adding Machine* (1923), produced by the Theatre Guild and revived recently by the Phoenix Theatre, is an allegory of a young man's experiences in a business civilization that has little respect for individual personalities.

As long as Rice confined himself to demonstrating the tragic implications of industrialization and commercialism, critics were willing to accept him. They had the precedents of Galsworthy in *Justice,* of Shaw and his imitators, of the young dramatists of the twenties and of O'Neill in *Beyond the Horizon.*

But Rice, after his great success with *Counsellor-at-Law* with its assortment of sharp portraits in a metropolitan law office, next tried to present his vision of the disintegrating effect of the depression in *We, the People*. The critics abandoned him. They had expected another series of portraits, not a passionate outburst against prejudiced judges, company unions, unscrupulous employers and other unpleasant features of Big Business.

The following year, Rice's anger at the persecution in Nazi Germany led him to portray the Reichstag Fire trials, in which such characters as Göring, Hitler and Van der

Lubbe appeared. The New York critics were even more dissatisfied. Granting that Rice was within his rights as a dramatist to be angry with the Nazis, they denied him the privilege of using the stage as a soapbox against Nazism. Here, they said, was a melodramatic harangue, not a play. Rice was accustomed to unfavorable criticism, and he went ahead with the presentation of another play that same year. This time the critics' disapproval proved too much, and *Between Two Worlds* closed quickly.

In 1936, his refusal to compromise with his principles caused him to resign as New York City Director of the Federal Theatre Project because the Government refused to permit the first edition of "The Living Newspaper," to include Mussolini and Haile Selassie.

One may admire a man's courage in undauntedly facing his adversaries and yet admit that he is an ineffective dramatist. That seems to explain the critics' attitude. Rice knew as well as any man in the theatre that any number of plays have become successes even after universal condemnation by the reviewers. *Abie's Irish Rose* and its competitor for the long-run record, *Tobacco Road,* are examples of this phenomenon.

One explanation for the lukewarm reception of Rice's later plays may be that New York audiences were not prepared for them. Only two years after *We, the People,* Clifford Odets' *Waiting for Lefty* made its astonishing appearance. The Theatre Union was born in 1933 and could offer such tendentious dramas as *Peace on Earth, Stevedore, The Black Pit* and *Sailors of Cattaro*. Rice's was that pioneering effort which seems always destined to fail because of its strangeness.

Today, in reading this early dramatic study of the American Depression, *We, the People,* one cannot help admitting the courage of its author. Rice, in 1931, had won great popular and critical success with *Counsellor-at-Law*. Perhaps only the appearance of *Of Thee I Sing* in the same season took the Pulitzer Prize out of his hands. He knew enough of New

York (his novel *Imperial City* has enough plot for ten plays) to have produced another genre painting. Yet he chose to write *We, the People*—something entirely different. Time will tell whether Rice lost himself as a dramatist while he found himself as a campaigner for social justice.

Rice has great gifts for comedy, but he does not resort to comedy simply because it is easier to accept than grim drama. When comedy appears in his plays, it usually derives from the characters. The mother of Mr. Simon, the district leader, the gum-chewing stenographer of *Counsellor-at-Law*, the Italian janitor, the Russian Socialist of *Street Scene*—these are comic characters because they are human, and their verisimilitude provokes the laughter of recognition, a frequent experience in the theatre.

Has Elmer Rice made any distinguished contributions to American drama, or is he another successful dramatist popular for the moment, writing but a paragraph in the history of American drama of the twentieth century? Rice has revealed certain gifts of characterization, which leads one to believe that his reputation will depend on the permanence of these characters. In the theatre, one easily comes under their spell and is quite willing to believe in their existence. Rice knows the souls of several people and can describe many more. Thus his portrait of Simon, the counsellor-at-law, is probably his masterpiece. Having worked in law offices and knowing as well as any practicing dramatist, the personality of the Jewish professional whose parents were humble immigrants, Rice naturally excels in such portraits. The mother of Simon, with her pride in her son's prominence and her repeated use of the expression, "I've got plenty of time," is a living portrait. Not many playwrights have succeeded in creating such characters.

With the dramatist's keen eye for revealing detail, Rice can create a character merely by giving him a distinctive walk. Thus, in *Counsellor-at-Law*, one of the secretaries had a gait the like of which had not been seen on the stage before. She walked as if all the world's sense of weariness and unappreciated excellence was locked up in her heart. Whenever she appeared, the audience was amused. It may have been merely a dramatic trick, but it was effective.

Next in importance among Rice's significant contributions is his skill in interpreting New York life. Among the favorite topics of conversation among playgoers when *Street Scene* was the hit of the town was the exact location of the street described. Some disputants went so far as to photograph three-story houses that they were certain had been the models for the one in the play. Only Rice's statement that his setting was a generalization of the many brownstone houses in Manhattan put an end to the discussion. The zeal of the debaters was an indication of that "willing suspension of disbelief" that Coleridge said was so necessary for complete enjoyment in the theatre. Very few stage pictures of daily life in New York City can compare with *Street Scene*.

Elmer Rice probably prefers to be judged, however, as a dramatist of social justice. To be sure, he is in a great company, which includes George Bernard Shaw, Gerhart Hauptmann and Sean O'Casey, to mention but a few of the most distinguished in the field.

The doctrine of Alexandre Dumas *fils* that art should be for man's sake motivates such writers. They do not measure out their emotions to be sure that their indignation does not overbalance their sense of the dramatic. Sometimes, as was the case with Galsworthy, whose temperament was controlled, the indignation is communicated to the spectator subtly without being stated explicitly in the play. It is ridiculous, of course, to chastise Rice because his temperament is unlike Galsworthy's, and hence frequently causes him to overstate when the restrained Englishman might have used understatement.

It is to Rice's credit that he refused to curry popular approval by continuing to turn out realistic portraits simply because they had been successful. What elevates Rice to the higher category of American dramatists is his refusal to limit himself to one proved type of play. Like O'Neill, who constantly experimented with new forms, Rice used different techniques. In *The Adding Machine,* he tried Expressionism at a time when it was the last word in Continental drama. In *We, the People,* Rice took the spectators into his confidence, particularly in the last act when he made the audience the jury before which his hero is tried.

Rice is a brave fighter who uses the stage as his vehicle. He is not a propagandist preaching universal unionization or revolution as a solution for the economic ills of our time. He preaches *against* rather than *for.* He is opposed to oppression, whether in Nazi Germany, in a Midwestern American town or in Czarist Russia. He is alive to the beauties of the world, one of which, young love, is tenderly portrayed in several of his plays. He has written about the ugliness of our impersonal business society, which makes possible such tragedies as those he describes in *The Adding Machine, Street Scene* and *We, the People.*

With the exception of *Dream Girl* (1945), Elmer Rice's later plays have not won the critical or popular acclaim that greeted *On Trial* (1914), *The Adding Machine* (1923) and *Street Scene* (1929). He is one of the few living playwrights whose dramatic career spans almost five decades. Most critics will agree that in these years he has made three noteworthy contributions to American drama. In *On Trial* he successfully used for the first time on the stage the flashback technique of the movies. In *The Adding Machine* he wrote the first American Expressionist play. In *Street Scene* he presented the most realistic portrait of New York City on the contemporary stage. In 1947, *Street Scene* was produced as an exciting musical, with music by Kurt Weill and lyrics by Langston Hughes. It has taken its place among the dozen or so serious musicals of the American theatre.

Elmer Rice may be admired for the skill with which he has employed a wide variety of styles—ranging from stark realism in *Street Scene* through expressionism in *The Adding Machine* to fantasy in *Dream Girl.* He has frequently been an advocate of liberal causes and freedom of expression. He is one of the few survivors of that exciting group of dramatists who came on the scene in the twenties and who did so much to raise the American drama from its low level in the early part of the century to its present-day leadership in world theatre. As an example of the realistic drama of the late twenties, *Street Scene* stands head and shoulders above the countless others that crowded the Broadway stage in the bountiful days of the boom era. It well deserves inclusion in the ANTA Series of Distinguished Plays.

FURTHER READING

Gagey, Edmond M. *Revolution in American Drama.* New York: Columbia, 1947, pp. 148–149.

Gassner, John. *Masters of the Drama.* New York: Dover, 1954, pp. 684–685.

Hewitt, Barnard W. *Theatre U.S.A.: 1668–1957.* New York: McGraw-Hill, 1959, pp. 377–379, 399, 479.

Krutch, Joseph Wood. *The American Drama Since 1918.* New York: Random House, 1938, pp. 232–235.

Kunitz, Stanley J. *Twentieth Century Authors: First Supplement.* New York: H. W. Wilson, 1955, pp. 826–827.

———, and Haycraft, Howard. *Twentieth Century Authors.* New York: H. W. Wilson, 1942, pp. 1166–1167.

Mantle, Burns. *American Playwrights Today.* New York: Dodd, Mead, 1929, pp. 175–180.

———. *Contemporary American Playwrights.* New York: Dodd, Mead, 1938, pp. 54–61.

Morehouse, Ward. *Matinee Tomorrow.* New York: McGraw-Hill, 1949, pp. 224–225, 284, 301.

Shipley, Joseph T. *Guide to Great Plays.* Washington: Public Affairs, 1956, pp. 544–546.

Short, Ernest. *Introducing the Theatre.* London: Eyre & Spottiswoode, 1949, pp. 158, 169–171, 248.

STREET SCENE

ELMER L. RICE

ACT I

SCENE: *The exterior of a walk-up apartment house, in a mean quarter of New York. It is of ugly brownstone and was built in the '90's. Between the pavement of large, gray flagstones and the front of the house, is a deep and narrow areaway, guarded by a rusted, ornamental iron railing. At the right, a steep flight of rotting wooden steps leads down to the cellar and to the janitor's apartment, the windows of which are just visible above the street level. Spanning the areaway is a stoop of four shallow, stone steps, flanked on either side by a curved stone balustrade. Beyond the broad fourth step, another step leads to the double wooden outer doors of the house; and as these are open, the vestibule, and the wide, heavy glass-paneled entrance door beyond are visible. Above the outer doors, is a glass fanlight, upon which appears the half-obliterated house number. At the left side of the doorway is a sign which reads: "Flat To-Let. 6 Rooms. Steam Heat."*

On either side of the stoop, are the two narrow windows of the ground-floor apartments. In one of the windows, at the left, is a sign bearing the legend: "Prof. Filippo Fiorentino. Music for all occasions: Also instruction." Above, are the six narrow windows of the first-floor apartments, and above that, the stone sills of the second-floor windows can just be seen.

To the left of the house, part of the adjoining building is visible: the motor entrance to a storage warehouse. Crude boarding across the large driveway and rough planks across the sidewalk and curb indicate that an excavation is in progress. On the boarding is painted in rude lettering: "Keep Out"; and at the curb is a small barrel bearing a sign with the words: "Street Closed." To the wall of the warehouse is affixed a brass plate, bearing the name: "Patrick Mulcahy Storage Warehouse Co. Inc."

To the right of the house, scaffolding and a wooden sidewalk indicate that the house next door is being demolished. On the scaffolding is a large, wooden sign reading: "Manhattan House-Wrecking Corp."

In the close foreground, below the level of the curb, is a mere suggestion of the street.

The house is seen in the white glare of an arc light, which is just offstage to the right. The windows in the janitor's apartment are lighted, as are also those of the ground-floor apartment, at the right, and the two windows at the extreme left of the first floor. A dim, red light is affixed to the boarding of the excavation at the left.

In the lighted ground-floor window, at the right of the doorway, ABRAHAM KAPLAN *is seated, in a rocking chair, reading a Yiddish newspaper. He is a Russian Jew, well past sixty: clean-shaven, thick gray hair, hooked nose, horn-rimmed spectacles. To the left of the doorway,* GRETA FIORENTINO *is leaning out of the window. She is forty, blond, ruddy-faced and stout. She wears a wrapper of light, flowered material and a large pillow supports her left arm and her ample, uncorseted bosom. In her right hand is a folding paper fan, which she waves languidly.*

Throughout the act and, indeed, throughout the play, there is constant noise. The noises of the city rise, fall, intermingle: the distant roar of "el" trains, automobile sirens and the whistles of boats on the river; the rattle of trucks and the indeterminate clanking of metals; fire engines, ambulances, musical instruments, a radio, dogs barking and human voices calling, quarreling and screaming with laughter. The noises are subdued and in the background, but they never wholly cease.

A moment after the rise of the curtain, an elderly man enters at the right and walks into the house, exchanging a nod with MRS. FIORENTINO. *A* MAN, *munching peanuts, crosses the stage from left to right.*

VOICE (*offstage*): Char-lie (EMMA JONES *appears at the left. She is middle-aged, tall and rather bony. She carries a small parcel.*)

MRS. FIORENTINO (*she speaks with a faint German accent*): Good evening, Mrs. Jones.

MRS. JONES (*stopping beneath Mrs. Fiorentino's window*): Good evenin', Mrs. F. Well, I hope it's hot enough for you.

MRS. FIORENTINO: Ain't it joost awful? When I was through with the dishes, you could take my clothes and joost wring them out.

MRS. JONES: Me, too. I ain't got a dry stitch on me.

MRS. FIORENTINO: I took off my shoes and my corset and made myself nice and comfortable, and tonight before I go to bed, I take a nice bath.

MRS. JONES: The trouble with a bath is, by the time you're all through, you're as hot as when you started. (*As* OLGA

OLSEN, *a thin, anemic Scandinavian, with untidy fair hair, comes up the cellar steps and onto the sidewalk.*) Good evenin', Mrs. Olsen. Awful hot, ain't it?

MRS. OLSEN (*coming over to the front of the stoop*): Yust awful. Mrs. Forentiner, my hoosban' say vill you put de garbage on de doom-vaider?

MRS. FIORENTINO: Oh, sure, sure! I didn't hear him vistle. (*As* MRS. JONES *starts to cross to the stoop.*) Don't go 'vay, Mrs. Jones. (*She disappears from the window.*)

MRS. OLSEN (*pushing back some wisps of hair*): I tank is more cooler in de cellar.

MRS. JONES (*sitting on the stoop and fanning herself with her parcel*): Phew! I'm just about ready to pass out.

MRS. OLSEN: My baby is crying, crying all day.

MRS. JONES: Yeah, I often say they mind the heat more'n we do. It's the same with dogs. My Queenie has jes' been layin' aroun' all day.

MRS. OLSEN: The baby get new teet'. It hurt her.

MRS. JONES: Don't tell me! If you was to know what I went t'roo with my Vincent. Half the time, he used to have convulsions. (WILLIE MAURRANT, *a disorderly boy of twelve, appears at the left, on roller skates. He stops at the left of the stoop and takes hold of the railing with both hands.*)

WILLIE (*raising his head and bawling*): Hey, Ma!

MRS. JONES (*disapprovingly*): If you want your mother, why don't you go upstairs, instead o' yellin' like that?

WILLIE (*without paying the slightest attention to her, bawls louder*): Hey, Ma!

MRS. MAURRANT (*appearing at one of the lighted first-floor windows*): What do you want, Willie? (*She is a fair woman of forty, who looks her age, but is by no means unattractive.*)

WILLIE: Gimme a dime, will ya? I wanna git a cone.

MRS. MAURRANT (*to* MRS. OLSEN *and* MRS. JONES): Good evening.

MRS. OLSEN and MRS. JONES: Good evenin', Mrs. Maurrant.

MRS. MAURRANT (*to* WILLIE): How many cones did you have today, already?

WILLIE (*belligerently*): I'm hot! All de other guys is havin' cones. Come on, gimme a dime.

MRS. MAURRANT: Well, it's the last one. (*She disappears.*)

MRS. JONES: You certainly don't talk very nice to your mother. (*To* MRS. OLSEN.) I'd like to hear one o' mine talkin' that way to me!

MRS. MAURRANT (*appearing at the window*): Remember, this is the last one.

WILLIE: Aw right. T'row it down. (MRS. FIORENTINO *reappears and leans out of the window again.*)

MRS. MAURRANT: Catch it! (*She throws out a twist of newspaper.* WILLIE *scrambles for it, hastily extracts the dime, drops the newspaper on the pavement and skates off, at the left.*)

MRS. FIORENTINO (*twisting her neck upwards*): Good evening, Mrs. Maurrant.

MRS. MAURRANT: Good evening, Mrs. Fiorentino. (*Calling after* WILLIE.) And don't come home too late, Willie! (*But* WILLIE *is already out of earshot.*)

MRS. FIORENTINO: Why don't you come down and be sociable?

MRS. MAURRANT: I'm keeping some supper warm for my husband. (*A slight pause.*) Well, maybe I will for just a minute. (*She leaves the window. The lights in her apartment go out.*)

MRS. FIORENTINO: She has her troubles with dot Willie.

MRS. JONES: I guess it don't bother her much. (*Significantly.*) She's got her mind on other things.

MRS. OLSEN (*looking about cautiously and coming over to the left of the stoop between the two women*): He vas comin' again today to see her.

MRS. JONES (*rising excitedly, and leaning over the balustrade*): Who—Sankey?

MRS. OLSEN (*nodding*): Yes.

MRS. FIORENTINO: Are you sure, Mrs. Olsen?

MRS. OLSEN: I seen him. I vas doostin' de halls.

MRS. FIORENTINO: Dot's terrible!

MRS. JONES: Wouldn't you think a woman her age, with a grown-up daughter—!

MRS. OLSEN: Two times already dis veek, I seen him here.

MRS. JONES: I seen him, meself, one day last week. He was comin' out o' the house, jest as I was comin' in wit' de dog. "Good mornin', Mrs. Jones," he says to me, as if butter wouldn't melt in his mouth. "Good mornin'," says I, lookin' him straight in the eye— (*Breaking off suddenly, as the vestibule door opens.*) Be careful, she's comin'. (MRS. MAURRANT *comes out of the house and stops, for a moment, on the top step.*)

MRS. MAURRANT: Goodness, ain't it hot! I think it's really cooler upstairs. (*She comes down the steps to the sidewalk.*)

MRS. JONES: Yeah, jes' what I was sayin', meself. I feel like a wet dishrag.

MRS. MAURRANT: I would have liked to go to the park concert tonight, if Rose had got home in time. I don't get much chance to go to concerts. My husband don't care for music. But Rose is more like me—just crazy about it.

MRS. JONES: Ain't she home yet?

MRS. MAURRANT: No. I think maybe she had to work overtime.

MRS. JONES: Well, all mine ever comes home for is to sleep.

MRS. FIORENTINO: The young girls nowadays—!

MRS. OLSEN: My sister was writin' me in Schweden is same t'ing—

MRS. JONES: It ain't only the young ones, either. (*A baby is heard crying in the cellar.*)

OLSEN'S VOICE (*from the cellar*): Olga! (*A* MAN, *in a dinner jacket and straw hat, appears at the left, whistling a jazz tune. He crosses the stage and goes off at the right.*)

MRS. OLSEN (*hurrying to the right*): I betcha the baby, she's cryin' again.

OLSEN'S VOICE: Ol-ga!

MRS. OLSEN: Yes. I come right away. (*She goes down the cellar steps.*)

126

MRS. JONES: What them foreigners don't know about bringin' up babies would fill a book.

MRS. FIORENTINO (*a little huffily*): Foreigners know joost as much as other people, Mrs. Jones. My mother had eight children and she brought up seven.

MRS. JONES (*tactfully*): Well, I'm not sayin' anythin' about the Joimans. The Joimans is different—more like the Irish. What I'm talkin' about is all them squareheads an' Polacks—(*with a glance in* KAPLAN's *direction*)—an' Jews.

BUCHANAN'S VOICE (*from a third-story window*): Good evening, ladies.

WOMEN (*in unison, looking upward*): Oh, good evening, Mr. Buchanan.

BUCHANAN'S VOICE: Well, is it hot enough for you?

MRS. JONES: I'll say!

BUCHANAN'S VOICE: I was just saying to my wife, it's not the heat I mind as much as it is the humidity.

MRS. JONES: Yeah, that's it! Makes everything stick to you.

MRS. MAURRANT: How's your wife feeling in this weather?

BUCHANAN'S VOICE: She don't complain about the weather. But she's afraid to go out of the house. Thinks maybe she couldn't get back in time, in case—you know.

MRS. JONES (*to the other women*): I was the same way, with my Vincent—afraid to take a step. But with Mae, I was up an' out till the very last minute.

MRS. FIORENTINO (*craning her neck upward*): Mr. Buchanan, do you think she would eat some nice minestrone—good Italian vegetable soup?

BUCHANAN'S VOICE: Why, much obliged, Mrs. F., but I really can't get her to eat a thing.

MRS. JONES (*rising and looking upward*): Tell her she ought to keep up her strength. She's got two to feed, you know.

BUCHANAN'S VOICE: Excuse me, she's calling.

MRS. JONES (*crossing to the railing, at the left of* MRS. FIOREN-TINO): You'd think it was him that was havin' the baby.

MRS. MAURRANT: She's such a puny little thing.

MRS. FIORENTINO (*with a sigh*): Well, that's the way it goes.

The little skinny ones have them and the big strong ones don't.

MRS. MAURRANT: Don't take it that way, Mrs. Fiorentino. You're a young woman, yet.

MRS. FIORENTINO (*shaking her head*): Oh, well!

MRS. JONES: My aunt, Mrs. Barclay, was forty-two— (*Breaking off.*) Oh, good evenin', Mr. Maurrant! (FRANK MAURRANT *appears, at the left, with his coat on his arm. He is a tall, powerfully built man of forty-five, with a rugged, grim face.*)

MRS. FIORENTINO: Good evening, Mr. Maurrant.

MAURRANT: 'Evenin'. (*He goes to the stoop and seats himself, mopping his face.*) Some baby of a day!

MRS. MAURRANT: Have you been working all this while, Frank?

MAURRANT: I'll say I've been workin'. Dress-rehearsin' since twelve o'clock, with lights—in this weather. An' tomorra I gotta go to Stamford, for the try-out.

MRS. MAURRANT: Oh, you're going to Stamford tomorrow?

MAURRANT: Yeah, the whole crew's goin'. (*Looking at her.*) What about it?

MRS. MAURRANT: Why, nothing. Oh, I've got some cabbage and potatoes on the stove for you.

MAURRANT: I just had a plate o' beans at the Coffee Pot. All I want is a good wash. I been sweatin' like a horse, all day. (*He rises and goes up the steps.*)

MRS. FIORENTINO: My husband, too; he's sweating terrible.

MRS. JONES: Mine don't. There's some people that just naturally do, and then there's others that don't.

MAURRANT (*to* MRS. MAURRANT): Is anybody upstairs?

MRS. MAURRANT: No. Willie's off playing with the boys. I can't keep him home.

MAURRANT: What about Rose?

MRS. MAURRANT: I think maybe she's working overtime.

MAURRANT: I never heard o' nobody workin' nights in a real-estate office.

MRS. MAURRANT: I thought maybe on account of the office

being closed tomorrow— (*To the others.*) Mr. Jacobson,
the head of the firm, died Tuesday, and tomorrow's the
funeral, so I thought maybe—

MRS. JONES: Yeah. Leave it to the Jews not to lose a workin'
day, without makin' up for it.

MAURRANT (*to* MRS. MAURRANT): She shouldn't be stayin'
out nights without us knowin' where she is.

MRS. MAURRANT: She didn't say a word about not coming
home.

MAURRANT: That's what I'm sayin', ain't it? It's a mother's
place to know what her daughter's doin'.

MRS. FIORENTINO (*soothingly*): Things are different nowadays, Mr. Maurrant, from what they used to be.

MAURRANT: Not in my family, they're not goin' to be no different. Not so long as I got somethin' to say.

GIRL'S VOICE (*offstage*): Red Rover! Red Rover! Let Freddie
come over! (GEORGE JONES, *a short, rather plump, red-faced
man, cigar in mouth, comes out of the house, as* MAURRANT
enters the vestibule.)

JONES: Hello, Mr. Maurrant.

MAURRANT (*curtly*): 'Evenin'. (*He enters the house.* JONES
looks after him in surprise, for a moment. MRS. MAURRANT
seats herself on the stoop.)

JONES: Good evenin', ladies.

MRS. FIORENTINO and MRS. MAURRANT: Good evening, Mr.
Jones.

JONES (*seating himself on the left balustrade*): What's the
matter with your hubby, Mrs. Maurrant? Guess he's feelin' the heat, huh?

MRS. MAURRANT: He's been working till just now and I guess
he's a little tired.

MRS. JONES: Men are all alike. They're all easy to get along
with, so long as everythin's goin' the way they want it to.
But once it don't—good night!

MRS. FIORENTINO: Yes, dot's true, Mrs. Jones.

JONES: Yeah, an' what about the women?

MRS. MAURRANT: I guess it's just the same with the women. I

often think it's a shame that people don't get along better, together. People ought to be able to live together in peace and quiet, without making each other miserable.

MRS. JONES: The way I look at it, you get married for better or worse, an' if it turns out to be worse, why all you can do is make the best of it.

MRS. MAURRANT: I think the trouble is people don't make allowances. They don't realize that everybody wants a kind word, now and then. After all, we're all human, and we can't just go along by ourselves, all the time, without ever getting a kind word. (*While she is speaking,* STEVE SANKEY *appears, at the right. He is in the early thirties, and is prematurely bald. He is rather flashily dressed, in a patently cheap, light-gray suit, and a straw hat, with a plaid band. As he appears,* MRS. JONES *and* MRS. FIORENTINO *exchange a swift, significant look.*)

SANKEY (*stopping at the right of the stoop and removing his hat*): Good evening, folks! Is it hot enough for you?

OTHERS: Good evening.

MRS. MAURRANT (*self-consciously*): Good evening, Mr. Sankey. (*Throughout the scene,* MRS. MAURRANT *and* SANKEY *try vainly to avoid looking at each other.*)

SANKEY: I don't know when we've had a day like this. Hottest June fifteenth in forty-one years. It was up to ninety-four at three P.M.

JONES: Six dead in Chicago. An' no relief in sight, the evenin' paper says. (MAURRANT *appears at the window of his apartment and stands there, looking out.*)

MRS. FIORENTINO: It's joost awful!

SANKEY: Well, it's good for the milk business. You know the old saying, it's an ill wind that blows nobody any good.

MRS. MAURRANT: Yes. You hardly get the milk in the morning, before it turns sour.

MRS. JONES: I'm just after pourin' half a bottle down the sink. (MAURRANT *leaves the window.*)

MRS. FIORENTINO: You shouldn't throw it away. You should make—what do you call it?—*schmier-käs'*.

SANKEY: Oh, I know what you mean—pot cheese. My wife makes it, too, once in a while.

MRS. MAURRANT: Is your wife all right again, Mr. Sankey? You were telling me last time, she had a cold. (MRS. JONES *and* MRS. FIORENTINO *exchange another look.*)

SANKEY: Was I? Oh, sure, sure. That was a couple weeks ago. Yes, sure, she's all right again. That didn't amount to anything much.

MRS. JONES: You got a family, too, ain't you?

SANKEY: Yes. Yes, I have. Two little girls. Well, I got to be going along. (*He goes to the left of the stoop and stops again.*) I told my wife I'd go down to the drugstore and get her some nice cold ginger ale. You want something to cool you off in this kind of weather.

MRS. JONES (*as* SANKEY *passes her*): If you ask me, all that gassy stuff don't do you a bit of good.

SANKEY: I guess you're right, at that. Still it cools you off. Well, good night, folks. See you all again. (*He strolls off, at the left, with affected nonchalance; but when he is almost out of sight, he casts a swift look back at* MRS. MAURRANT. *A dowdy* WOMAN, *wheeling a dilapidated baby carriage, appears at the left, and crosses the stage.*)

JONES: What's his name—Sankey?

MRS. JONES: Yeah—Mr. Sankey.

MRS. MAURRANT: He's the collector for the milk company. (AGNES CUSHING *comes out of the house. She is a thin, dried-up woman, past fifty.*)

MISS CUSHING (*coming down the steps*): Good evening.

OTHERS: Good evening, Miss Cushing.

MRS. MAURRANT: How is your mother today, Miss Cushing?

MISS CUSHING (*pausing at the left of the stoop*): Why, she complains of the heat. But I'm afraid it's really her heart. She's seventy-two, you know. I'm just going down to the corner to get her a little ice cream. (*As she goes off at the left,* OLSEN, *the janitor, a lanky Swede, struggles up the cellar steps with a large, covered, tin garbage barrel. The others look around in annoyance, as he bangs the garbage barrel upon the pavement.*)

OLSEN: Phew! Hot! (*He mops his face and neck with a dingy handkerchief, then lights his pipe and leans against the railing.*)

MRS. JONES (*significantly, as she crosses to the center of the stoop and sits*): Between you and I, I don't think her mother's got long for this world. Once the heart starts goin' back on you—!

MRS. FIORENTINO: It's too bad.

MRS. MAURRANT: Poor soul! She'll have nothing at all when her mother dies. She's just spent her whole life looking after her mother.

MRS. JONES: It's no more than her duty, is it?

MRS. FIORENTINO: You could not expect that she should neglect her mother.

VOICE (*offstage*): Char-lie!

MRS. MAURRANT: It's not a matter of neglecting. Only—it seems as if a person should get more out of life than just looking after somebody else.

MRS. JONES: Well, I hope to tell you, after all I've done for mine, I expect 'em to look after me, in my old age.

MRS. MAURRANT: I don't know. It seems to me you might just as well not live at all, as the way she does. (*Rising, with affected casualness.*) I don't know what's become of Willie. I think I'd better walk down to the corner and look for him. My husband don't like it if he stays out late. (*She goes off, at the left. They all watch her, in dead silence, until she is out of earshot. Then the storm breaks.*)

MRS. JONES (*rising excitedly*): Didja get that? Goin' to look for Willie! Can ya beat it?

MRS. FIORENTINO: It's joost terrible!

JONES: You think she's just goin' out lookin' for this guy Sankey?

MRS. JONES (*scornfully*): Ain't men the limit? What do you think he come walkin' by here for? (*Mincingly.*) Just strolled by to get the wife a little ginger ale. A fat lot he cares whether his wife has ginger ale!

MRS. FIORENTINO: Two little girls he's got, too!

JONES: Yeah, that ain't right—a bird like that, wit' a wife an' two kids of his own.

MRS. FIORENTINO: The way he stands there and looks and looks at her!

MRS. JONES: An' what about the looks she was givin' him! (*Seating herself again.*) You'd think he was the Prince of Wales, instead of a milk-collector. And didja get the crack about not seein' him for two weeks?

MRS. FIORENTINO: And joost today he was upstairs, Mrs. Olsen says. (OLSEN *approaches the stoop and removes his pipe from his mouth.*)

OLSEN (*pointing upwards*): Some day, her hoosban' is killing him. (*He replaces his pipe and goes back to his former position.*)

MRS. FIORENTINO: Dot would be terrible!

JONES: He's li'ble to, at that. You know, he's got a wicked look in his eye, dat baby has.

MRS. JONES: Well, it's no more than he deserves, the little rab- bit—goin' around breakin' up people's homes. (*Mockingly.*) Good evenin', folks! Jes' like Whozis on the radio.

JONES: D'ya think Maurrant is wise to what's goin' on?

MRS. JONES: Well, if he ain't, there must be somethin' the matter with him. But you never can tell about men. They're as blind as bats. An' what I always say is, in a case like that, the husband or the wife is always the last one to find out. (MISS CUSHING, *carrying a small paper bag, hurries on, at the left, in a state of great excitement.*)

MISS CUSHING (*breathlessly, as she comes up the left of the stoop*): Say what do you think! I just saw them together— the two of them!

MRS. JONES (*rising excitedly*): What did I tell you?

MRS. FIORENTINO: Where did you see them, Miss Cushing?

MISS CUSHING: Why, right next door, in the entrance to the

133

warehouse. They were standing right close together. And he had his hands up on her shoulders. It's awful, isn't it?

JONES: Looks to me like this thing is gettin' pretty serious.

MRS. JONES: You didn't notice if they was kissin' or anythin', did you?

MISS CUSHING: Well, to tell you the truth, Mrs. Jones, I was so ashamed for her, that I hardly looked at all.

JONES (*sotto voce, as the house door opens*): Look out! Maurrant's comin'. (*A conspirators' silence falls upon them, as* MAURRANT, *pipe in mouth, comes out of the house.*)

MISS CUSHING (*tremulously*): Good evening, Mr. Maurrant.

MAURRANT (*on the top step*): 'Evenin'. (*To the others.*) What's become of me wife?

MRS. JONES: Why, she said she was goin' around the corner to look for Willie.

MAURRANT (*grunts*): Oh.

MRS. JONES: They need a lot of lookin' after, when they're that age. (*A momentary silence.*)

MISS CUSHING: Well, I think I'd better get back to my mother. (*She goes up the steps.*)

MRS. JONES, MRS. FIORENTINO and JONES: Good night, Miss Cushing.

MISS CUSHING: Good night. (*As she passes* MAURRANT.) Good night, Mr. Maurrant.

MAURRANT: 'Night. (*She looks at him swiftly, and goes into the vestibule.*)

BOY'S VOICE (*offstage*): Red Rover! Red Rover! Let Mary come over! (*As* MISS CUSHING *enters the house,* SHIRLEY KAPLAN *appears at the ground-floor window, at the extreme right, with a glass of steaming tea in her hand. She is a dark, unattractive Jewess, past thirty. She wears a light house dress.* KAPLAN *goes on reading.*)

SHIRLEY (*to the neighbors outside; she speaks with the faintest trace of accent*): Good evening.

OTHERS (*not very cordially*): Good evenin'.

SHIRLEY: It's been a terrible day, hasn't it?

JONES and MRS. JONES: Yeah.

SHIRLEY (*going to the other window*): Papa, here's your tea. Haven't you finished your paper yet? It makes it so hot, with the lights on.

KAPLAN (*lowering his newspaper*): Oll right! Oll right! Put it out! Put it out! There is anahoo, notting to read in de papers. Notting but deevorce, skendal, and moiders. (*He speaks with a strong accent, overemphatically and with much gesticulation. He puts his paper away, removes his glasses, and starts to drink his tea.*)

SHIRLEY: There doesn't seem to be a breath of air, anywhere. (*No one answers.* SHIRLEY *goes away from the window and puts out the lights.*)

MRS. JONES (*sotto voce*): You wouldn't think anybody would want to read that Hebrew writin', would ya? I don't see how they make head or tail out of it, meself.

JONES: I guess if you learn it when you're a kid—

MRS. JONES (*suddenly*): Well, will you look at your hubby, Mrs. F.! He's sure got his hands full! (*She looks towards the left, greatly amused.* SHIRLEY *reappears at the window at the extreme right, and seats herself on the sill.*)

MRS. FIORENTINO (*leaning far out*): Joost look at him! (*Calling.*) Lippo, be careful you don't drop any!

LIPPO (*offstage*): 'Allo, Margherita! (*They all watch in amusement, as* FILIPPO FIORENTINO, *a fat Italian, with thick black hair and mustache, comes on at the left. He is clutching a violin in his left arm and balancing five ice-cream cones in his right hand.*) Who wantsa da ice-cream cone? Nice fresha ice-cream cone!

MRS. FIORENTINO: Lippo, you will drop them!

MRS. JONES (*going to him*): Here, gimme your violin. (*She relieves him of the violin and he shifts two of the cones to his left hand.*)

LIPPO (*as* MRS. JONES *hands the violin to* MRS. FIORENTINO): T'ank you, Meeses Jones. 'Ere's for you a nica, fresha ice-cream cone. (MRS. FIORENTINO *puts the violin on a chair behind her.*)

MRS. JONES (*taking a cone*): Why thank you very much, Mr. F.

LIPPO (*going to the window*): Meeses Fiorentino, 'ere's for you a nica, fresha ice-cream cone.

MRS. FIORENTINO (*taking the cone*): It makes me too fat.

LIPPO: Ah, no! Five, ten poun' more, nobody can tell da deef! (*He laughs aloud at his own joke and crosses to the stoop.*)

MRS. JONES (*enjoying her cone*): Ain't he a sketch, though?

LIPPO: Meester Jones, you eata da cone, ha?

JONES: Why, yeah, I will at that. Thanks. Thanks.

LIPPO: Meester Maurrant?

MAURRANT: Naw; I got me pipe.

LIPPO: You lika better da pipe den da ice cream? (*Crossing the stoop.*) Meesa Kaplan, nica, fresha cone, yes?

SHIRLEY: No, thanks. I really don't want any.

LIPPO: Meester Kaplan, yes?

KAPLAN (*waving his hand*): No, no! Tenks, tenks!

MRS. JONES (*to* JONES): You oughta pay Mr. F. for the cones.

JONES (*reluctantly reaching into his pocket*): Why, sure.

LIPPO (*excitedly*): Ah, no, no! I don' taka da mon'. I'm treata da whole crowd. I deedn' know was gona be such a biga crowd or I bringa doz'. (*Crossing to* OLSEN.) Meester Olsen, you lika da cone, ha?

OLSEN: Sure. Much oblige'. (*He takes the pipe from his mouth and stolidly licks the cone.*)

LIPPO (*seating himself on the stoop, with a long sigh of relaxation*): Aaah! (*He tastes the cone and smacking his lips, looks about for approval.*) Ees tasta good, ha?

JONES (*his mouth full*): You betcha!

MRS. JONES: It cools you off a little.

LIPPO: Sure. Dassa right. Cool you off. (*He pulls at his clothing and sits on the stoop.*) I'ma wat, wat—like I jus' come outa da bad-tub. Ees 'ota like hal in da Park. Two, t'ree t'ousan' people, everybody sweatin'—ees smal lika menageria. (*While he is speaking,* ALICE SIMPSON, *a tall, spare spinster, appears at the right. She goes up the steps, enters*

136

the vestibule, and is about to push one of the buttons on the side wall.)

MRS. JONES (*sotto voce*): She's from the Charities. (*Coming over to the stoop and calling into the vestibule.*) If you're lookin' for Mrs. Hildebrand, she ain't home yet.

MISS SIMPSON (*coming to the doorway*): Do you know when she'll be back?

MRS. JONES: Well, she oughta be here by now. She jus' went aroun' to the Livingston. That's the pitcher-theayter.

MISS SIMPSON (*outraged*): You mean she's gone to a moving-picture show?

OLSEN (*calmly*): She's comin' now.

LIPPO (*rising to his feet and calling vehemently*): Mees Hil'-brand! Hurry up! Hurry up! Ees a lady here. (*He motions violently to her to hurry.* LAURA HILDEBRAND *appears at the right, with her two children,* CHARLIE *and* MARY. *She is a small, rather young woman, with a manner of perpetual bewilderment. Both children are chewing gum, and* MARY *comes on skipping a rope and chanting:* "Apple, peach, pear, plum, banana." CHARLIE *carefully avoids all the cracks in the sidewalk.*)

MISS SIMPSON (*coming out on the steps*): Well, good evening, Mrs. Hildebrand!

MRS. HILDEBRAND (*flustered*): Good evening, Miss Simpson.

MISS SIMPSON: Where have you been?—to a moving-picture show?

MRS. HILDEBRAND: Yes ma'am.

MISS SIMPSON: And where did you get the money?

MRS. HILDEBRAND: It was only seventy-five cents.

MISS SIMPSON: Seventy-five cents is a lot, when you're being dispossessed and dependent upon charity. I suppose it came out of the money I gave you to buy groceries with.

MRS. HILDEBRAND: We always went, Thursday nights, to the pictures when my husband was home.

MISS SIMPSON: Yes, but your husband isn't home. And as far as anybody knows, he has no intention of coming home.

137

KAPLAN (*leaning forward out of his window*): Ees dis your conception of cherity?

SHIRLEY: Papa, why do you interfere?

MISS SIMPSON (*to* KAPLAN): You'll please be good enough to mind your own business.

KAPLAN: You should go home and read in your Bible de life of Christ.

MRS. JONES (*to* MRS. FIORENTINO): Will you listen to who's talkin' about Christ!

MISS SIMPSON (*turning her back on* KAPLAN *and speaking to* MRS. HILDEBRAND): You may as well understand right now that nobody's going to give you any money to spend on moving-picture shows.

LIPPO: Ah, wotsa da matter, lady? (*He thrusts his hand into his pocket and takes out a fistful of coins.*) 'Ere, you taka da mon', you go to da pitcha, ever' night. (*He forces the coins into* MRS. HILDEBRAND'S *hand.*) An' here's for da bambini. (*He gives each child a nickel.*)

MRS. FIORENTINO (*to* MRS. JONES): Dot's why we never have money.

MRS. HILDEBRAND (*bewildered*): I really oughtn't to take it.

LIPPO: Sure! Sure! I got plenta mon'.

MISS SIMPSON (*disgustedly*): We'd better go inside. I can't talk to you here, with all these people.

MRS. HILDEBRAND (*meekly*): Yes ma'am. (*She follows* MISS SIMPSON *into the house, her children clinging to her.*)

MRS. JONES: Wouldn't she give you a pain?

LIPPO: I tella you da whola troub'. She's a don' gotta nobody to sleepa wit'. (*The men laugh.*)

MRS. JONES (*to* MRS. FIORENTINO): Ain't he the limit!

MRS. FIORENTINO (*greatly pleased*): Tt!

LIPPO: Somebody go sleepa wit' her, she's alla right, Meester Jones, 'ow 'bout you? (*SHIRLEY, embarrassed, leaves the window.*)

JONES (*with a sheepish grin*): Naw, I guess not.

LIPPO: Wot'sa matter? You 'fraid you' wife, ha? Meester Maurrant, how 'bout you? (*MAURRANT emits a short laugh.*)

MRS. FIORENTINO (*delighted*): Lippo, you're joost awful.

LIPPO (*enjoying himself hugely*): Alla ri'. Ahma gonna go myself! (*He laughs boisterously. The others laugh too.*)

MRS. JONES (*suddenly*): Here's your wife, now, Mr. Maurrant. (*A sudden silence falls upon them all, as* MRS. MAURRANT *approaches at the left. A swift glance apprises her of* MAUR-RANT'S *presence.*)

LIPPO: 'Allo, Meeses Maurrant. Why you don' come to da concerto?

MRS. MAURRANT: Well, I was waiting for Rose, but she didn't get home. (*To* MAURRANT, *as she starts to go up the steps.*) Is she home yet, Frank?

MAURRANT: No, she ain't. Where you been all this while?

MRS. MAURRANT: Why, I've been out looking for Willie.

MAURRANT: I'll give him a good fannin', when I get hold of him.

MRS. MAURRANT: Ah, don't whip him, Frank, please don't. All boys are wild like that, when they're that age.

JONES: Sure! My boy Vincent was the same way. An' look at him, today—drivin' his own taxi an' makin' a good livin'.

LIPPO (*leaning on the balustrade*): Ees jussa same t'ing wit' me. W'en Ahm twelva year, I run away—I don' never see my parents again.

MAURRANT: That's all right about that. But it ain't gonna be that way in my family.

MRS. MAURRANT (*as* MISS SIMPSON *comes out of the house*): Look out, Frank. Let the lady pass.

MISS SIMPSON: Excuse me. (*They make way for her, as she comes down the steps.* MRS. MAURRANT *seats herself on the stoop.*)

LIPPO: Meeses Hil'brand, she gotta de tougha luck, ha? To-morra, dey gonna t'row 'er out in da street, ha?

MISS SIMPSON (*stopping at the right of the stoop and turning towards him*): Yes, they are. And if she has any place to sleep, it will only be because the Charities find her a place. And you'd be doing her a much more neighborly act, if you helped her to realize the value of money, instead of encouraging her to throw it away.

LIPPO (*with a deprecatory shrug*): Ah, lady, no! I give 'er coupla dollar, maka 'er feel good, maka me feel good—dat don' 'urt nobody. (SHIRLEY *reappears at the window.*)

MISS SIMPSON: Yes it does. It's bad for her character.

KAPLAN (*throwing away his cigarette and laughing aloud*): Ha! You mek me leff!

MISS SIMPSON (*turning, angrily*): Nobody's asking your opinion.

KAPLAN: Dot's oll right. I'm taling you wit'out esking. You hoid maybe already dot poem:
>   "Orgenized cherity, measured and iced,
>   In der name of a kushus, stetistical Christ."

MISS SIMPSON (*fiercely*): All the same, you Jews are the first to run to the Charities. (*She strides angrily off at the right.* LIPPO, *affecting a mincing gait, pretends to follow her.*)

KAPLAN (*leaning out of the window*): Come back and I'll tal you somet'ing will maybe do good your kerecter.

MRS. FIORENTINO: Lippo!

MRS. JONES (*highly amused*): Look at him, will ya?

LIPPO (*laughing and waving his hand*): Gooda-bye, lady! (*He comes back to the stoop.*)

KAPLAN (*to the others*): Dey toin out in de street a mudder vit' two children, and dis female comes and preaches to her bourgeois morelity.

MRS. JONES (*to* MRS. FIORENTINO): He's shootin' off his face again.

SHIRLEY: Papa, it's time to go to bed!

KAPLAN (*irritably*): Lat me alone, Shoiley. (*Rising and addressing the others.*) Dees cherities are notting but anudder dewise for popperizing de verking-klesses. W'en de lendlords steal from de verkers a million dollars, dey give to de Cherities a t'ousand.

MAURRANT: Yeah? Well, who's puttin' her out on the street? What about the lan'lord here? He's a Jew, ain't he?

MRS. JONES: I'll say he's a Jew! Isaac Cohen!

KAPLAN: Jews oder not Jews—wot has dis got to do vit' de quastion? I'm not toking releegion, I'm toking economics. So long as de kepitalist klesses—

MAURRANT (*interrupting*): I'm talkin' about if you don't pay your rent, you gotta move.

MRS. MAURRANT: It doesn't seem right, though, to put a poor woman out of her home.

MRS. FIORENTINO: And for her husband to run away—dot vos not right either.

LIPPO: I betcha 'e's got 'nudder woman. He find a nice blonda chicken, 'e run away.

MRS. JONES: There ought to be a law against women goin' around, stealin' other women's husbands.

MRS. FIORENTINO: Yes, dot's right, Mrs. Jones.

MAURRANT: Well, what I'm sayin' is, it ain't the landlord's fault.

KAPLAN: Eet's de folt of our economic system. So long as de institution of priwate property exeests, de verkers vill be at de moicy of de property-owning klesses.

MAURRANT: That's a lot o' bushwa! I'm a woikin' man, see? I been payin' dues for twenty-two years in the Stage-Hands Union. If we're not gettin' what we want, we call a strike, see?—and then we get it.

LIPPO: Sure! Ees same wit' me. We gotta Musician Union. We getta pay for da rehears', we getta pay for da overtime—

SHIRLEY: That's all right when you belong to a strong union. But when a union is weak, like the Teachers' Union, it doesn't do you any good.

MRS. JONES (*to* MRS. FIORENTINO): Can y' imagine that?—teachers belongin' to a union!

KAPLAN (*impatiently*): Oll dese unions eccomplish notting wotever. Oll dis does not toch de fondamental problem. So long as de tuls of industry are in de hands of de kepitalist klesses, ve vill hev exploitation and sloms and—

MAURRANT: T' hell wit' all dat hooey! I'm makin' a good livin' an' I'm not doin' any kickin'.

OLSEN (*removing his pipe from his mouth*): Ve got prosperity, dis coontry.

JONES: You said somethin'!

KAPLAN: Sure, for de reech is planty prosperity! Mister Morgan rides in his yacht and upstairs dey toin a voman vit' two children in de street.

MAURRANT: And if you was to elect a Socialist president tomorra, it would be the same thing.

MRS. FIORENTINO: Yes, dot's right, Mr. Maurrant.

JONES: You're right!

KAPLAN: Who's toking about electing presidents? Ve must put de tuls of industry in de hends of de vorking-klesses and dis ken be accomplished only by a sushal revolution!

MAURRANT: Yeah? Well, we don't want no revolutions in this country, see? (*General chorus of assent.*)

MRS. JONES: I know all about that stuff—teachin' kids there ain't no Gawd an' that their gran'fathers was monkeys.

JONES (*rising, angrily*): Free love, like they got in Russia, huh? (KAPLAN *makes a gesture of impatient disgust, and sinks back into his chair.*)

MAURRANT: There's too goddam many o' you Bolshevikis runnin' aroun' loose. If you don't like the way things is run here, why in hell don't you go back where you came from?

SHIRLEY: Everybody has a right to his own opinion, Mr. Maurrant.

MAURRANT: Not if they're against law and order, they ain't. We don't want no foreigners comin' in, tellin' us how to run things.

MRS. FIORENTINO: It's nothing wrong to be a foreigner. Many good people are foreigners.

LIPPO: Sure! Looka Eetalians. Looka Cristoforo Colombo! 'E'sa firs' man discov' America—'e's Eetalian, jussa like me.

MAURRANT: I'm not sayin' anythin' about that—

OLSEN (*removing his pipe*): Firs' man is Leif Ericson.

LIPPO (*excitedly, going towards* OLSEN): Wassa dat?

OLSEN: Firs' man is Leif Ericson.

LIPPO: No! No! Colombo! Cristoforo Colomb'—'e'sa firs' man discov' America—ever'body know dat! (*He looks about appealingly.*)

MRS. JONES: Why, sure, everybody knows that.

JONES: Every kid learns that in school.

SHIRLEY: Ericson was really the first discoverer—

LIPPO (*yelling*): No! Colomb!

SHIRLEY: But Columbus was the first to open America to settlement.

LIPPO (*happily, as he goes back to the stoop*): Sure, dassa wot Ahm say—Colomb' is firs'.

OLSEN: Firs' man is Leif Ericson. (LIPPO *taps his forehead, significantly.*)

LIPPO: Looka wot Eetalian do for America—'e build bridge, 'e build railroad, 'e build subway, 'e dig sewer. Wit' out Eetalian, ees no America.

JONES: Like I heard a feller sayin': the Eye-talians built New York, the Irish run it an' the Jews own it. (*Laughter.*)

MRS. FIORENTINO (*convulsed*): Oh! Dot's funny!

JONES (*pleased with his success*): Yep; the Jews own it all right.

MAURRANT: Yeah, an' they're the ones that's doin' all the kickin'.

SHIRLEY: It's no disgrace to be a Jew, Mr. Maurrant.

MAURRANT: I'm not sayin' it is. All I'm sayin' is, what we need in this country is a little more respect for law an' order. Look at what's happenin' to people's homes, with all this divorce an' one thing an' another. Young girls goin' around smokin' cigarettes an' their skirts up around their necks. An' a lot o' long-haired guys talkin' about free love an' birth control an' breakin' up decent people's homes. I tell you it's time somethin' was done to put the fear o' God into people!

MRS. JONES: Good for you, Mr. Maurrant!

JONES: You're damn right.

MRS. FIORENTINO: Dot's right, Mr. Maurrant!

MRS. MAURRANT: Sometimes, I think maybe they're only trying to get something out of life.

MAURRANT: Get somethin', huh? Somethin' they oughtn't to have, is that it?

MRS. MAURRANT: No; I was only thinking—

MAURRANT: Yeah, you were only thinkin', huh?

KAPLAN (*rising to his feet again*): De family is primerily an economic institution.

MRS. JONES (*to* MRS. FIORENTINO): He's in again.

KAPLAN: W'en priwate property is ebolished, de family will no longer hev eny reason to exeest.

SHIRLEY: Can't you keep quiet, papa?

MAURRANT (*belligerently*): Yeah? Is that so? No reason to exist, huh? Well, it's gonna exist, see? Children respectin' their parents an' doin' what they're told, get me? An' husbands and wives, lovin' an' honorin' each other, like they said they would, when they was spliced—an' any dirty sheeny that says different is li'ble to get his head busted open, see?

MRS. MAURRANT (*springing to her feet*): Frank!

SHIRLEY (*trying to restrain* KAPLAN): Papa!

KAPLAN: Oll right! I should argue vit' a low-kless gengster.

MAURRANT (*raging*): Who's a gangster? Why, you goddam—! (*He makes for the balustrade.*)

MRS. MAURRANT (*seizing his arm*): Frank!

JONES (*seizing the other arm*): Hey! Wait a minute! Wait a minute!

MAURRANT: Lemme go!

SHIRLEY (*interposing herself*): You should be ashamed to talk like that to an old man! (*She slams down the window.*)

MAURRANT: Yeah? (*To* MRS. MAURRANT *and* JONES) All right, lemme go! I ain't gonna do nothin'. (*They release him.* SHIRLEY *expostulates with* KAPLAN *and leads him away from the window.*)

MRS. JONES (*who has run over to the right of the stoop*):

144

Maybe if somebody handed him one, he'd shut up with his talk for a while.

LIPPO: 'E talka lika dat een Eetaly, Mussolini's gonna geeve 'eem da castor oil.

MRS. JONES (*laughing*): Yeah? Say, that's a funny idea! (*Still chuckling, she goes back to the railing at the left of the stoop.*)

JONES: No kiddin', is that what they do?

MRS. FIORENTINO: Yes, dot's true. My husband read it to me in the Italian paper.

MRS. MAURRANT: Why must people always be hurting and injuring each other? Why can't they live together in peace?

MAURRANT (*mockingly*): Live in peace! You're always talkin' about livin' in peace!

MRS. MAURRANT: Well, it's true, Frank. Why can't people just as well be kind to each other?

MAURRANT: Then let 'im go live with his own kind.

JONES (*coming down the steps*): Yeah, that's what I say. (*As MRS. JONES laughs aloud.*) What's eatin' you?

MRS. JONES: I was just thinkin' about the castor oil. (*MAUR-RANT seats himself on the right balustrade.*)

LIPPO: Sure, 'esa funny fell', Mussolini. (*Doubling up in mock pain.*) 'E geeve 'em da pain in da belly, dey no can talk. (*Suddenly.*) Look! 'Eresa da boy. 'Esa walk along da street an' reada da book. Datsa da whola troub': reada too much book. (*While LIPPO is speaking, SAMUEL KAPLAN appears at the left. He is twenty-one, slender, with dark, unruly hair and a sensitive, mobile face. He is hatless, and his coat is slung over one shoulder. He walks along slowly, absorbed in a book. As he approaches the stoop, SHIRLEY, in a kimono, appears at the closed window, opens it, and is about to go away again, when she sees SAM.*)

SHIRLEY (*calling*): Sam!

SAM (*looking up*): Hello, Shirley.

SHIRLEY: Are you coming in?

SAM: No, not yet. It's too hot to go to bed.

SHIRLEY: Well, I'm tired. And Papa's going to bed, too. So don't make a noise when you come in.

SAM: I won't.

SHIRLEY: Good night.

SAM: Good night. (SHIRLEY *goes away from the window; to the others, as he seats himself on the curb to the right of the stoop*): Good evening!

SEVERAL: 'Evening.

LIPPO (*approaching* SAM): 'Ow you lika da concerto? I see you sittin' in da fronta seat.

SAM: I didn't like it. Why don't they play some real music, instead of all those Italian organ-grinder's tunes?

LIPPO (*excitedly*): Wotsa da matter? You don't like da Verdi?

SAM: No, I don't. It's not music!

LIPPO: Wot you call music—da Tschaikov', ha? (*He hums derisively a few bars from the first movement of the* Symphonie Pathétique.)

SAM: Yes, Tschaikovsky—and Beethoven. Music that comes from the soul.

MRS. MAURRANT: The one I like is— (*She hums the opening bars of Mendelssohn's "Spring Song."*)

LIPPO: Dotsa da "Spreeng Song" from da Mendelson.

MRS. MAURRANT: Yes! I love that. (*She goes on humming softly.*)

MRS. FIORENTINO: And the walzer von Johann Strauss. (*She hums the "Wienerwald Waltz."*)

MRS. JONES: Well, gimme a good jazz band, every time.

LIPPO (*protesting*): Ah, no! Ees not music, da jazz. Ees breaka your ear. (*He imitates the discordant blaring of a saxophone.*)

JONES (*bored*): Well, I guess I'll be on me way.

MRS. JONES: Where are *you* goin'?

JONES: Just around to Callahan's to shoot a little pool. Are you comin' along, Mr. Maurrant?

MAURRANT: I'm gonna wait awhile. (*A* MAN, *with a club-foot, appears at the right and crosses the stage.*)

MRS. JONES (*as* JONES *goes toward the right*): Don't be comin' home lit, at all hours o' the mornin'.

JONES (*over his shoulder*): Aw, lay off dat stuff! I'll be back in a half an hour. (*He goes off, at the right.*)

VOICE (*offstage*): Char-lie!

MRS. JONES: Him an' his pool! Tomorra he won't be fit to go to work, again.

SAM (*who has been awaiting a chance to interrupt*): When you hear Beethoven, it expresses the struggles and emotions of the human soul.

LIPPO (*waving him aside*): Ah, ees no good, da Beethoven. Ees alla time sad, sad. Ees wanna maka you cry. I don' wanna cry, I wanna laugh. Eetalian music ees make you 'appy. Ees make you feel good. (*He sings several bars of "La donna é mobile."*)

MRS. MAURRANT (*applauding*): Yes, I like that, too.

LIPPO: Ah, ees bew-tiful! Ees maka you feela fine. Ees maka you wanna dance. (*He executes several dance steps.*)

MRS. FIORENTINO (*rising*): Vait, Lippo, I vill give you music. (*She goes away from the window. The lights go on, in the Fiorentino apartment.*)

LIPPO (*calling after her*): Playa Puccini, Margherita! (*He hums an air from* Madame Butterfly. *Then as* MRS. FIORENTINO *begins to play the waltz from* La Bohème *on the piano.*) Ah! *La Bohème!* Bew-tiful! Who'sa gonna dansa wit' me? Meeses Maurrant, 'ow 'bout you?

MRS. MAURRANT (*with an embarrassed laugh*): Well, I don't know. (*She looks timidly at* MAURRANT, *who gives no sign.*)

LIPPO: Ah, come on! Dansa wit' me! (*He takes her by the hand.*)

MRS. MAURRANT: Well, all right, I will.

LIPPO: Sure, we hava nica dance. (*They begin to dance on the sidewalk.*)

LIPPO (*to* MAURRANT): Your wife ees dansa swell.

MRS. MAURRANT (*laughing*): Oh, go on, Mr. Fiorentino! But I always loved to dance! (*They dance on.* SANKEY *appears, at the left, carrying a paper bag, from which the neck of a ginger-ale bottle protrudes.* MAURRANT *sees him and rises.*)

MRS. JONES (*following* MAURRANT's *stare and seeing* SANKEY): Look out! You're blockin' traffic!

SANKEY (*stopping at the left of the stoop*): I see you're having a little dance. (MRS. MAURRANT *sees him and stops dancing.* LIPPO *leans against the right balustrade, panting. The music goes on.*) Say, go right ahead. Don't let me stop you.

MRS. MAURRANT: Oh, that's all right. I guess we've danced about enough. (*She goes up the steps, ill at ease.*)

SANKEY: It's a pretty hot night for dancing.

MRS. MAURRANT: Yes, it is.

SANKEY (*going towards the right*): Well, I got to be going along. Good night, folks.

OTHERS (*except* MAURRANT): Good night.

LIPPO (*as he seats himself at the left of the stoop*): Stoppa da music, Margherita! (*The music stops.* SANKEY *goes off, at the right.* MRS. MAURRANT *goes quickly up the steps.*)

MAURRANT (*stopping her*): Who's that bird?

MRS. MAURRANT: Why, that's Mr. Sankey. He's the milk-collector.

MAURRANT: Oh, he is, is he? Well, what's he hangin' around here for?

MRS. MAURRANT: Well, he lives just down the block, somewhere.

MRS. JONES: He's just been down to the drugstore, gettin' some ginger ale for his wife.

MAURRANT: Yeah? Well, what I want to know is, why ain't Rose home yet?

MRS. MAURRANT: I told you, Frank—

MAURRANT: I know all about what you told me. What I'm sayin' is, you oughta be lookin' after your kids, instead of doin' so much dancin'.

MRS. MAURRANT: Why, it's the first time I've danced, in I don't know when.

MAURRANT: That's all right, about that. But I want 'em home, instead o' battin' around the streets, hear me? (*While he is speaking,* WILLIE *appears sobbing, at the left, his clothes torn and his face scratched. He is carrying his skates.*)

MRS. MAURRANT (*coming down the steps*): Why, Willie, what's the matter? (*Reproachfully, as* WILLIE *comes up to her, sniffling.*) Have you been fighting again?

WILLIE (*with a burst of indignation*): Well, dat big bum ain't gonna say dat to me. I'll knock da stuffin's out o' him, dat's what I'll do!

MAURRANT (*tensely, as he comes down the steps*): Who's been sayin' things to you?

WILLIE: Dat big bum, Joe Connolly, dat's who! (*Blubbering.*) I'll knock his goddam eye out, next time!

MRS. MAURRANT: Willie!

MAURRANT (*seizing* WILLIE'S *arm*): Shut up your swearin', do you hear? Or I'll give you somethin' to bawl for. What did he say to you, huh? What did he say to you?

WILLIE (*struggling*): Ow! Leggo my arm!

MRS. MAURRANT: What difference does it make what a little street-loafer like that says?

MAURRANT: Nobody's askin' you! (*To* WILLIE.) What did he say? (*He and* MRS. MAURRANT *exchange a swift involuntary look; then* MAURRANT *releases the boy.*) G'wan up to bed now, an' don't let me hear no more out o' you. (*Raising his hand.*) G'wan now. Beat it! (*WILLIE ducks past* MAURRANT *and hurries up the steps and into the vestibule.*)

MRS. MAURRANT: Wait, Willie, I'll go with you. (*She goes up the steps, then stops and turns.*) Are you coming up, Frank?

MAURRANT: No I ain't. I'm goin' around to Callahan's for a drink, an' if Rose ain't home, when I get back, there's gonna be trouble. (*Without another glance or word, he goes off at the right.* MRS. MAURRANT *looks after him for a moment, with a troubled expression.*)

MRS. MAURRANT (*entering the vestibule*): Well, good night, all.

OTHERS: Good night. (SAM *rises. As* MRS. MAURRANT *and* WILLIE *enter the house,* MRS. FIORENTINO *reappears at the window.*)

MRS. FIORENTINO: Lippo! (*She sees that something is wrong.*)

MRS. JONES: Say, you missed it all! (SAM, *about to go up the steps, stops at the right of the stoop.*)

MRS. FIORENTINO (*eagerly*): Vat?

MRS. JONES (*volubly*): Well, they was dancin', see? An' who should come along but Sankey!

MRS. FIORENTINO: Tt! (*A light appears in the Maurrant apartment.*)

MRS. JONES: Well, there was the three o' them—Mr. Maurrant lookin' at Sankey as if he was ready to kill him, an' Mrs. Maurrant as white as a sheet, an' Sankey, as innocent as the babe unborn.

MRS. FIORENTINO: Did he say something?

MRS. JONES: No, not till after Sankey was gone. Then he wanted to know who he was an' what he was doin' here. "He's the milk-collector," she says.

MRS. FIORENTINO: It's joost awful.

MRS. JONES: Oh, an' then Willie comes home.

LIPPO: Da boy tella 'eem 'is mamma ees a whore an' Weelie leeck 'im.

MRS. JONES: Well, an' what else is she?

SAM (*unable longer to restrain himself*): Stop it! Stop it! Can't you let her alone? Have you no hearts? Why do you tear her to pieces, like a pack of wolves? It's cruel, cruel! (*He chokes back a sob, then dashes abruptly into the house.*)

LIPPO (*rising to his feet and yelling after him*): Wotsa matter you?

MRS. JONES: Well, listen to him, will you! He must be goin' off his nut, too.

LIPPO: 'Esa reada too mucha book. Ees bad for you.

MRS. FIORENTINO: I think he is loving the girl.

MRS. JONES: Yeah? Well, that's all the Maurrants need is to have their daughter get hooked up wit' a Jew. It's a fine house to be livin' in, ain't it, between the Maurrants upstairs, an' that bunch o' crazy Jews down here. (*A GIRL appears at the left, glancing apprehensively, over her shoulder, at a MAN who is walking down the street behind her. They cross the stage and go off, at the right.*)

MRS. JONES (*as MRS. OLSEN comes up the cellar steps and over to the stoop*): Well, good night.

MRS. FIORENTINO: Good night, Mrs. Jones.

LIPPO: Goo' night, Meeses Jones.

MRS. JONES: Wait a minute, Mrs. Olsen. I'll go with you. (*MRS. JONES and MRS. OLSEN enter the house. OLSEN yawns mightily, knocks the ashes from his pipe, and goes down the cellar steps. WILLIE MAURRANT leans out of the window and spits into the areaway. Then he leaves the window and turns out the light. A POLICEMAN appears, at the right, and strolls across the stage.*)

LIPPO (*who has gone up the steps*): Margherita, eef I ever ketcha you sleepin' wit' da meelkaman, Ahm gonna breaka your neck.

MRS. FIORENTINO (*yawning*): Stop your foolishness, Lippo, and come to bed! (*LIPPO laughs and enters the house. MRS. FIORENTINO takes the pillow off the window sill, closes the window, and starts to pull down the shade. ROSE MAURRANT and HARRY EASTER appear at the left. ROSE is a pretty girl of twenty, cheaply but rather tastefully dressed. EASTER is about thirty-five, good-looking, and obviously prosperous.*)

MRS. FIORENTINO: Good evening, Miss Maurrant.

ROSE (*as they pass the window*): Oh, good evening, Mrs. Fiorentino. (*ROSE and EASTER cross to the stoop. MRS. FIORENTINO looks at them a moment, then pulls down the shade and turns out the lights.*)

ROSE (*stopping at the foot of the steps*): Well, this is where

I live, Mr. Easter. (*She extends her hand.*) I've had a lovely time.

EASTER (*taking her hand*): Why, you're not going to leave me like this, are you? I've hardly had a chance to talk to you.

ROSE (*laughing*): We've been doing nothing but talking since six o'clock. (*She tries gently to extricate her hand.*)

EASTER (*still holding it*): No, we haven't. We've been eating and dancing. And now, just when I want to talk to you—(*he puts his other arm around her*)—Rose—

ROSE (*rather nervously*): Please don't, Mr. Easter. Please let go. I think there's somebody coming. (*She frees herself, as the house door opens and* MRS. OLSEN *appears in the vestibule. They stand in silence, as* MRS. OLSEN *puts the door off the latch, tries it to see that it is locked, dims the light in the vestibule and comes out on the stoop.*)

MRS. OLSEN (*as she comes down the steps*): Goot evening, Miss Maurrant. (*She darts a swift look at* EASTER *and crosses to the cellar steps.*)

ROSE: Good evening, Mrs. Olsen. How's the baby?

MRS. OLSEN: She vas cryin' all the time. I tank she vas gettin' new teet'.

ROSE: Oh, the poor little thing! What a shame!

MRS. OLSEN (*as she goes down the steps*): Yes, ma'am. Goot night, Miss Maurrant.

ROSE: Good night, Mrs. Olsen. (*To* EASTER.) She's got the cutest little baby you ever saw.

EASTER (*rather peevishly*): Yeah? That's great. (*Taking* ROSE's *hand again.*) Rose, listen—

ROSE: I've really got to go upstairs now, Mr. Easter. It's awfully late.

EASTER: Well, can't I come up with you, for a minute?

ROSE (*positively*): No, of course not!

EASTER: Why not?

ROSE: Why, we'd wake everybody up. Anyhow, my father wouldn't like it.

EASTER: Aren't you old enough to do what you like?

ROSE: It's not that. Only I think when you're living with people, there's no use doing things you know they don't like. (*Embarrassed.*) Anyhow, there's only the front room and my little brother sleeps there. So good night, Mr. Easter.

EASTER (*taking both her hands*): Rose—I'm crazy about you.

ROSE: Please let me go, now.

EASTER: Kiss me good night.

ROSE: No.

EASTER: Why not, hm?

ROSE: I don't want to.

EASTER: Just one kiss.

ROSE: No.

EASTER: Yes! (*He takes her in his arms and kisses her. ROSE frees herself and goes to the right of the stoop.*)

ROSE (*her bosom heaving*): It wasn't nice of you to do that.

EASTER (*going over to her*): Why not? Didn't you like it? Hm?

ROSE: Oh, it's not that.

EASTER: Then what is it, hm?

ROSE (*turning and facing him*): You know very well what it is. You've got a wife, haven't you?

EASTER: What of it? I tell you I'm clean off my nut about you.

ROSE (*nervously, as the house door opens*): Look out! Somebody's coming. (*EASTER goes to the other side of the stoop and they fall into a self-conscious silence, as MRS. JONES comes out of the house, leading an ill-conditioned dog.*)

MRS. JONES (*as she comes down the steps*): Oh, good evenin'. (*She stares at EASTER, then goes towards the right.*)

ROSE: Good evening, Mrs. Jones. It's been a terrible day, hasn't it?

MRS. JONES: Yeah. Awful. (*Stopping.*) I think your father's been kinda worried about you.

ROSE: Oh, has he?

MRS. JONES: Yeah. Well, I gotta give Queenie her exercise. Good night. (*She stares at* EASTER *again, then goes off at right.*)

ROSE: Good night, Mrs. Jones. (*To* EASTER.) I'll soon have all the neighbors talking about me.

EASTER (*going over to her again*): What can they say, hm? That they saw you saying good night to somebody on the front doorstep?

ROSE: They can say worse than that—and what's more, they will, too.

EASTER: Well, why not snap out of it all?

ROSE: Out of what?

EASTER (*indicating the house*): This! The whole business. Living in a dirty old tenement like this; working all day in a real-estate office, for a measly twenty-five a week. You're not going to try to tell me you like living this way, are you?

ROSE: No, I can't say that I like it, especially. But maybe it won't always be this way. Anyhow, I guess I'm not so much better than anybody else.

EASTER (*taking her hand*): Do you know what's the matter with you? You're not wise to yourself. Why, you've got just about everything, you have. You've got looks and personality and a bean on your shoulders—there's nothing you haven't got. You've got "It," I tell you.

ROSE: You shouldn't keep looking at me, all the time, at the office. The other girls are beginning to pass hints about it.

EASTER (*releasing her hand, genuinely perturbed*): Is that a fact? You see, that shows you! I never even knew I was looking at you. I guess I just can't keep my eyes off you. Well, we've got to do something about it.

ROSE (*nervously snapping the clasp of her handbag*): I guess the only thing for me to do is to look for another job.

EASTER: Yes, that's what I've been thinking, too. (*As she is about to demur.*) Wait a minute, honey! I've been doing a little thinking and I've got it all doped out. The first thing you do is throw up your job, see?

ROSE: But—

EASTER: Then you find yourself a nice, cozy little apartment somewhere. (*As she is about to interrupt again.*) Just a minute, now! Then you get yourself a job on the stage.

ROSE: How could I get a job on the stage?

EASTER: Why, as easy as walking around the block. I've got three or four friends in the show business. Ever hear of Harry Porkins?

ROSE: No.

EASTER: Well, he's the boy that put on *Mademoiselle Marie* last year. He's an old pal of mine, and all I'd have to say to him is—(*putting his arm around her shoulder*)— "Harry, here's a little girl I'm interested in," and he'd sign you up in a minute.

ROSE: I don't think I'd be any good on the stage.

EASTER: Why, what are you talking about, sweetheart? There's a dozen girls, right now, with their names up in electric lights, that haven't got half your stuff. All you got to do is go about it in the right way—put up a little front, see? Why, half the game is nothing but bluff. Get yourself a classy little apartment, and fill it up with trick furniture, see? Then you doll yourself up in a flock of Paris clothes and you throw a couple or three parties and you're all set. (*Taking her arm.*) Wouldn't you *like* to be on Broadway?

ROSE: I don't believe I ever could be.

EASTER: Isn't it worth trying? What have you got here, hm? This is no kind of a racket for a girl like you. (*Taking her hand.*) You do like me a little, don't you?

ROSE: I don't know if I do or not.

EASTER: Why, sure you do. And once you get to know me better, you'd like me even more. I'm no Valentino, but I'm not a bad scout. Why, think of all the good times we could have together—you with a little apartment and all. And maybe we could get us a little car—

Rose: And what about your wife?

Easter (*letting go her hand*): The way I figure it is, she doesn't have to know anything about it. She stays up there in Bronxville, and there are lots of times when business keeps me in New York. Then, in the summer, she goes to the mountains. Matter of fact, she's going next week and won't be back until September.

Rose (*shaking her head and going towards the stoop*): I don't think it's the way I'd want things to be.

Easter: Why, there's nothing really wrong about it.

Rose: Maybe there isn't. But it's just the way I feel about it, I guess.

Easter: Why, you'd get over that in no time. There's lots of girls—

Rose: Yes, I know there are. But you've been telling me all along I'm different.

Easter: Sure, you're different. You're in a class by yourself. Why, sweetheart— (*He tries to take her in his arms.*)

Rose (*pushing him away*): No. And you mustn't call me sweetheart.

Easter: Why not?

Rose: Because I'm not your sweetheart.

Easter: I want you to be— (*A sudden yell of pain is heard from upstairs. They both look up, greatly startled.*)

Easter: My God, what's that—a murder?

Rose: It must be poor Mrs. Buchanan. She's expecting a baby.

Easter: Why does she yell like that? God, I thought somebody was being killed.

Rose: The poor thing! (*With sudden impatience, she starts up the steps.*) I've got to go, now. Good night.

Easter (*taking her hand*): But, Rose—

Rose (*freeing her hand quickly*): No, I've got to go. (*Suddenly.*) Look, there's my father. There'll only be an argument, if he sees you.

Easter: All right, I'll go. (*He goes towards the left, as* Maurrant *appears at the right.*)

ROSE (*going up to the top step*): Good night.

EASTER: Good night. (*He goes off, at the left.* ROSE *begins searching in her handbag for her latchkey.*)

ROSE (*as* MAURRANT *approaches*): Hello, Pop.

MAURRANT (*stopping at the foot of the steps*): Who was that you was talkin' to?

ROSE: That's Mr. Easter. He's the manager of the office.

MAURRANT: What's he doin' here? You been out wit' him?

ROSE: Yes, he took me out to dinner.

MAURRANT: Oh, he did, huh?

ROSE: Yes, I had to stay late to get out some letters. You see, Pop, the office is closed tomorrow, on account of Mr. Jacobson's funeral—

MAURRANT: Yeah, I know all about that. This is a hell of a time to be gettin' home from dinner.

ROSE: Well, we danced afterwards.

MAURRANT: Oh, you danced, huh? With a little pettin' on the side, is that it?

ROSE (*rather angrily, as she seats herself on the left balustrade*): I don't see why you can never talk to me in a nice way.

MAURRANT: So you're startin' to go on pettin' parties, are you?

ROSE: Who said I was on a petting party?

MAURRANT: I suppose he didn't kiss you or nothin', huh?

ROSE: No, he didn't! And if he did—

MAURRANT: It's your own business, is that it? (*Going up the steps.*) Well, I'm gonna make it my business, see? Is this bird married? (ROSE *does not answer.*) I t'ought so! They're all alike, them guys—all after the one thing. Well, get this straight. No married men ain't gonna come nosin' around my family, get me?

ROSE (*rising agitatedly, as the house door opens*): Be quiet, Pop! There's somebody coming.

MAURRANT: I don't care! (BUCHANAN *hurries out of the house. He is a small and pasty young man—a typical "white-collar* slave." *He has hastily put on his coat and trousers over his pajamas and his bare feet are in slippers.*)

BUCHANAN (*as he comes down the steps*): I think the baby's coming!

ROSE (*solicitously*): Can I do anything, Mr. Buchanan?

BUCHANAN (*as he hurries towards the left*): No, I'm just going to phone for the doctor.

ROSE (*coming down the steps*): Let me do it, and you go back to your wife.

BUCHANAN: Well, if you wouldn't mind. It's Doctor John Wilson. (*Handing her a slip of paper.*) Here's his number. And the other number is her sister, Mrs. Thomas. And here's two nickels. Tell them both to come right away. She's got terrible pains. (*Another scream from upstairs.*) Listen to her! I better go back. (*He dashes up the steps and into the house.*)

ROSE: Oh, the poor woman! Pop, tell Ma to go up to her. Hurry!

MAURRANT: Aw, all right. (*He follows* BUCHANAN *into the house.* ROSE *hurries off at the left, just as* MAE JONES *and* DICK MCGANN *appear.* MAE *is a vulgar shopgirl of twenty-one;* DICK, *a vacuous youth of about the same age.* MAE *is wearing* DICK's *straw hat and they are both quite drunk.*)

MAE (*to* ROSE): Hello, Rose. What's your hurry?

ROSE (*without stopping*): It's Mrs. Buchanan. I've got to phone to the doctor. (*She hurries off.*)

DICK (*as they approach the stoop*): Say, who's your little friend?

MAE: Oh, that's Rose Maurrant. She lives in the house.

DICK: She's kinda cute, ain't she?

MAE (*seating herself on the stoop*): Say, accordin' to you, anythin' in a skirt is kinda cute—providin' the skirt is short enough.

DICK: Yeah, but they ain't any of 'em as cute as you, Mae.

MAE (*yawning and scratching her leg*): Yeah?

DICK: Honest, I mean it. How 'bout a little kiss? (*He puts*

158

*his arms about her and plants a long kiss upon her lips.
She submits, with an air of intense boredom.*)

DICK (*removing his lips*): Say, you might show a little en-
thoo-siasm.

MAE (*rouging her lips*): Say, you seem to think I oughta
hang out a flag, every time some bozo decides to wipe
off his mouth on me.

DICK: De trouble wit' you is you need another little snifter.
(*He reaches for his flask.*)

MAE: Nope! I can't swaller any more o' that rotten gin o'
yours.

DICK: Why, it ain't so worse. I don't mind it no more since
I had that brass linin' put in me stomach. Well, happy
days! (*He takes a long drink.*)

MAE (*rising indignantly*): Hey, for God's sake, what are you
doin'—emptyin' the flask?

DICK (*removing the flask from his lips*): I t'ought you didn't
want none.

MAE: Can't you take a joke? (*She snatches the flask from him
and drains it, kicking out at* DICK, *to prevent his taking it
from her.*)

DICK (*snatching the empty flask*): Say, you wanna watch
your step, baby, or you're li'ble to go right up in a puff o'
smoke.

MAE (*whistling*): Phew! Boy! I feel like a t'ree alarm fire! Say,
what de hell do dey make dat stuff out of?

DICK: T'ree parts dynamite an' one part army-mule. Dey use
it for blastin' out West.

MAE (*bursting raucously into a jazz tune*): Da-da-da-da-dee!
Da-da-da-da-dee! (*She executes some dance steps.*)

DICK: Say, shut up, will ya? You'll be wakin' the whole neighborhood.

MAE (*boisterously*): What the hell do I care? Da-da-da-da-
dee! Da-da-da-da-dee! (*Suddenly amorous, as she turns an
unsteady pirouette.*) Kiss me, kid!

DICK: I'll say! (*They lock in a long embrace.* SAM, *coatless,
his shirt collar open, appears at the window, watches the*

pair for a moment, and then turns away, obviously disgusted. They do not see him.)

DICK (*taking* MAE's *arm*): Come on!

MAE: Wait a minute! Where y' goin'?

DICK: Come on, I'm tellin' ya! Fred Hennessy gimme de key to his apartment. Dere won't be nobody dere.

MAE (*protesting feebly*): I oughta go home. (*Her hand to her head.*) Oh, baby! Say, nail down dat sidewalk, will ya?

DICK: Come on! (ROSE *appears, at the left.*)

MAE: Sweet Papa! (*She kisses* DICK *noisily; then bursts into song again.*) Da-da-da-da-dee! Da-da-da-da-dee! (*As they pass* ROSE.) Hello, Rose. How's de milkman?

DICK (*raising his hat with drunken politeness*): Goo' night, sweetheart. (*They go off, at the left,* MAE's *snatches of song dying away in the distance.* ROSE *stands still, for a moment, choking back her mortification.*)

BUCHANAN'S VOICE: Miss Maurrant, did you get them?

ROSE (*looking up*): Why yes, I did. The doctor will be here right away. And Mrs. Thomas said it would take her about an hour. (VINCENT JONES *appears at the right and stops near the stoop. He is a typical New York taxicab driver, in a cap.* ROSE *does not see him.*)

BUCHANAN'S VOICE: She's got terrible pains. Your mother's up here, with her. (MRS. BUCHANAN *is heard calling faintly.*) I think she's calling me. (ROSE *goes towards the stoop and sees* VINCENT.)

VINCENT: Hello, Rosie.

ROSE: Good evening. (*She tries to pass, but he blocks her way.*)

VINCENT: What's your hurry?

ROSE: It's late.

VINCENT: You don' wanna go to bed, yet. Come on, I'll take you for a ride in me hack. (*He puts his arm about her.*)

ROSE: Please let me pass. (SAM *appears at the window. They do not see him.*)

VINCENT (*enjoying* ROSE's *struggle to escape*): You got a lot o' stren'th, ain't you? Say, do you know, you're gettin' fat? (*He passes one hand over her body.*)

ROSE: Let me go, you big tough.

SAM (*simultaneously*): Take your hands off her! (*He climbs quickly out of the window and onto the stoop.* VINCENT, *surprised, releases* ROSE *and steps to the sidewalk.* ROSE *goes up the steps.* SAM, *trembling with excitement and fear, stands on the top step.* VINCENT *glowers up at him.*)

VINCENT: Well, look who's here! (*Mockingly.*) Haster gesehn de fish in de Bowery? (*Menacingly.*) What de hell do you want?

SAM (*chokingly*): You keep your hands off her!

VINCENT: Yeah? (*Sawing the air with his hands.*) Oi, Jakie! (*He suddenly lunges forward, seizes* SAM's *arm, pulls him violently by the right hand down the steps and swings him about, so that they stand face to face, to the left of the stoop.* ROSE *comes down between them.*) Now what o' ya got t' say?

ROSE: Let him alone!

SAMS (*inarticulately*): If you touch her again—

VINCENT (*mockingly*): If I touch her again—! (*Savagely.*) Aw, shut up, you little kike bastard! (*He brushes* ROSE *aside and putting his open hand against* SAM's *face, sends him sprawling to the pavement.*)

ROSE (*her fists clenched*): You big coward.

VINCENT (*standing over* SAM): Get up, why don't you?

ROSE (*crossing to* SAM): If you hit him again, I'll call my father.

VINCENT (*as* MRS. JONES *and the dog appear at the right*): Gee, don't frighten me like dat. I got a weak heart. (*He is sobered, nevertheless.* SAM *picks himself up.*)

VINCENT (*as* MRS. JONES *approaches*): Hello, Ma.

MRS. JONES (*with maternal pride*): Hello, Vincent. What's goin' on here?

VINCENT: Oh, jus' a little friendly argument. Ikey Finkelstein don't like me to say good evenin' to his girl friend.

ROSE: You'd better keep your hands to yourself, hereafter.

161

VINCENT: Is dat so? Who said so, huh?

MRS. JONES: Come on, Vincent. Come on upstairs. I saved some stew for you.

VINCENT: All right, I'm comin'. (*To* ROSE.) Good night, dearie. (*He makes a feint at* SAM, *who starts back in terror.* VINCENT *laughs.*)

MRS. JONES: Aw, let 'im alone, Vincent.

VINCENT (*as he goes up the steps*): Who's touchin' him? A little cockroach like dat, ain't woit' my time (*To* ROSE.) Some sheik you picked out for yourself! (*He enters the vestibule and opens the door with his latchkey.*)

MRS. JONES (*going up the steps*): You seem to have plenty of admirers, Miss Maurrant. (*Pausing on the top step.*) But I guess you come by it natural. (ROSE *does not reply.* MRS. JONES *follows* VINCENT *into the house.* ROSE *averts her head to keep back the tears.* SAM, *stands facing the house, his whole body quivering with emotion. Suddenly he raises his arms, his fists clenched.*)

SAM (*hysterically, as he rushes to the foot of the stoop*): The dirty bum! I'll kill him!

ROSE (*turning and going to him*): It's all right, Sam. Never mind.

SAM (*sobbing*): I'll kill him. I'll kill him! (*He throws himself on the stoop and, burying his head in his arms, sobs hysterically.* ROSE *sits beside him and puts her arm about him.*)

ROSE: It's all right, Sam. Everything's all right. Why should you pay any attention to a big tough like that? (SAM *does not answer.* ROSE *caresses his hair and he grows calmer.*) He's nothing but a loafer, you know that. What do you care what he says?

SAM (*without raising his head*): I'm a coward.

ROSE: Why, no, you're not, Sam.

SAM: Yes, I am. I'm a coward.

ROSE: Why, he's not worth your little finger, Sam. You wait and see. Ten years from now, he'll still be driving a taxi and you—why, you'll be so far above him, you won't even remember he's alive.

SAM: I'll never be anything.

ROSE: Why, don't talk like that, Sam. A boy with your brains and ability. Graduating from college with honors and all that! Why, if I were half as smart as you, I'd be just so proud of myself!

SAM: What's the good of having brains, if nobody ever looks at you—if nobody knows you exist?

ROSE (*gently*): I know you exist, Sam.

SAM: It wouldn't take much to make you forget me.

ROSE: I'm not so sure about that. Why do you say that, Sam?

SAM: Because I know. It's different with you. You have beauty —people look at you—you have a place in the world—

ROSE: I don't know. It's not always so easy, being a girl—I often wish I were a man. It seems to me that when you're a man, it's so much easier to sort of—be yourself, to kind of be the way you feel. But when you're a girl, it's different. It doesn't seem to matter what you are, or what you're thinking or feeling—all that men seem to care about is just the one thing. And when you're sort of trying to find out, just where you're at, it makes it hard. Do you see what I mean? (*Hesitantly.*) Sam, there's something I want to ask you— (*She stops.*)

SAM (*turning to her*): What is it, Rose?

ROSE: I wouldn't dream of asking anybody but you. (*With a great effort.*) Sam, do you think it's true—what they're saying about my mother? (SAM *averts his head, without answering.*)

ROSE (*wretchedly*): I guess it is, isn't it?

SAM (*agitatedly*): They were talking here, before—I couldn't stand it any more! (*He clasps his head and, springing to his feet, goes to the right of the stoop.*) Oh, God, why do we go on living in this sewer?

ROSE (*appealingly*): What can I do, Sam? (SAM *makes a helpless gesture.*) You see, my father means well enough, and all that, but he's always been sort of strict and—I don't know—sort of making you freeze up, when you really wanted to be nice and loving. That's the whole trouble, I guess; my mother never had anybody to really love her. She's sort of gay and happy-like—you know, she likes having a good time and all that. But my father is different. Only—the way things are now—everybody talking and making remarks, all the neighbors spying and whispering—it sort of makes me feel—(*she shudders*)—I don't know—!

SAM (*coming over to her again*): I wish I could help you, Rose.

ROSE: You do help me, Sam—just by being nice and sympathetic and talking things over with me. There's so few people you can really talk to, do you know what I mean? Sometimes, I get the feeling that I'm all alone in the world and that— (*A scream of pain from* MRS. BUCHANAN.)

ROSE (*springing to her feet*): Oh, just listen to her!

SAM: Oh, God!

ROSE: The poor thing! She must be having terrible pains.

SAM: That's all there is in life—nothing but pain. From before we're born, until we die! Everywhere you look, oppression and cruelty! If it doesn't come from Nature, it comes from humanity—humanity trampling on itself and tearing at its own throat. The whole world is nothing but a blood-stained arena, filled with misery and suffering. It's too high a price to pay for life—life isn't worth it! (*He seats himself despairingly on the stoop.*)

ROSE (*putting her hand on his shoulder*): Oh, I don't know, Sam. I feel blue and discouraged, sometimes, too. And I get a sort of feeling of, oh, what's the use. Like last night. I hardly slept all night, on account of the heat and on account of thinking about—well, all sorts of things. And this morning, when I got up, I felt so miserable. Well, all of a sudden, I decided I'd walk to the office. And when I got to the park, everything looked so green and fresh, that I got a kind of feeling of, well, maybe it's not so bad, after all. And then, what do you think?—all of a sudden, I saw a big lilac-bush, with some flowers still on it. It made me think about the poem you said for me—remember?—the one about the lilacs.

SAM (*quoting*):

"When lilacs last in the dooryard bloom'd,

And the great star early droop'd in the western sky in the
night,

I mourn'd, and yet shall mourn, with ever-returning spring."

(*He repeats the last line*)—"I mourned and yet shall
mourn, with ever-returning spring?" Yes!

ROSE: No, not that part. I mean the part about the farmhouse.
Say it for me, Sam. (*She sits at his feet.*)

SAM:

In the dooryard fronting an old farmhouse, near the white-
wash'd palings,

Stands the lilac-bush tall-growing with heart-shaped leaves
of rich green,

With many a pointed blossom rising delicate, with the per-
fume strong I love,

With every leaf a miracle—and from this bush in the dooryard,

With delicate-color'd blossoms and heart-shaped leaves of
rich green,

A sprig with its flower I break.

ROSE (*eagerly*): Yes, that's it! That's just what I felt like doing
—breaking off a little bunch of the flowers. But then I
thought, maybe a policeman or somebody would see me,
and then I'd get into trouble; so I didn't.

BUCHANAN'S VOICE: Miss Maurrant! Miss Maurrant! (SAM *and*
ROSE *spring to their feet and look up*).

ROSE: Yes?

BUCHANAN'S VOICE: Do you mind phoning to the doctor
again? She's getting worse.

ROSE: Yes, sure I will. (*She starts to go.*) Wait! Maybe this
is the doctor now.

BUCHANAN'S VOICE (*excitedly as* DR. WILSON *appears at the
left*): Yes, that's him. Mrs. Maurrant! Tell her the doctor's
here! Doctor, I guess you're none too soon.

DR. WILSON (*a seedy, middle-aged man in a crumpled Pana-
ma*): Plenty of time. Just don't get excited. (*He throws*

away his cigarette and enters the vestibule. The mechanical clicking of the doorlatch is heard as DR. WILSON *goes into the house.*)

ROSE: I hope she won't have to suffer much longer.

MAURRANT (*appearing at the window, in his undershirt*): Rose!

ROSE (*rather startled*): Yes, Pop, I'll be right up.

MAURRANT: Well, don't be makin' me call you again, d'ya hear?

ROSE: I'm coming right away. (MAURRANT *leaves the window.*)

ROSE: I'd better go up now, Sam.

SAM: Do you have to go to bed, when you're told, like a child?

ROSE: I know, Sam, but there's so much wrangling goes on, all the time, as it is, what's the use of having any more? Good night, Sam. There was something I wanted to talk to you about, but it will have to be another time. (*She holds out her hand.* SAM *takes it and holds it in his.*)

SAM (*trembling and rising to his feet*): Rose, will you kiss me?

ROSE (*simply*): Why, of course I will, Sam. (*She offers him her lips. He clasps her in a fervent embrace, to which she submits but does not respond.*)

ROSE (*freeing herself gently*): Don't be discouraged about things, Sam. You wait and see—you're going to do big things, some day. I've got lots of confidence in you.

SAM (*turning away his head*): I wonder if you really have, Rose?

ROSE: Why, of course I have! And don't forget it! Good night. I hope it won't be too hot to sleep.

SAM: Good night, Rose. (*He watches her, as she opens the door with her latchkey and goes into the house. Then he goes to the stoop and seating himself, falls into a reverie. A* POLICEMAN *appears at the right and strolls across, but* SAM *is oblivious to him. In the distance, a homecomer sings drunkenly. A light appears, in the Maurrant hall bedroom, and a moment later,* Rose *comes to the window and leans out.*)

Rose (*calling softly*): Hoo-hoo! Sam! (Sam *looks up, then rises.*) Good night, Sam. (*She wafts him a kiss.*)

Sam (*with deep feeling*): Good night, Rose dear. (*She smiles at him. Then she pulls down the shade.* Sam *looks up for a moment, then resumes his seat. A scream from* Mrs. Buchañan *makes him shudder. A deep rhythmic snoring emanates from the Fiorentino apartment. A steamboat whistle is heard. The snoring in the* Fiorentino *apartment continues.* Sam *raises his clenched hands to heaven. A distant clock begins to strike twelve.* Sam's *arms and head drop forward.*)

ACT II

SCENE: *Daybreak, the next morning. It is still quite dark and comparatively quiet. The rhythmic snoring in the Fiorentino apartment is still heard, and now and then, a distant "el" train or speeding automobile. A moment after the rise of the curtain,* JONES *appears, at the right, on his way home from the speakeasy. He reels, slightly, but negotiates the steps and entrance-door, without too much difficulty. It grows lighter—and noisier. The street light goes out. The* OLSEN *baby begins to cry. An alarm clock rings. A dog barks. A canary begins to sing. Voices are heard in the distance. They die out and other voices are heard. The house door opens and* DR. WILSON *comes out, passing* JONES, *at the top of the stoop.* DR. WILSON *stands on the steps and yawns the yawn of an overtired man. Then he lights a cigarette and goes towards the left.)*

BUCHANAN'S VOICE: Doctor!

DR. WILSON (*stopping and looking up*): Well?

BUCHANAN'S VOICE: What if she does wake up?

DR. WILSON (*sharply*): She won't, I've told you! She's too exhausted. The best thing you can do is lie down and get some sleep yourself. (*As he goes off at the left,* MAE *and* DICK *appear. They walk slowly and listlessly and far apart.*)

DICK (*as they reach the stoop*): Well, goo' night.

MAE (*with a yawn, as she find her latchkey*): Goo' night. (*Going up the steps and looking towards the Fiorentino apartment*): Aw, shut up, you wop!

168

DICK (*his dignity wounded*): How 'bout kissin' me good
night?

MAE (*venomously, from the top step*): For God's sake, ain't
you had enough kissin' for one night! (*She enters the vestibule and puts the key in the lock. The ringing of an alarm
clock is heard.*)

DICK (*raising his voice*): Well, say, if that's the way you feel
about it—

MAE: Aw, go to hell! (*She enters the house. The alarm clock
has stopped ringing.*)

DICK: You dirty little tart! (*He stands, muttering to himself,
for a moment, then goes off at the right, passing the* POLICE-
MAN, *who looks at him, suspiciously. The sounds of a Swed-
ish quarrel are heard from the janitor's apartment. The baby
is still crying. As the* POLICEMAN *goes left, a* MILKMAN *appears, whistling and carrying a rack of full milk bottles.*)

POLICEMAN: Hello, Louie. (*The snoring in the Fiorentino
apartment stops.*)

MILKMAN: Hello, Harry. Goin' to be another scorcher.

POLICEMAN: You said it. (*He goes off at the left. The* MILK-
MAN *crosses to the cellar steps.* MAE *appears, at the hall
bedroom window of the Jones apartment, and removes her
dress over her head. The* MILKMAN, *about to go down the
steps, sees her and stops to watch.* MAE, *about to slip out of
her step-in, sees him, throws him an angry look and pulls
down the shade. The* MILKMAN *grins and goes down the
cellar steps.* CHARLIE HILDEBRAND *comes out of the house.
He is chewing gum and as he comes out to the top of the
stoop, he scatters the wrappings of the stick of gum on the
stoop. Then he jumps down the four steps of the stoop, in
one jump, and goes off at the left, pulling the chewing gum
out in a long ribbon, and carefully avoiding all the cracks
in the pavement. A* YOUNG WORKMAN, *carrying a kit of
tools and a tin lunchbox, appears at the left, extinguishes
the red light on the excavation, and opening the door, goes
in. A* TRAMP *comes on at the right and shuffles across. He
sees a cigar butt on the pavement, picks it up and pockets*

it, as he exits at the left. ROSE, *in her nightgown, appears at the window, yawns slightly and disappears. It is daylight now. The baby stops crying.* MRS. OLSEN *comes up the cellar steps. She goes up the stoop, turns out the light in the vestibule, and takes the door off the latch. The* MILKMAN *comes up the cellar steps, his tray laden with empty bottles and goes off, whistling, at the left.* SAM, *coatless, a book in his hand, appears at the window. He looks out for a moment, then climbs out on the stoop, looks up at* ROSE'S *window, then seats himself and begins to read.* WILLIE *comes out of the house.*)

WILLIE (*chanting, as he comes down the steps*): Fat, Fat the water rat, fifty bullets in his hat.

SAM: Hello, Willie. Is Rose up yet?

WILLIE (*without stopping or looking at him*): Yeah. I don't know. I guess so. (*He turns a somersault and goes off at left, continuing his chanting.* SAM *glances at* ROSE'S *window again, and then resumes his book.* MRS. JONES *and her dog come out of the house.*)

MRS. JONES (*haughtily, as she comes down the steps*): Mornin'.

SAM (*scarcely looking up from his book*): Good morning. (MRS. JONES *and dog go off at the right. A middle-aged workman, carrying a large coil of wire, appears at the left and goes to the door of the excavation.* MRS. OLSEN *comes out of the house and exits into the basement.*)

WORKMAN (*calling*): You down there, Eddie?

VOICE (*from the depths*): Yeah!

WORKMAN: All right! (*He climbs down into the excavation.* ROSE *comes to window and pulls up the shade.* WILLIE *and* CHARLIE *can be heard, offstage left, engaged in an earnest conversation.*)

CHARLIE (*offstage*): He could not!

WILLIE (*offstage*): He could so! (*They appear at left. Each has under his arm, a paper bag, from which a loaf of bread protrudes.*)

CHARLIE: I'll betcha he couldn't.

WILLIE: I'll betcha he could.

CHARLIE: I'll betcha a million dollars he couldn't.

WILLIE: I'll betcha five million dollars he could. Hold that! (*He hands Charlie his loaf of bread and turns a cartwheel.*) Bet you can't do it.

CHARLIE: Bet I can. (*He puts both loaves of bread on the pavement, attempts a cartwheel and fails.*)

WILLIE (*laughing raucously*): Haw-haw! Told you you couldn't!

CHARLIE: Can you do this? (*He turns a back somersault.*)

WILLIE: Sure—easy! (*He turns a back somersault. They pick up their loaves again.* WILLIE's *drops out of the bag, but he dusts it, with his hand, and replaces it.*) How many steps can you jump up?

CHARLIE: Three. (*He jumps up three steps.*)

WILLIE: I can do four.

CHARLIE: Let's see you. (WILLIE, *the bread under his arm, jumps up the four steps, undisturbed by* SAM's *presence. He drops the bread, and is about to replace it in the bag, but gets a better idea. He inflates the bag and explodes it with a blow of his fist.* CHARLIE *looks on, in admiration and envy.*)

ROSE (*appearing at the window*): Willie, we're waiting for the bread.

WILLIE (*holding it up*): All right! Cantcha see I got it? (*He enters the house, followed by* CHARLIE.)

SAM (*rising*): Hello, Rose.

ROSE: Hello, Sam.

SAM: Come down.

ROSE: I haven't had breakfast yet. (*Calling into the room.*) Yes! He's on his way up.

MISS CUSHING (*coming out of the house*): Good morning. (*She looks inquiringly from* SAM *to* ROSE.)

SAM (*impatiently*): Good morning. (*A middle-aged nun appears at the right, accompanied by a scrawny child of about fourteen. They walk across the stage.*)

ROSE: Good morning, Miss Cushing. (MISS CUSHING *goes off, at the left, glancing back at* ROSE *and* SAM.)

ROSE: I'm going to Mr. Jacobson's funeral. (*Calling into the room.*) Yes, I'm coming. (*To* SAM.) Breakfast's ready. I'll be down as soon as the dishes are done. (*She disappears.* SAM *looks up at the window, for a moment, then begins to read again.* MRS. FIORENTINO *appears at the window, at the extreme left, with a double armful of bedding, which she deposits upon the window sill. Then she goes away again.*)

SHIRLEY (*appearing at the window*): Sam, breakfast is ready.

SAM: I don't want any breakfast.

SHIRLEY: What do you mean, you don't want any breakfast? What kind of a business is that, not to eat breakfast?

SAM: Do I have to eat breakfast, if I don't want to?

SHIRLEY: You've got your head so full of that Rose Maurrant upstairs, that you don't want to eat or sleep or anything, any more.

SAM: If I don't feel like eating, why should I eat? (*Bursting out.*) You're always telling me: "Eat!" "Don't eat!" "Get up!" "Go to bed!" I know what I want to do, without being told.

SHIRLEY: I don't see, just when you're graduating from college, why you want to get mixed up with a little *batzimer* like that!

SAM: It's always the same thing over again with you. You never can get over your race prejudice. I've told you a hundred times that the Jews are no better than anybody else.

SHIRLEY: I'm not talking about that! Look at the kind of family she comes from. What's her father? Nothing but an illiterate roughneck. And her mother—

SAM (*indignantly*): Are you starting, too?

KAPLAN'S VOICE: Shoi-ley!

SHIRLEY: Wait a minute, Papa's calling. (*Into the room.*) All right, Papa! (*To* SAM.) Come in, Sam, or Papa will be making long speeches again.

SAM (*impatiently*): All right! All right! I'll come. (*A young*

*shopgirl, smiling to herself, appears at the right and walks
across the stage.* SAM *rises and goes into the house.* SHIRLEY
leaves the window. BUCHANAN, *emerging from the house,
collarless and unshaven, encounters* SAM *in the vestibule.*)

BUCHANAN (*eagerly*): Good morning.

SAM (*abruptly*): Good morning. (*He enters the house.*
BUCHANAN *looks back at him, then comes down the steps.*
MRS. FIORENTINO *raises the drawn shade and opens the
window.*)

MRS. FIORENTINO: Good morning, Mr. Buchanan.

BUCHANAN: Oh, good morning, Mrs. Fiorentino. (*Going over
to the left balustrade.*) I guess you know that the baby
came last night, don't you?

MRS. FIORENTINO: No! I did not hear a vord about it.

BUCHANAN: Why, I thought she'd wake up the whole neighborhood, the way she was yelling. Three-thirty this morning, the baby came. I been up the whole night. (*An old*
LETTER CARRIER, *coatless, appears at the right.*)

MRS. FIORENTINO: A boy, is it?

BUCHANAN: No, it's a little girl. I guess we'll call her Mary,
after my mother.

LETTER CARRIER (*going up the steps*): Mornin'.

MRS. FIORENTINO: Good morning. Any letters for me?

LETTER CARRIER (*from the top of the steps*): No, not a thing.

BUCHANAN (*turning toward him*): I was just telling Mrs. Fiorentino, I had a little addition to my family last night.

LETTER CARRIER: Your first, is it?

BUCHANAN (*hastening to explain*): Well, we've only been married a little over a year.

LETTER CARRIER: Well, I've had seven, an' I'm still luggin' a
mailbag at sixty-two. (*He goes into the vestibule and puts
the mail into the letter boxes.*)

MRS. FIORENTINO: How is your wife?

BUCHANAN: Well, she had a pretty hard time of it. Her sister's
up there with her. And Mrs. Maurrant was up, nearly all
night. I don't know what we'd have done without her.

LETTER CARRIER (*coming down the steps*): It don't pay to

let 'em have their own way, too much. That's where I made my mistake. (*As the* LETTER CARRIER *goes off, at the left,* LIPPO *appears at the window behind his wife, and tickles her.*)

MRS. FIORENTINO (*startled*): Lippo!

BUCHANAN: Morning. I was just telling your wife—

MRS. FIORENTINO: Lippo, what do you think? Mr. Buchanan has a little girl!

LIPPO: Ah, dotsa fine! Margherita, why you don' have da baby, ha?

MRS. FIORENTINO (*abruptly*): I must go and make the coffee. (*She goes away from the window.* OLSEN *comes halfway up the steps and leans against the railing, smoking his pipe.*)

VOICE (*offstage left*): Oh-h! Corn! Sweet corn!

LIPPO: Ees funny t'ing. You gotta da leetle, skeeny wife an' she's hava da baby. My Margherita, she's beeg an' fat an' she no can hava da baby.

BUCHANAN: Well, that's the way o' the world, I guess. (*As he goes off, at the left, an* ICEMAN *appears, trundling a three-wheeled cart, filled with ice.*)

LIPPO: Buon giorno, Mike.

MIKE: Buon giorno, signore. Come sta?

LIPPO: Benissimo. Fa molto caldo ancora, oggi.

MIKE: Si, si, signore. Bisognera abbastanza ghiaccio. Twen'y fi' cent, ha?

LIPPO: No, no, é troppo.

MIKE: Twen'y cent? Eesa melta fas'.

LIPPO: Alla right. Gimme twen'y cent.

MIKE: Si, si, signore. Sure. (*As he wheels the cart to the cellar entrance and begins to chop a block of ice, a* MAN *in shirt sleeves strides in from the left and stops at the curb, as though seeing someone in a house across the street.*)

MAN (*angrily*): Well, what about it? We've been waiting a half an hour!

VOICE: I'll be right over!

MAN: Yeah? Well, make it snappy! (*He strides off at the left,*

174

muttering angrily. ROSE *comes out of the house and stands in the doorway, looking for* SAM. *Then she comes out on the stoop and peers into the* KAPLAN *apartment. As she turns away, she see* LIPPO.)

ROSE (*crossing to the left of the stoop*): Good morning.

LIPPO: Gooda mornin', Meesa Maurrant. (MIKE *goes down into the cellar, with a chunk of ice.*)

ROSE: It's awful hot again, isn't it?

LIPPO: You don' like?

ROSE: I don't sleep very well, when it's so hot.

LIPPO: No? Ahm sleepa fine. Een Eetaly, where Ahm born, is much more 'ot like 'ere. Een summer, ees too 'ot for workin'. Ees too 'ot only for sleepin'. W'en Ahm leetla boy, Ahm sleepa, sleepa, whola day. I don't wear no clo's—nawthin' only leetle short pair pants. I lay down on groun' under da lemon tree, Ahm sleepa whola day.

ROSE: Under a lemon tree! That must have been nice.

LIPPO: Ees smella sweet, lemon tree. Where Ahm born ees thousan' lemon tree. Lemon an' olive an' arancia.

ROSE: Oh, that must be lovely!

LIPPO: Ah, ees bew-tiful! Ees most bewtiful place in whole worl'. You hear about Sorrent', ha?

ROSE: No, I don't think I ever did.

LIPPO (*incredulously*): You never hear about Sorrent'?

ROSE: No, I don't know much about geography. Is it a big place?

LIPPO: Ees not vera beeg—but ever'body know Sorrent'. Sorrento gentile! La bella Sorrento! You hear about Napoli— Baia di Napoli?

ROSE: Oh yes, the Bay of Naples! Is it near there?

LIPPO: Sure, ees on Bay of Napoli. Ees bew-tiful! Ees alla blue. Sky blue, water blue, sun ees shine alla time.

ROSE: Oh, how lovely. (MIKE *comes up the cellar steps, chops another block of ice, and goes down the cellar steps with it.*)

LIPPO: An' ees Vesuvio, too. You hear about Vesuvio?—ees beeg volcano.

175

ROSE: Oh yes, sure. I saw a picture once, called *The Last Days of Pompeii*, and it showed Mount Vesuvius, with smoke coming out of the top.

LIPPO: Da's right. An' nighttime, ees fire come out, maka da sky red.

ROSE: Didn't it frighten you?

LIPPO: Ah no, ees nawthin' to be afraid. Ees jus' volcano.

ROSE: I'd love to go to Italy. It must be awfully pretty. But I don't suppose I ever will.

LIPPO: W'y sure! Some day you gonna marry reech fella; 'e's taka you Eetaly—ever'where.

ROSE: I guess there's not much chance of that. Rich fellows aren't going around looking for girls like me to marry. Anyhow, I don't think money is everything, do you?

LIPPO: Ees good to hava money. Da's w'y Ahm come to America. Een Eetaly, ees bewtiful, but ees no money. 'Ere ees not bewtiful, but ees plenty money. Ees better to 'ave money. (*An elderly* MAN, *in the gray uniform of a special officer, comes out of the house, filling his pipe from a tobacco box.*)

MAN: Good mornin'.

ROSE: Good morning, Mr. Callahan. (*The* MAN *drops the empty tobacco tin on the sidewalk and goes off slowly at the left.*) I don't think I'd be happy, just marrying a man with money, if I didn't care for him, too.

LIPPO (*laughing*): Wotsa matter, ha? You lova da leetla kike, ha?

ROSE: Why no, I don't. I don't love anybody—at least, I don't think I do. But it's not on account of his being a Jew.

LIPPO: No, ees no good—Jew. 'E's only t'ink about money, money—alla time money.

ROSE: But Sam isn't like that, a bit. He's only interested in poetry and things like that. (*The* ICEMAN *comes up out of the cellar and trundles off his cart at the right.*)

MRS. FIORENTINO (*calling*): Lippo! Breakfast!

LIPPO (*calling*): Alla right, Margherita! (*To* ROSE.) You marry fella wit' lot o' money. Ees much better. (*He goes away from the window, as* MISS CUSHING *appears, at the left, carrying a paper bag.*)

ROSE: How's your mother today, Miss Cushing?

MISS CUSHING: She's not feeling so good today.

ROSE: It's too bad she's not feeling well.

MISS CUSHING: I'm afraid it's her heart. At her age, you know— (*As she enters the house, two* COLLEGE GIRLS *of nineteen appear at the right.*)

FIRST GIRL (*as they appear*): I don't understand it.

SECOND GIRL: Convex is this way; and concave is this way.

FIRST GIRL: That I know.

SECOND GIRL: When you're nearsighted, they give you convex glasses, and when you're farsighted, they give you concave.

FIRST GIRL: That I didn't know.

SECOND GIRL: Of course, you know it. Didn't we have it in psychology?

FIRST GIRL (*as they disappear at the left*): I don't remember. (WILLIE *comes out of the house, on his way to school. He is hatless, and carries his books under his arm.*)

ROSE (*intercepting him at the top of the stoop*): Why, Willie, the way you look! Your collar's all open.

WILLIE: I know it! De button came off.

ROSE: Why didn't you ask Ma to sew it on for you?

WILLIE: She ain't dere. She's up at Buchanan's.

ROSE: Well, wait till I see if I have a pin. (*She searches in her handbag.*)

WILLIE (*starting down the steps*): Aw, it's all right de way it is.

ROSE (*following him to the sidewalk*): No, it isn't. You can't go to school like that. (*Producing a safety pin.*) Now, hold still, while I fix it.

WILLIE (*squirming*): Aw, fer de love o' Mike—!

ROSE: You'll get stuck, if you don't hold still. There, that looks better, now. And you didn't comb your hair, either.

WILLIE (*trying to escape*): Say, lemme alone, cantcha?

ROSE (*taking a comb out of her handbag and combing his*

hair): You can't go to school looking like a little street-loafer.

WILLIE: Aw, you gimme a pain in de—

ROSE: You're getting big enough to comb your own hair, without being told. There! Now you look very nice.

WILLIE: So's your old man! (*He runs towards the left kicking the empty tobacco tin ahead of him, then stops, turns and deliberately rumples his hair.*)

ROSE (*indignantly, as* WILLIE *runs off*): Why, Willie! (MRS. JONES *and the dog appear at the right.* OLSEN *knocks the ashes out of his pipe and goes down into the cellar.* MRS. MAURRANT *comes out of the house.*)

ROSE: Hello, Ma.

MRS. JONES (*at the steps*): Good mornin'.

ROSE and MRS. MAURRANT: Good morning, Mrs. Jones.

MRS. JONES: How's little Mrs. Buchanan gettin' on?

MRS. MAURRANT: Well, she's sleeping now, poor thing. She was so worn out, she just went off into a sound sleep. I really didn't think, last night, she'd have the strength to pull through it.

MRS. JONES: Well, it's somethin' we all got to go through. I been through enough with mine, I hope to tell you. Not that they didn't turn out all right.

MRS. MAURRANT: I wouldn't give up having mine for anything in the world.

MRS. JONES: Well, after all, what more does any woman want than watchin' her kids grow up an' a husband to look out for her?

MRS. MAURRANT: Yes, that's true.

MRS. JONES: Yes, and the world would be a whole lot better off, if there was more that lived up to it. (*Starting up the steps.*) Well, I gotta get my Mae up out o' bed. Gawd knows what time she got in, this mornin'. (*She enters the vestibule, then stops and turns.*) If you don't mind my bein' so bold, Mrs. Maurrant—an' I don't mind sayin' it in front of your daughter, either—I'd think twice before I'd let any child o' mine bring a Jew into the family.

178

Rose (*with a show of temper*): I don't see what it has to do with you, Mrs. Jones.

Mrs. Jones: There's no need to get huffy about it. I'm only advisin' you for your own good. I'm sure it don't make no difference to me what you do. Come on, Queenie. (*She goes into the house.*)

Rose: Well, of all the nerve I ever heard in my life—! She and those wonderful children of hers!

Mrs. Maurrant (*coming halfway down the steps*): The best way is not to pay any attention to her. There's lots of people like that, in the world—they never seem to be happy, unless they're making trouble for somebody. Did Willie go to school?

Rose: Yes, he did. It's awful the way he goes around, looking like a little tough. And the language he uses, too.

Mrs. Maurrant: I know. I just don't seem able to manage him, any more.

Rose: I sometimes wonder if it wouldn't be better for us all, if we moved out to the suburbs somewhere—you know, some place in Jersey or Staten Island.

Mrs. Maurrant: I don't think Pop would do it. (*As Maurrant comes out of the house, carrying a much-battered satchel.*) Are you leaving now, Frank?

Maurrant (*from the top of the stoop*): Looks like it, don't it. Where you been all this while?

Mrs. Maurrant: Why, you know where I've been, Frank— up to Mrs. Buchanan's.

Maurrant: Yeah? An' where you goin' now?

Mrs. Maurrant: Just around to Kraus's to get a chicken. I thought I'd make her some chicken soup, to give her strength.

Maurrant: Say, how about lookin' after your own home an' lettin' the Buchanans look after theirs.

Mrs. Maurrant: All I'm trying to do is to be a little neighborly. It's the least anybody can do, with the poor thing hardly able to lift her hand.

Maurrant: That's all right about that! (*Coming down the*

steps.) A woman's got a right to stay in her own home, lookin' after her husband an' children.

MRS. MAURRANT (*going towards him*): What else have I been doing all these years, I'd like to know?

MAURRANT: Well, just see that you don't forget it, that's all— or there's li'ble to be trouble.

MRS. MAURRANT (*putting her hand on his arm*): All right, Frank. Don't say any more, please. When will you be back —tomorrow?

MAURRANT: I don' know when I'll be back. Whenever I'm t'roo wit' me work—that's when. What are you so anxious to know for, huh?

MRS. MAURRANT: Why, I just asked, that's all.

MAURRANT: Oh, you just asked, huh? Just in case somebody wanted to come aroun' callin', is that it?

MRS. MAURRANT: No, it isn't. It isn't anything of the kind. You got no right to talk to me like that, in front of my own daughter. You got no right. No, you haven't! (*She turns away and hurries off, abruptly, at the left.*)

ROSE: Ma! (*She starts to run after her mother.*)

MAURRANT (*imperiously*): Come back here, you! (ROSE *hesitates.*) Come back, hear me? (ROSE *turns and comes slowly back.*) You stay right here. (*He puts down his satchel and takes a flask from his pocket.*)

ROSE: Why do you talk to her like that?

MAURRANT: Nobody's askin' you.

ROSE: If you were only a little nicer to her, maybe everything would be different.

MAURRANT: Yeah? Where's she got any kick comin'. Ain't I always been a good husband to her? Ain't I always looked after her? (*He takes a drink.*)

ROSE: It's not that, Pop. It's somebody to be sort of nice to her that she wants—sort of nice and gentle, the way she is to you. That's all it is.

MAURRANT (*turning to her*): So she's got you headed the same way, has she? Goin' out nights with married men, huh?

180

ROSE: You don't need to worry about me, Pop. I can take care of myself, all right.

MAURRANT: No daughter o' mine ain't gonna go that way. I seen too many o' those kind around the theayter.

ROSE: Things are different, nowadays, Pop. I guess maybe you don't realize that. Girls aren't the way they used to be —sort of soft and helpless. A girl nowadays knows how to look out for herself. But not her, Pop; she needs somebody to look after her.

MAURRANT: Aw, can all that talk! You been listenin' to them Bolshevikis, that's the trouble. But I'm gonna keep you straight, by God, or I'll know the reason why.

ROSE: I guess I've got a right to think about things for myself.

MAURRANT: Yeah? Well, don't let me ketch that other bozo comin' around here, either—that's all I got to say.

ROSE (*hesitantly, going up to him*): Pop, listen—couldn't we get a little house somewhere—Queens or somewhere like that?

MAURRANT: What's the idea?

ROSE: Well, I don't know. I sort of thought it would be nice for all of us. And maybe if Ma had a nice little home and some real nice neighbors—do you see what I mean?

MAURRANT: This place suits me all right.

ROSE: You can get some real nice little houses, that don't cost such an awful lot. And I wouldn't mind helping to pay for it. And once we had it all fixed up—

MAURRANT: Forget it! I don' know when I'll be back. (*As he starts to go right.*) An' remember what I tol' you, hear?

MRS. JONES (*appearing at her window, with a tin dustpan*): Good mornin', Mr. Maurrant. You off on a little trip?

MAURRANT (*curtly*): Yeah! (*He goes off. MRS. JONES empties the dustpan out of the window and goes away. KAPLAN comes out of the house, a bundle of newspapers under his arm. He walks slowly and painfully, with the aid of a heavy stick.*)

KAPLAN (*at the foot of the steps*): Vy do you look so sed, hm?

ROSE (*turning, and sitting on the right balustrade*): Oh, good
morning, Mr. Kaplan.

KAPLAN: A young girl, like you, should not look so sed.

ROSE: I'm not sad, especially, only—

KAPLAN: You got troubles, hm?

ROSE: I don't know. It's just sort of everything.

KAPLAN: Velt-schmerz you got, hm? Vit' my boy Sem is de
same t'ing. Dees vay you feel only ven you are yong. Ven
you gat old like me, you tink only: "Moch longer I von't
be here."

ROSE: Why should things be the way they are, Mr. Kaplan?
Why must people always be fighting and having troubles,
instead of just sort of being happy together.

KAPLAN: My dear yong leddy, ef I could enser dis quastion, I
would be de greatest benefactor thet de verld hes ever
known. Dees is som't'ing, vich all de philosophers hev been
unable to enser. De ones thet believe in God, say de davil
is responsible; and de ones thet don't believe in God, say
'uman nature is responsible. It is my opinion thet most un-
heppiness can be traced to economic cosses and thet—
(CHARLIE *and* MARY HILDEBRAND *have come out of the
house, carrying their schoolbooks.*)

MARY: Hello.

ROSE: Hello, Mary. Hello, Charlie.

CHARLIE: Hello.

MARY (*chattily, as they reach the sidewalk*): We're going to
be dispossessed today.

ROSE: What a shame!

MARY: Yes, ma'am. My father went away and so we couldn't
pay the rent.

CHARLIE (*tugging at her arm*): Aw, come on, Mary.

ROSE: Have you another place to live, Mary?

MARY: No ma'am. But Miss Simpson, from the Charities, says
she'll find us a place. She says we must learn to be less extravagant.

CHARLIE: Come ahead, will you?

MARY: I'm going to school now. Good-bye.

ROSE: Good-bye. (*The children go off, at the left.*)

KAPLAN: More trobles!

ROSE: I know. Isn't it awful to think of them being turned out in the street like that?

KAPLAN: In a ciwilized verld, soch t'ings could not heppen.

ROSE: You mean if there were different laws?

KAPLAN: Not laws! We got already too many laws. Ve must hev ection, not laws. De verking-klesses must t'row off de yoke of ke*pit*alism, and ebolish wage-slevery.

ROSE: But wouldn't people still be unkind to each other and fight and quarrel among themselves?

KAPLAN: My dear young leddy, so long as ve keep men in slevery, dey vill behave like sleves. But wance ve establish a verld based upon 'uman needs and not upon 'uman greed—

ROSE: You mean people will begin being nice to each other and making allowances and all?

KAPLAN: All dees vill come. Wot ve hev now is a wicious soicle. On de one hend, ve hev a rotten economic system—

ROSE: Excuse me, here's my mother. (*She goes towards the left, as* MRS. MAURRANT *approaches, a paper package in her hand.* KAPLAN *goes off, at the right.*)

MRS. MAURRANT (*as* ROSE *comes up to her*): Did he go? (*They stop on the pavement, at the left of the stoop.*)

ROSE: Yes.

MRS. MAURRANT: I got a little chicken, to make Mrs. Buchanan some soup.

ROSE: He had a flask with him, Ma. I hope he doesn't start drinking.

MRS. MAURRANT: What did he say—anything?

ROSE: No, only the way he always talks. I tried to talk to him about buying a house, somewhere, but he wouldn't listen.

MRS. MAURRANT: No, I knew he wouldn't.

ROSE: It doesn't seem to be any use trying to get him to listen to anything.

MRS. MAURRANT: It's always been that way. I've always tried to be a good wife to him, Rose. But it never seemed to make any difference to him.

Rose: I know, Ma.

Mrs. Maurrant: And I've tried to be a good mother, too.

Rose: I know, Ma. I know just the way you feel about it.

Mrs. Maurrant (*appealingly*): Do you, Rose?

Rose: Yes, Ma, I do. Honest I do.

Mrs. Maurrant: I've always tried to make a nice home for him and to do what's right. But it doesn't seem to be any use.

Rose: I know, Ma. (*Hesitantly.*) But it's on account of— (*She stops.*)

Mrs. Maurrant: Are you going to start, too? Are you going to start like all the others? (*She turns away and bursts into tears.*)

Rose (*fondling her*): Don't Ma. Please don't.

Mrs. Maurrant: I thought you'd be the one that would feel different.

Rose: I do, Ma—really I do.

Mrs. Maurrant: What's the good of being alive, if you can't get a little something out of life? You might just as well be dead.

Rose: Look out, Ma. Somebody's coming. (*A smartly dressed girl, with one side of her face covered with cotton and adhesive tape, appears at the left and crosses the stage. At the same time,* Jones *comes out of the house.* Rose *and* Mrs. Maurrant *stand in awkward silence, as he comes down the stoop and approaches them.*)

Jones: Well, is it hot enough for you, today?

Rose: It's awful, isn't it?

Jones (*as he goes towards the left*): You said it. Still along about January, we'll all be wishin' we had a little o' this weather. (*He exits.* Mrs. Maurrant *goes towards the stoop.*)

Rose: Ma, listen. If I say something, will you listen to me?

Mrs. Maurrant: Yes, sure I will, Rose. I'll listen to anything you say, only—

Rose: Well, what I was thinking was, if he didn't come around here so much, maybe. Do you see what I mean, Ma?

MRS. MAURRANT (*constrainedly*): Yes, Rose.

ROSE (*putting her arm around her*): It's on account of all that's going around—everybody in the whole house. You see what I mean, don't you, Ma?

MRS. MAURRANT: Every person in the world has to have somebody to talk to. You can't live without somebody to talk to. I'm not saying that I can't talk to you, Rose, but you're only a young girl and it's not the same thing.

ROSE: It's only on account of Pop. I'm scared of what he's likely to do, if he starts drinking.

MRS. MAURRANT: Well, I'll see, Rose. Sometimes I think I'd be better off if I was dead.

ROSE: If there was only something I could do.

MRS. MAURRANT: There isn't anything anybody could do. It's just the way things are, that's all. (BUCHANAN *appears at the left. They turn and face him, as he approaches.*)

MRS. MAURRANT: Oh, Mr. Buchanan, I got a little chicken, so that I could make her some good, nourishing soup.

BUCHANAN: Well, say, you got to let me pay you for it.

MRS. MAURRANT: Oh, never mind about that. We'll have the chicken for supper tonight. Did you have her medicine made up?

BUCHANAN: Yes, I got it right here. I called up the office and they told me not to come down today.

MRS. MAURRANT: Well, that's very nice. It'll be a comfort to her to have you around.

BUCHANAN: Yes, that's what I thought, too. Well, I'd better be getting upstairs. (*He goes up the steps.*)

MRS. MAURRANT: I'll be up later, with the soup.

BUCHANAN: Well, thanks. (*Stopping at the top of the stoop and turning to her.*) You've been a mighty good neighbor, Mrs. Maurrant. (*He enters the house.*)

MRS. MAURRANT: He's an awful nice, young feller—so nice and gentle. And he's always trying to be so helpful. It makes you feel sort of sorry for him. (SHIRLEY *comes out of the house, carrying a large wicker bag, which contains her*

185

lunch and schoolbooks. She takes a post card out of the mailbox.)

MRS. MAURRANT (*going up the steps*): Well, I'd better go and start this chicken. Are you coming home for lunch, Rose?

ROSE: Yes. I'll be back, as soon as the funeral's over.

MRS. MAURRANT: Oh, all right. (*As she sees* SHIRLEY.) Good morning.

SHIRLEY (*coming out of the vestibule, reading the post card*): Good morning.

ROSE: Good morning. (MRS. MAURRANT *goes into the house. The shade of* MAE's *window flies up and she is seen, for an instant, dressed only in her step-in. She yawns noisily and turns away from the window.*)

ROSE (*seating herself on the stoop*): It's another awful day, isn't it?

SHIRLEY: Yes, and when you have to keep forty children quiet—! Well, thank goodness, in two weeks, school closes. Otherwise, I think I'd go crazy.

ROSE: Well, you get a nice, long vacation, anyhow.

SHIRLEY: Not much vacation for me. I'm taking summer courses at Teachers' College. (*She looks at* ROSE *a moment, hesitates, and then comes down the steps.*) Miss Maurrant, if you don't mind, I want to talk to you about my brother, Sam.

ROSE: Why certainly, Miss Kaplan.

SHIRLEY: I guess you know he's only finishing college, this month—

ROSE: Yes, of course, I do.

SHIRLEY: Then he has to go three years to law school and pass the bar examination, before he can be a full-fledged lawyer.

ROSE: Yes, it takes a long time.

SHIRLEY: A long time and lots of money. And before a young lawyer begins to make his own living, that takes a long time, too. It will be ten years, maybe, before he's making enough to support himself and a family. (*Looking away.*) Then, it's time enough for him to think about marriage.

ROSE: You don't mean me and Sam, Miss Kaplan?

SHIRLEY: Yes, that's just what I mean.

ROSE: Why, we're just good friends, that's all.

SHIRLEY: I know how it is with a boy like Sam, Miss Maurrant. He thinks he's a man, already; but he's nothing but a boy. If you're such a good friend, you shouldn't take his mind away from his work.

ROSE: But I haven't meant to, Miss Kaplan—honest I haven't.

SHIRLEY: I've had to work hard enough to get him as far as he is. And I have my father to take care of, too. The few dollars he makes, writing for the radical papers, don't even pay the rent. Believe me, every dollar I make goes.

ROSE: I know. Sam's often told me how much he owes to you.

SHIRLEY: He doesn't owe me anything. I don't care about the money. Only he should be thinking about his work and not about other things.

ROSE: Yes, he should be thinking about his work. But don't you think there are other things in the world, too, besides just work?

SHIRLEY: Don't you think I know that? I know that just as well as you do. Maybe, you think I'm only an old-maid schoolteacher, without any feelings.

ROSE: Oh, I don't—really I don't!

SHIRLEY (*turning her head away*): Maybe I'm not a movie vamp, with dimples—but I could have had my chances, too. Only, I wanted to give Sam an education.

ROSE: I haven't tried to vamp Sam, honestly I haven't. We just seemed sort of naturally to like each other.

SHIRLEY: Why must you pick out Sam? You could get other fellows. Anyhow, it's much better to marry with your own kind. When you marry outside your own people, nothing good ever comes of it. You can't mix oil and water.

ROSE: I don't know. I think if people really care about each other—

SHIRLEY: He's nothing but a baby. He sees a pretty face and, right away, he forgets about everything else.

ROSE (*with a flash of temper*): I know I haven't as much brains as Sam, or as you, either, if that's what you mean.

SHIRLEY (*contritely, going towards her*): I didn't mean to hurt your feelings. I haven't got anything against you. Only, he's all I've got in the world. What else have I got to live for?

SAM (*appearing at the extreme right window, with a cup of coffee and a piece of coffee cake*): Hello, Rose.

ROSE: Hello, Sam.

SHIRLEY (*in a low tone*): Please don't tell him what I said. (SAM *goes to the other window.*)

ROSE: Oh, no I won't. (SHIRLEY *hurries off, at the left.*)

ROSE (*rising and turning towards SAM*): Sam—

SAM (*holding out the coffee cake*): Want some coffee cake?

ROSE: No. (*Going up the steps.*) Sam, there's something I want to ask you, before I forget. Is there any special way you have to act in a synagogue?

SAM (*eating throughout*): In a synagogue?

ROSE: Yes. The funeral I'm going to, is in a synagogue, and I thought there might be some special thing you have to do. Like in church, you know, a girl is always supposed to keep her hat on.

SAM: I don't know. I've never in my life been in a synagogue.

ROSE: Didn't you ever go to Sunday school, or anything like that?

SAM: No.

ROSE: That's funny. I thought everybody went, once in a while. How about when your mother died?

SAM: She was cremated. My parents were always rationalists.

ROSE: Didn't they believe in God or anything?

SAM: What do you mean by God?

ROSE (*puzzled*): Well—you know what I mean. What anybody means—God. Somebody that sort of loves us and looks after us, when we're in trouble.

SAM (*sitting on the window sill*): That's nothing but superstition—the lies that people tell themselves, because reality is too terrible for them to face.

ROSE: But, Sam, don't you think it's better to believe in something that makes you a little happy, than not to believe in anything and be miserable all the time?

SAM: There's no such thing as happiness. That's an illusion, like all the rest.

ROSE: Then, what's the use of living?

SAM (*brushing the last crumbs off his hands*): Yes, what is the use?

ROSE: Why, you oughtn't to talk like that, Sam—a person with all the talent and brains that you've got. I know things aren't just the way you want them to be. But they aren't for anybody. They aren't for me, either.

SAM: Then, why don't we get out of it, together?

ROSE: I don't see just how we could do that, Sam.

SAM: It would be easy enough—ten cents' worth of carbolic acid.

ROSE: Why, Sam, you don't mean kill ourselves!

SAM: Is your life so precious to you that you want to cling to it?

ROSE: Well, yes. I guess it is.

SAM: Why? Why? What is there in life to compensate for the pain of living?

ROSE: There's a lot. Just being alive—breathing and walking around. Just looking at the faces of people you like and hearing them laugh. And seeing the pretty things in the store windows. And roughhousing with your kid brother. And—oh, I don't know—listening to a good band, and dancing—Oh, I'd hate to die! (*Earnestly.*) Sam, promise you won't talk about killing yourself, any more.

SAM: What difference would it make to you, if I did?

ROSE: Don't talk like that, Sam! You're the best friend I've ever had. (*She puts her hand on his.*)

SAM: I can't think of anything but you.

ROSE: There's something I want to ask your advice about, Sam. It's about what I started to tell you about, last night. A man I know wants to put me on the stage.

SAM (*releasing her hand and drawing back*): What man?

ROSE: A man that works in the office. He knows a manager

and he says he'll help me get started. You see, what I thought was, that if I could only get out of here and have a decent place to live and make a lot of money, maybe everything would be different, not only for me, but for Ma and Pop and Willie.

SAM: But don't you know what he wants, this man?

ROSE: Nobody gives you anything for nothing, Sam. If you don't pay for things in one way, you do in another.

SAM: Rose, for God's sake, you mustn't! (VINCENT JONES *comes out of the house.*)

ROSE (*seeing* VINCENT *in the vestibule*): Look out, Sam, here's that tough, from upstairs. (*She goes over to the left of the stoop.*)

VINCENT (*in the doorway*): Hello, Rosie. Been here all night, talkin' to the little yit? (ROSE *does not answer.*)

VINCENT (*turning to Sam*): Hello, motzers! Shake! (*He leans over the balustrade and seizes* SAM's *hand, in a crushing grip.*)

SAM (*writhing with pain*): Let me go!

ROSE: Let him alone! (VINCENT *gives* SAM's *hand another vicious squeeze and then releases him.* SAM *cowers back in the window, nursing his hand.*)

VINCENT (*waving his hand about in mock pain*): Jesus, what a grip dat little kike's got! I'd hate to get into a mix-up wit' him. (*To* ROSE.) Got a date for tonight, kid?

ROSE: Yes, I have.

VINCENT: Yeah? Gee, ain't dat too bad. I'll give you two dollars, if you let me snap your garter.

ROSE: Shut up, you! (VINCENT *laughs.* SAM *makes an inarticulate sound.*)

VINCENT (*threateningly*): Whadja say? I t'ought I hoid you say sumpin. (*He makes a threatening gesture.* SAM *shrinks back.*)

VINCENT (*with a loud laugh, as he goes down the steps*): Fightin' Kaplan, de pride o' Jerusalem! (*He looks at them both, then laughs again.*) Fer cryin' out loud! (*He goes off at the left.*)

ROSE: Oh, if there was only some way of getting out of here! (SAM *puts the back of his hand to his forehead and turns away.*) I sometimes think I'd just like to run away.

SAM (*without turning*): Yes!

ROSE: Anywhere—it wouldn't matter where—just to get out of this.

SAM (*turning*): Why shouldn't we do it?

ROSE (*rather startled coming over to the right balustrade*): Would you go with me, Sam?

SAM: Yes—anywhere.

ROSE: I've heard that people are much nicer and friendlier, when you get outside of New York. There's not so much of a mad rush, other places. And being alone, you could sort of work things out for yourself. (*Suddenly.*) Only, what would you do, Sam?

SAM: I could get a job, too.

ROSE: And give up your law work?

SAM: I'd give up everything, to be with you.

ROSE: No. I wouldn't let you do that, Sam. It's different with me— (EASTER *appears at the right.*)

EASTER (*stopping at the right of the stoop*): Good morning, Miss Maurrant. (*Startled,* ROSE *turns and sees him, for the first time.*)

ROSE (*none too pleased*): Oh, good morning, Mr. Easter. What brings you in this neighborhood?

EASTER (*not very plausibly*): Well, I just happened to have a little business, right around the corner. So, I thought as long as you were going to the funeral, we might just as well go together.

ROSE: Well, I hardly expected to see you around here. (*An awkward pause.*) Oh, I'd like you to meet my friend, Mr. Kaplan.

EASTER: How do you do, Mr. Kaplan? Glad to know you. (SAM *murmurs something inaudible. An awkward silence.*)

ROSE (*to* SAM): Mr. Easter is the manager of the office. (SAM *does not reply. Another silence.*)

ROSE (*to* EASTER): It's awful hot again, isn't it?

EASTER: Worse than yesterday. (*Approaching the stoop.*) Tell you what I was thinking. I was thinking, that after the funeral, we might take a run down to the beach, somewhere, and cool off a little.

ROSE: I can't today. I've got a lot of things I want to do.

EASTER: Oh, you can do 'em some other day.

ROSE: No, really, I can't. (*Looking at her watch.*) Well, I guess it's time we got started. (*She comes down the steps.*)

EASTER: Yes, it is. We'll pick up a cab at the corner. (MRS. MAURRANT *appears at her window, looks out, and sees* ROSE *and* EASTER.)

ROSE: Why, I thought I'd walk. It's not far.

EASTER: Too hot, today, for any walking.

ROSE (*starting to go towards the left*): Not if you keep in the shade.

EASTER: Much more comfortable taking a cab.

ROSE: I'd rather walk.

EASTER: Well, whatever you say. Good morning, Mr. Kaplan. Glad to have met you. (SAM *murmurs an inaudible reply.*)

ROSE: Good-bye, Sam. I'll see you, later. (SAM *does not answer.* ROSE *and* EASTER *go towards the left, in silence.* SAM *watches them, intently, trembling with jealousy.* MRS. MAURRANT, *surprised and disturbed, watches* ROSE *and* EASTER.)

ROSE (*to* EASTER, *as they disappear*): It's a lucky thing my father wasn't around. (SAM *suddenly turns and goes into the house.* MRS. MAURRANT *remains at the window, looking out, with obvious expectancy.*)

DISTANT VOICE (*offstage left*): Straw-berries! Straw-berries! (*An anemic girl of eighteen, with a music-roll under her arm, appears at the left. She enters the house and pushes one of the buttons, in the vestibule, then goes to the entrance door and waits. A moment later,* MRS. FIORENTINO *appears hastily, at the window, and whisks away the bed-clothes. After another moment, the latch clicks and the girl enters the house.*)

VOICE (*a little nearer*): Oh-h! Straw-berries! Straw-berries!

(SANKEY *appears at the right. He carries a pencil behind his ear, wears a round cap with a metal name plate and a stiff visor, and carries a large black-covered billholder. He and* MRS. MAURRANT *see each other and both become tense with excitement.* MRS. MAURRANT *beckons to him and he comes over to the railing, under her window.*)

MRS. MAURRANT (*in a low, tense voice*): Come up.

SANKEY (*looking about, nervously*): Now?

MRS. MAURRANT: Yes. I got to talk to you.

SANKEY: Is it all right?

MRS. MAURRANT: Yes. He's gone to Stamford.

SANKEY: How about later?

MRS. MAURRANT: No. Rose'll be home in a hour. She's not working today.

SANKEY: All right. (*He looks about again, then goes quickly towards the steps.* SAM *appears, at the entrance door. He is about to step out, when he sees* SANKEY. *He stops and looks at him.* SANKEY *sees* SAM, *hesitates a moment, then goes quickly into the house. Meanwhile,* MRS. MAURRANT *has closed both windows and pulled down the shades.* SAM *takes a periodical out of the mailbox, then comes out of the house and down the steps. He looks up at the* MAURRANT *windows, sees the drawn shades, and looks about, in perturbed perplexity, not knowing what to do. At length, he sits down on the steps of the stoop, tears the wrapper off the periodical—*The Nation—*and begins to read. The girl in* LIPPO'S *apartment begins playing the piano. This continues throughout the scene. Two untidy and rather coarse-looking men appear, at the left and approach the stoop:* JAMES HENRY, *a city marshal, and* FRED CULLEN, *his assistant. They stop in front of the house.* SAM *pays no attention to them.*)

MARSHAL (*crossing to the left of the stoop, and taking a paper from his pocket*): Dis is it (*To* SAM.) Hildebrand live here?

SAM (*startled*): What?

MARSHAL: I'm askin' you if Hildebrand lives here.

SAM: Yes. Fourth floor.

MARSHAL: Better give de janitor a buzz, Fred. (*Fred goes up the steps and rings the janitor's bell, then leans over the left balustrade.*)

FRED (*bawling*): Hey, janitor.

OLSEN (*below*): Vell?

FRED: Come on out, a minute. (*As* OLSEN *appears below.*) We got a warrant for Hildebrand.

OLSEN: Fourt' floor—Hildebrand.

FRED: Yeah, I know. We got a warrant for her.

MARSHAL: I'm City Marshal Henry. We got a dispossess warrant.

OLSEN (*coming up the steps*): Oh, sure. You gonna put 'em out?

MARSHAL: Yeah, dat's it. Has she got anybody to take de foinicher away?

OLSEN (*with a shrug*): I don' know.

MARSHAL: Well, we'll have t' dump it on de sidewalk, den. Go ahead, Fred. (*They enter the house.* OLSEN *leans his elbows on the coping, and smokes his pipe.* SAM *sits on the steps, deep in troubled thought. A grocery boy, with a full basket, appears at the right, and goes down the cellar steps.* MAE JONES *comes out of the house. She stands on the top step, yawns noisily, and goes off, at left. She and* SAM *do not pay the slightest attention to each other.*)

VOICE (*a little nearer*): Straw-berries! Straw-berries! (MRS. OLSEN *comes up the cellar steps, with a heavy pail of water.* OLSEN *leans forward to make room for her. She staggers over to the stoop, almost dropping the pail, and goes up the steps, into the vestibule.* OLSEN *yawns and goes down into the cellar.* MRS. JONES *appears, at the window, her hair wet and stringy, a towel pinned about her shoulders, and leans out to dry her hair.*)

OLD-CLOTHES MAN (*appearing at left*): I kesh ko! I kesh ko! (*He wears a battered derby and carries a folded newspaper under his arm.* MRS. OLSEN, *on her knees, begins washing up the vestibule.* FRED *comes out of the house, carrying a worn chair and a large gilt-framed picture, which he de-*

posits on the sidewalk, against the railing, to the left of the
stoop.)

OLD-CLOTHES MAN (*as if to someone across the street*): Kesh
ko? (*To* SAM.) Any old klose, mister? (SAM *pays no attention to him.* FRED *re-enters the house.*)

OLD-CLOTHES MAN (*to* MRS. JONES): Any ol' klose, leddy?

MRS. JONES: Naw, nawthin'.

OLD-CLOTHES MAN: Hets? Shoes? Ol' stockings?

MRS. JONES: Nawthin', I tell you. (*As the* OLD-CLOTHES MAN
goes off, at the right, MAURRANT *appears, still carrying his
satchel.*)

MRS. JONES: Why, hello, Mr. Maurrant. (MAURRANT *looks up
without replying and comes over to the stoop.*) I thought
you was off to Stamford.

MAURRANT: I changed me— (*He stops, to the right of the
stoop, and looks up at the drawn shades of his apartment.
SAM rises, slowly and rigidly, his eyes glued in fascination,
upon* MAURRANT. MAURRANT'S *movements take on a lithe
and catlike quality. Then, slowly and deliberately, he goes
towards the steps, his back arched, like a tiger ready to
spring.*)

SAM (*suddenly blocking the steps*): No! No! For God's sake—!

MAURRANT (*raging*): Out o' me way, you goddam little rat!
(*He flings* SAM *violently aside, almost knocking him down.
MRS. OLSEN, terrified, rises and shrinks into a corner, as
MAURRANT with swift stealthiness, enters the house. MRS.
JONES leans out, to see what is wrong. SAM rushes down the
steps and stands under the* MAURRANT *windows. The* MAR-
SHAL *comes out of the house, carrying a wash-boiler, filled
with pots.*)

SAM (*hysterically*): Mrs. Maurrant! Mrs. Maurrant!

MRS. JONES: What's the matter? (*The* MARSHAL *puts the wash-
boiler on the balustrade and looks on, in amazement.*)

SAM (*to* MRS. JONES): Quick! Run and tell her! Quick!

MRS. JONES: What is it? (*Suddenly.*) Oh, Gawd, is he in there?
(*She leaves the window, hastily.*)

SAM: Yes! Mrs. Maurrant! Mrs. Maurrant! (*A scream of terror is heard, from the* MAURRANT *apartment.*)

MRS. MAURRANT'S VOICE: Frank! Frank! (*Two shots are heard, in quick succession, and then a heavy fall.* MRS. OLSEN *runs out of the vestibule and down into the cellar.* SANKEY'S *voice is heard, inarticulate with fear. Then, one of the shades shoots up, and* SANKEY *appears at the window, coatless, his face deformed by terror. He tries to open the window, but succeeds only in shattering the pane with his elbow.* MAURRANT *appears behind him and pulls him away from the window. Then another shot is heard.*)

MARSHAL: For Chris' sake, what's happenin'? Get an ambulance, you! (*He pushes* SAM *towards the left, then hurries off, at the right. As* SAM *runs off, a crowd begins to form.* OLSEN *comes up from the cellar, followed by the* GROCERY BOY. *The two workmen come up, out of the excavation. Two or three of the workmen from the demolished building, run on at the right.*)

WORKMAN: What's happening?

MAN: What is it? A murder? (*Still others join the crowd: A huckster, a janitor from a neighboring house, a mulatto girl, six or eight women of the neighborhood, some in street dresses, others in house dresses or dingy wrappers.* LIPPO'S PUPIL *appears, at the window, badly frightened. The crowd surges about, uncertainly, not knowing what has happened, and buzzing with questions, which nobody can answer. While the crowd is still forming,* FRED, *the* MARSHAL'S *assistant, appears at the broken window.*)

FRED (*excitedly*): Grab dat boid! He's comin' down!

WORKMAN: What boid?

MAN: Here he is, now! (*The crowd murmurs with excitement and surges about the stoop, as the house door opens and* MAURRANT *appears. His coat is open and his shirt is torn almost to shreds. His face, hands and clothing are covered with blood. He stands in the doorway for a moment, surveying the crowd, his eyes glaring.*)

FRED: Grab him! Don't let him get away! (*As the crowd*

makes a concerted movement towards MAURRANT, *he whips
out an automatic revolver and levels it. The crowd shrinks
back. Some of the women scream.*)

MAURRANT: Git back! Git back, all o' you! (*The crowd falls
back towards the left, to make way for him. With his back
to the balustrade, he comes quickly down the steps, and
still leveling his revolver at the crowd, retreats backwards
to the cellar steps. A man, approaching at the right, comes
stealthily up behind him, but* MAURRANT *senses his presence
in time, wheels quickly, menaces the man with his revolver,
then rushes down the cellar steps. While all this is happening, the other shade in the* MAURRANT *apartment flies up
and* MISS CUSHING *opens the window and leans out.*)

MISS CUSHING: Hurry up! Get an ambulance! (*No one pays
any attention to her, as they are all watching* MAURRANT.
As MAURRANT *runs down the cellar steps, the crowd surges
forward to the railing, on both sides of the stoop and leans
over. A scream from* MRS. OLSEN *is heard from the basement.* FRED *goes away from the window.*)

MISS CUSHING: Get an ambulance, somebody! (*Unable to at-
tract anyone's attention, she leaves the window.*)

OLSEN: Olga! (*He hurries down the cellar steps.*)

MAN (*calling*): Here's a cop! (*The crowd looks to the right.*)
Hey! Hurry up! (*A* POLICEMAN *runs on from the right.*)

POLICEMAN: Where is he?

VOICES IN THE CROWD: He's down the cellar! He ran down
the cellar! He went down the steps!

POLICEMAN: Get out of the way! (*The* POLICEMAN *and two
men in the crowd go down the cellar steps.*)

VOICES IN THE CROWD: Watch yourself! Look out, he's got a
gun! He's a big guy with his shirt torn! (*The rest of the
crowd peers over the railing.*)

MISS CUSHING (*leaning out of* ROSE'S *window*): Hey, don't
you hear me? Get an ambulance!

ANOTHER MAN (*looking up*): What's de matter? You want de
ambulance?

MISS CUSHING: Yes! Right away!

ANOTHER MAN (*to the* GROCERY BOY): Run aroun' de corner
to de horspital, Johnny, an' tell 'em to send de ambulance!

GROCERY BOY: Sure!

MISS CUSHING: Run! (*The* GROCERY BOY *runs off swiftly at the
left.* MISS CUSHING *leaves the window. Meanwhile, as the
POLICEMAN and the two MEN have gone down the cellar
steps, the MARSHAL has run on, from the right, panting.*)

MARSHAL (*as the* GROCERY BOY *runs off*): Did dey git 'm?

MAN: He beat it down de cellar.

WORKMAN: De cop's gone after him.

MARSHAL: Why de hell didn' you stop 'em? (FRED *comes out
of the house.*)

WORKMAN: He had a gun.

FRED: Did somebody go for de ambulance?

MAN: Yeah. De kid went.

WOMAN: It's only aroun' de corner.

ANOTHER MAN: Dey'll be here, right away. (*The crowd moves
over towards* FRED.)

THE MARSHAL (*pushing his way through the crowd and up
the steps*): What de hell happened, Fred?

FRED (*as the crowd moves toward the stoop*): It's a moider.
Dis boid's wife an' some other guy. Jesus, you oughta see
de blood. (*Another* POLICEMAN *runs up, at left, closely followed by* SAM.)

FRED: Upstairs, officer! Dere's two of 'em got shot.

POLICEMAN (*elbowing his way through the crowd*): Look out
o' de way, youse! (*He goes up the stoop and crosses to the
door.*) Where's de guy dat did it?

VOICES IN THE CROWD: Down de cellar! He beat it down de
steps!

FRED: Dere's another cop after 'im. You better look after dem,
upstairs. Foist floor.

SAM (*agonized*): Are they dead? (*No one pays any attention
to him.*)

MARSHAL (*stopping the* POLICEMAN, *and exhibiting his
badge*): I'm City Marshal Henry. Kin I do anythin'?

POLICEMAN: Don' let anybody in or out! Hear?

MARSHAL: Yeah, sure! (*The* POLICEMAN *exits quickly, into the house.*)

SAM: Are they dead? (*No one notices him. The* MARSHAL *takes up his position in the doorway.*)

BUCHANAN (*appearing at the* MAURRANT *window*): Where's the ambulance?

MARSHAL: It'll be here, right away. Dere's a cop on his way up.

SAM: Mr. Buchanan! Mr. Buchanan! Are they dead? (*But* BUCHANAN *has already disappeared. The* TWO MEN, *who followed the first* POLICEMAN *into the cellar, now come up the steps. The crowd moves over to the railing, at the right.*)

MARSHAL: Did you get him, boys?

ONE OF THE MEN: He must be hidin', somewheres. De cop's lookin' for 'im.

ANOTHER MAN: Somebody better call de resoives. (SAM *runs up the steps and tries to enter the house.*)

MARSHAL (*seizing him roughly*): You can't get in now! Get back dere! (*He pushes* SAM *back into the crowd, at the foot of the steps.*)

POLICEMAN (*appearing at the* MAURRANT *window*): Hey, call up headquarters an' tell 'em to send the resoives. Make it quick! (*He goes away from the window.*)

MARSHAL: You go, Fred.

FRED: Sure!

MAN: Dere's a phone in de warehouse. (*An ambulance bell is heard at the left, as* FRED *goes quickly towards the left. Another spectator hurries on and joins the crowd.*)

VOICES IN THE CROWD: Dere it is! Dere's de ambulance now! Here dey come! (*The crowd moves over towards the left.*)

MAN: Dey won't be able to git past.

POLICEMAN (*reappearing at the window*): Is dat de ambulance?

MARSHAL: Yeah. (BUCHANAN *and* MRS. JONES *crowd to the window, behind the* POLICEMAN, *and, at the other window,* LIPPO, MISS CUSHING *and* MRS. HILDEBRAND *appear. A hos-*

pital interne and an ambulance driver come on at the left.)

POLICEMAN: Hurry up, Doc! She's still breathin'.

INTERNE (*forcing his way through the crowd*): All right! Better bring the stretcher, Harry.

AMBULANCE DRIVER: Yes, sir. (*He hurries off, at the left. The* INTERNE *goes quickly into the house. The crowd attempts to follow, several of its members going up the steps.*)

MARSHAL (*pushing them back*): Keep back, now! Back off de stoop, everybody! (*The crowd forms a compact mass, about the foot of the steps. The persons at the* MAURRANT *windows have disappeared.* FRED *hurries on, at the left.*)

FRED (*pushing his way through the crowd and up the steps*): I got 'em. Dey'll be right up. Anudder cop jes' wen' in t'roo de warehouse cellar.

MARSHAL: Dey'll git 'im all right. (*Looking at his watch.*) Better git busy wit' dat foinicher, Fred. We got two udder jobs today.

FRED: Yeah, sure, Jimmy. (*He enters the house. The* AMBULANCE DRIVER *appears at the left, carrying a canvas stretcher.*)

AMBULANCE DRIVER: Get out o' the way!

MARSHAL: Git back, can't youse? What de hell's de matter wit' youse? (*He comes down the steps and violently pushes the crowd back. The* AMBULANCE DRIVER *enters the house.*)

POLICEMAN (*at the window*): Are dey bringin' dat stretcher?

MARSHAL: On de way up! (*To the crowd.*) Keep back! (*The* POLICEMAN *leaves the window.* LIPPO'S PUPIL, *her music-roll under her arm, appears timidly in the doorway.*)

MARSHAL (*grabbing her arm roughly*): Where you goin'?

GIRL (*nervously*): I'm going home.

MARSHAL: Home? Where do you live?

GIRL: Ninety-first Street.

MARSHAL: What are you doin' here?

GIRL: I just came for a music lesson, that's all.

MARSHAL: Yeah? Well, you can't go now.

GIRL (*beginning to whimper*): I want to go home.

MARSHAL: You can't go, now. Nobody can't leave de house, now.

POLICEMAN (*coming out of the house*): Who's dis kid?

MARSHAL: Says she come here to take a music lesson an' she wants to go home.

POLICEMAN (*to the girl*): Do you know anythin' about this killin'?

GIRL: No, I don't. I just heard some shooting, that's all. My mother will be worried, if I don't come home.

POLICEMAN: Well, you can't go, now. Get inside dere, out o' de way. Dey'll be bringin' her down, in a minute. (*He pushes the girl inside the house and comes down the steps.*) Come on, git back from dem steps! Back now, all o' youse! (*He and the* MARSHAL *push the crowd back to the right of the stoop, leaving the steps and the sidewalk in front of them clear. Then he goes up the steps again.*)

MARSHAL: What did he do? Shoot two of 'em?

POLICEMAN: I'll say he did! His wife an' her sweetie. A guy named Sankey. He was dead when I got up dere.

MARSHAL: I seen him tryin' to climb out t'roo de winder. An' dis guy grabs 'im an' pulls 'im back.

INTERNE (*from the* MAURRANT *window*): Officer! Come on up! (*He leaves the window, as the* POLICEMAN *exits into the house. Suddenly,* SAM *utters an exclamation of anguish and, pushing his way out of the crowd, hurries over to the left.*)

MARSHAL: Hey, you! Where you goin'? (SAM *ignores him and hurries on.*)

WOMAN: Look! There's the Maurrant girl!

ANOTHER WOMAN: Who?

WOMAN: It's her daughter. (*The crowd murmurs, excitedly, as* ROSE *comes on quickly, at the left.*)

ROSE: What's the matter, Sam? What's the ambulance for? Did anybody get hurt?

SAM: Go away, Rose. Go away.

ROSE: Who is it, Sam? What's the matter? Is it my mother? It's not my mother, is it? (*Clinging to him.*) Sam, is it?

SAM: There's been an accident. Go away, Rose. (*He tries to force her away.*)

ROSE: Tell me what's happened! Tell me!

MISS CUSHING (*appearing at the window*): They're bringing her down!

ROSE (*with a cry*): It *is* my mother!

MISS CUSHING (*seeing her*): Oh, my God, there's Rose! (MRS. FIORENTINO, MRS. JONES, MRS. HILDEBRAND, LIPPO *and* BUCHANAN *crowd to the* MAURRANT *windows.*)

SAM: Rose! Go away! (*She pays no attention to him, but stands watching the door, transfixed. The* INTERNE *comes briskly out of the house.*)

INTERNE (*to the* MARSHAL): Hold the door open, will you? (*He comes down the steps.*)

MARSHAL: Sure, doc! (*He hurries into the vestibule.*)

INTERNE (*to the crowd*): Keep back, now!

ROSE (*seizing the* INTERNE'S *arm*): Doctor! Is she dead?

INTERNE: Who are you? Her daughter?

ROSE: Yes, sir. I'm her daughter.

INTERNE: She's pretty badly hurt. Step aside, now! (*They step aside, as the* AMBULANCE DRIVER *and the* POLICEMAN *come out of the house, carrying* MRS. MAURRANT *on the stretcher. There is a low murmur from the crowd.*)

AMBULANCE DRIVER: Easy, now.

POLICEMAN: All right. (*They come down the steps and go towards the left.*)

ROSE (*running forward and gripping the side of the stretcher*): Mother! Mother!

MRS. MAURRANT (*opening her eyes, feebly*): Rose! (*She tries to lift her hand, but it falls back.*)

INTERNE (*pulling* ROSE *back*): You mustn't talk to her, now. (SAM *takes her about the shoulders. They and the* INTERNE *follow the stretcher off, at the left. The crowd swarms after them.* FRED *comes out of the house, carrying one end of an iron bedstead.*)

ACT III

SCENE: *Mid-afternoon of the same day. At the left of the stoop, is a large roll of bedding. Before the rise of the curtain, and continuing faintly thereafter, a woman can be heard singing scales.* OLSEN, *pipe in mouth, is leaning against the railing. Two* MEN, *furniture-movers appear at the left.*

ONE OF THE MEN (*picking up the bedding*): All right. Dat's all, Charlie! (*The* MEN *exit left. A* POLICEMAN *comes out of the house, carrying the bloodstained dress of* MRS. MAURRANT, *and* SANKEY's *coat, cap, and billholder. He comes down the steps, and exits at the right. At the left, two young* NURSEMAIDS, *in smart uniforms, appear, each wheeling a de luxe baby carriage.*)

FIRST NURSEMAID (*seeing the house number*): This must be the place, right here—346. (*They stop, under the* MAURRANT *windows.*)

SECOND NURSEMAID: Yes, I guess it is.

FIRST NURSEMAID: Yes, this is it, all right. (*Looking up.*) Must be right up there, on the first floor, see?

SECOND NURSEMAID: Yes, sure. (*Excitedly.*) Say, look! You can see where the glass is out of the window. That's where this feller what's-his-name tried to climb out.

FIRST NURSEMAID: Oh, yes, I see it! Say, what do you know about that!

SECOND NURSEMAID (*taking a pink tabloid newspaper from under the hood of the baby buggy*): Wait! There's a picture of it, somewhere. (*Turning the pages.*) Here it is. (*They excitedly examine it together, as she reads.*) "Composograph showing Sankey, scantily clad, in a last vain attempt to escape the vengeance of the jealousy-crazed husband, whose home he had destroyed." And there's Maurrant pulling him back. And Mrs. Maurrant trying to get the pistol away from him, see? Look at the blood running down her face, will you?

FIRST NURSEMAID: It's worse than awful! Can you *imagine* what those two must have felt like, when he walked in on them like that?

SECOND NURSEMAID: Well, he just happened to be one of the ones that finds out! Believe me, there's lots and lots of husbands that don't know the half of what goes on uptown, while they're downtown making a living.

FIRST NURSEMAID: Say, you're not telling me, are you? If I was to spill all I know, there'd be many a happy home busted up. I wonder if they caught him.

SECOND NURSEMAID (*as her baby begins a thin wailing*): Oh, God, he's in again! (*To the unseen baby.*) Shut up, a little while, can't you? (*She shakes the carriage.*)

POLICEMAN (*appearing at the Maurrant windows, a tabloid in his hand*): Keep movin' ladies. No loiterin' aroun' here.

FIRST NURSEMAID (*eagerly*): Say, have they caught him, yet?

POLICEMAN: Why, ain't you hoid? He was last seen, flyin' over Novia Scotia, on his way to Paris.

FIRST NURSEMAID: Who are you trying to string, anyhow?

SECOND NURSEMAID (*coquettishly*): Say, will you let us come up and look around?

POLICEMAN: Why, sure, sure! Bring de babies, too. De commissioner is soivin' tea, up here, at four-thoity.

SECOND NURSEMAID: You're awful smart, aren't you?

POLICEMAN: Yeah, dat's why dey put me on de entertainment committee. I'm Handsome Harry Moiphy, de boy comedian o' Brooklyn.

FIRST NURSEMAID (*looking at her watch*): Oh, say, I ought to be getting back. (*Turning her carriage.*) Clarice darling would throw a duck-fit, if she knew I brought her precious Dumplings to a neighborhood like this.

SECOND NURSEMAID (*turning her carriage*): There's not so much to see, anyhow. It's nothing but a cheap, common dump. (*They go towards the left.*)

POLICEMAN: Over de river, goils. See you in de funny papers.

SECOND NURSEMAID: Don't you get so fresh.

POLICEMAN: Drop in again, when you're in de neighborhood. An' tell Mrs. Vanderbilt, Harry was askin' for her. (*As the NURSEMAIDS go off, at the left, EASTER hurries on at the right, several folded newspapers under his arm.*)

EASTER (*to the POLICEMAN, going to the left of the stoop*): Is Miss Maurrant up there, officer?

POLICEMAN: No. There ain't nobody up here but me.

EASTER: You don't happen to know where she is, do you?

POLICEMAN: No, I don't. Are you a reporter?

EASTER: Who, me? I'm just a friend of hers. I've got to see her.

POLICEMAN: Well, I ain't seen her since she went off to the horspital this mornin'. She ain't been back since. (*He starts to leave the window.*)

EASTER: Oh, officer!

POLICEMAN: Yeah?

EASTER: Have they caught him, yet?

POLICEMAN: Naw, not yet. But we'll get 'im, all right! (*He leaves the window. EASTER remains at the left of the stoop, uncertain whether to go or not. MRS. JONES appears, at the right, carrying several newspapers.*)

MRS. JONES (*to OLSEN*): Have they caught him yet?

OLSEN (*shaking his head*): No.

MRS. JONES: I been down at Police Headquarters, all this while— (*Breaking off, as she notices EASTER.*) Say, what's he want here? (*OLSEN shrugs his shoulders.*)

EASTER (*approaching them*): Pardon me, but maybe you can tell me where I can find Miss Maurrant? (*OLSEN shakes his head.*)

MRS. JONES: Why, no, I can't. I jus' this minute got back from Police Headquarters. Maybe she's aroun' at the horspital.

EASTER: No, I just came from there.

MRS. JONES: Well, I really couldn't say where she is. Was there somethin' special you wanted to see her about?

EASTER: I'm a friend of hers—

MRS. JONES: Yeah, I noticed you talkin' to her, last night, when I took the dog out. (*Staring at him.*) Well, I guess she'll need all the friends she's got, now. Imagine a thing like that happenin' right here in this house, at ten o'clock in the mornin'! Everythin' goin' on just as usual, and then, all of a sudden, before you know it, there's two people murdered.

OLSEN: I tal everybody some day he kill her.

MRS. JONES: Well, I ain't sayin' it's right to kill anybody, but if anybody had a reason, he certainly had. You oughta heard some o' the questions they was askin' me down at the Police. I could feel myself gettin' redder an' redder. "Say," I says, "how do you expect me to know things like that?" (*Suddenly, as she looks left.*) Here's Rose now!

EASTER: Where? (*He turns quickly and hurries to the left, as* ROSE *appears, carrying four or five packages.*)

MRS. JONES (*to* OLSEN): He seems to take a pretty friendly interest in her. (OLSEN *nods.*)

ROSE (*anxiously, as she comes up to* EASTER, *at the left of the stoop*): Have they caught him yet?

EASTER: Why, no, they haven't. I just asked the officer, upstairs.

ROSE: Oh, I hope he got away! If they get him, there's no telling what they'll do to him. And what would be the good of that? He never would have done it, if he'd been in his right mind.

EASTER: I only heard about it, a little while ago. So I went right around to the hospital. But they said you'd left.

ROSE (*going to the steps*): She never opened her eyes again. They did everything they could for her, but it didn't help.

EASTER: Here, let me take your bundles.

ROSE: No, it's all right. I think I'll just sit down for a minute. (*She sits on the stoop and puts the packages beside her.*)

EASTER: Can't I get you something? A drink or something?

ROSE: No, I'm all right. It's so hot. (*She puts her hand to her head.*) And all those people asking me a lot of questions.

MRS. JONES (*approaching the stoop*): Are you feelin' dizzy or anythin'?

ROSE: No, I'll be all right in a minute.

MRS. JONES: Well, I was gonna say, if you want to go up to my flat an' lay down for a minute—

ROSE: No, thanks! I don't want to lie down. I've got to go upstairs to get some things.

EASTER: Why, say, you don't want to go up there!

ROSE: I've got to; there's some things I need.

EASTER: Well, let me get them for you. Or this lady here.

MRS. JONES: Yeah, sure. The place is a sight, up there. You're li'ble to go into a faint or somethin'.

ROSE: I guess nothing can be any worse than what's happened already. (*Indicating the bundles.*) I got to change my dress. I bought a white dress for her. And white silk stockings. I want her to look pretty.

MRS. JONES: Yeah, white is the nicest.

ROSE: She looks so quiet and natural. You'd think she was asleep.

MRS. JONES: It was the same way with my mother. You'd of thought she was gonna get up, the next minute. (*Starting to go up the steps.*) Well, I gotta go up an' get me some lunch. Between everythin' happenin' an' goin' down to Police Headquarters an' all, I ain't had a bite to eat since breakfast. (*Stopping on the top step, and looking from* ROSE *to* EASTER.) Well, you certainly never know, when you get up in the mornin', what the day is gonna bring. (*She enters the house.*)

ROSE (*rising*): Well, I'd better be going up, too. There's a lot of things to attend to.

EASTER: You better let me come up with you.

ROSE: Why thanks, Mr. Easter. But I'd rather go alone, if you don't mind.

EASTER: But, listen here—you can't go through all this alone —a kid like you. That's why I came around. I knew you'd be needing a helping hand.

ROSE: That's awfully nice of you, Mr. Easter. But I don't need any help, honest I don't. (*She opens one of the packages.*)

EASTER: Why, you can't handle everything yourself! What about a place to live and all that?

ROSE (*taking a rosette of black crepe out of the package*): Well, I don't exactly know, yet. I'll have to find some place where Willie and I can live. I'd like it to be some place where he wouldn't be running around the streets all the time. You see, there's nobody but me to look out for him, now. (OLSEN *crosses to the cellar.* MRS. JONES *appears at her window and furtively peeps out, at* ROSE *and* EASTER.)

ROSE (*as she sees that* OLSEN *is about to descend the cellar steps*): Oh, Mr. Olsen!

OLSEN (*stopping*): Yes ma'am.

ROSE: Would you mind lending me a hammer and some tacks? I want to put up this crepe.

OLSEN: Yes ma'am; I bring 'em right away. (*He goes down into the cellar.* MRS. JONES *leaves the window.*)

EASTER (*insistently*): But why won't you let me help you out?

ROSE: It's terribly nice of you, Mr. Easter. But I'll be able to manage alone, really I will. It isn't as if I wasn't young and strong and able to take care of myself. But as it is, I'd sort of rather not be under obligations.

EASTER: Why, you wouldn't be under any obligations. I just mean it in a friendly way, that's all.

ROSE: You've been very nice to me and all that, Mr. Easter. But—well, I've been sort of thinking things over—you know, about what we talked about last night and all. And I honestly don't think I'd care about going on the stage.

EASTER: Say, you've got me all wrong, Rose! Just forget all about that, will you? I just want to help you out, that's all. (*Taking a step towards her.*) I think you're one swell kid, and I want to do something for you. I'm not trying to put anything over on you. (SHIRLEY *appears, at the left, carrying her schoolbag, from which a newspaper protrudes.*)

ROSE: Well, that's nice and friendly of you, Mr. Easter. And if I ever do need any help—

SHIRLEY (*catching sight of* ROSE): Rose! You poor thing! (*She runs up to* ROSE *and throws her arms about her.*) It's terrible—terrible!

ROSE: Yes, it is. But I sort of had a feeling, all along, that something terrible was going to happen. (OLSEN *comes up the steps, with a hammer and a box of tacks.*)

SHIRLEY: How could he do such a thing! I couldn't believe it when I read it.

ROSE: He was out of his mind, when he did it. Oh, I only hope he got away! (*As* OLSEN *approaches.*) Oh, thanks, Mr. Olsen.

OLSEN: I do it.

ROSE (*giving him the crepe*): Oh, would you, please? Right up there, I think. (*She indicates the left of the doorway.*)

OLSEN (*going up the steps*): Sure.

ROSE (*going to* EASTER *and extending her hand*): Thanks for coming around, Mr. Easter. I don't know when I'll be able to get back to the office.

EASTER: Why, that's all right about that. Only, in the meantime, I wish—

ROSE: If I need any help, I'll let you know. (*With a tone of finality in her voice.*) Good-bye.

EASTER: All right; but don't forget. (*He hesitates, then decides to go.*) Well, good-bye. (*He goes off at left.*)

ROSE: I've got to go up and get some things that Willie and I need. Sam went to call for him at school and take him around to my aunt's. You see, I didn't want him coming back here. He's only a kid, after all.

SHIRLEY: Oh, it's such a terrible thing! I can't believe it yet.

OLSEN (*holding up the crepe*): Dis vay?

ROSE: Yes, like that. (*Hesitantly, as she picks up her bundles.*) Miss Kaplan, it's sort of silly of me, I guess. But I'm kind of afraid to go up there alone. I wonder if you'd mind coming up with me. (OLSEN *tacks up the crepe*.)

SHIRLEY: Anything I can do for you, poor child! (*She and* ROSE *go up the steps*.)

ROSE: Thanks ever so much. (*To* OLSEN.) Thanks, Mr. Olsen. It's awfully nice of you. (*She and* SHIRLEY *enter the house.* OLSEN *exits down the cellar steps.* KAPLAN *appears, at his window, and seating himself, begins to read a newspaper. An undersized* MAN *and a tall, athletic* WOMAN *appear at the right. They are dressed for tennis and carry tennis rackets*.)

MAN (*as they cross*): He *would* say that.

WOMAN: So I just looked at him for a moment, without saying anything. And then, I said: "My dear boy," I said. "What do you expect anyhow, in this day and age?" I said, "Why even Frankl has to do a black bathroom, occasionally," I said.

MAN (*as they disappear at the left*): Exactly! And what did he say to that? (BUCHANAN *comes out of the house, and, seeing* KAPLAN *at the window, stops at the right balustrade*.)

BUCHANAN: Well, there's been *some* excitement around here, today.

KAPLAN (*looking up from his paper*): Dees is a terrible t'ing vich hes heppened.

BUCHANAN: I'll say it is! You know, the way I look at it, he didn't have a right to kill the both of them like that. Of course I'm not saying what she did was right, either.

KAPLAN: How ken ve call ourselves ciwilized, ven ve see thet sax jealousy hes de power to avaken in us de primitive pessions of de sevege?

BUCHANAN (*rather bewildered by this*): Yes, that's true, too. Of course, you can't expect a man to stand by and see his home broken up. But murdering them, like that, is going a little too far. Well, I got to go and phone the doctor. This thing's given my wife a kind of a *relapse*. She thought a lot of Mrs. Maurrant. (*He goes down the steps, and off at the left, as* LIPPO *appears, at the right*.)

LIPPO (*stopping in front of* KAPLAN'S *window*): Dey don' ketcha Maurrant, ha?

KAPLAN: I hevn't hoid anyt'ing foider.

LIPPO: He'sa gonna gat da 'lectrica chair, ha?

KAPLAN: De blood-lust of our enlightened population must be setisfied! De Chreestian state will kerry out to de last letter de Mosaic law.

LIPPO: Eef Ahm ketcha my wife sleepin' wit' 'nudder man, Ahm gonna keela 'er, too. (SAM *hurries on at the left.*)

KAPLAN: So you t'ink thet merriage should give to de hosband de power of life and det' and thet—

SAM (*going up the steps*): Papa, is there any news of Maurrant?

KAPLAN: I hev heard notting.

SAM: The police are going to make me testify against him. What can I do, Papa?

KAPLAN: You ken do notting.

SAM: How can I send a man to the electric chair? How can I? I tried to stop him, Papa. I tried to warn her— (*He stops short, as several shots are heard offstage, at the left.*) What's that?

LIPPO (*excitedly*): Dey finda 'im! (*He runs off, at the left, followed by* SAM. KAPLAN *leans out of the window. At the same moment,* MRS. JONES *leans out of her window and, a moment later,* MRS. FIORENTINO *out of hers. In the* MAURRANT *apartment, the* POLICEMAN *leans out and* ROSE *and* SHIRLEY *appear in the hall bedroom window.* ROSE *is wearing a mourning dress.* OLSEN *comes up the cellar steps and runs off at the left.* MRS. OLSEN *comes up the steps. Several* MEN *and* WOMEN *appear, at the right, and run off, at the left.*)

ROSE (*agitatedly*): Is that him?

POLICEMAN: Must be! (VOICES *are heard shouting, in the distance, and then another shot. The* POLICEMAN *leaves the window.*)

ROSE: Oh, God! They wouldn't shoot him, would they? (*She leaves the window.*)

SHIRLEY (*following her*): Rose! (*Two or three more persons appear at the right and run off at the left. The* POLICEMAN *runs out of the house, as* BUCHANAN *appears at the left.*)

BUCHANAN (*excitedly*): They got him! (*The* POLICEMAN *runs off, at the left.* SHIRLEY *reappears at the* MAURRANT *window.*)

MRS. JONES (*calling*): Have they got him?

BUCHANAN: Yes! He was hiding in the furnace, down at 322. (*As* ROSE *comes out of the house.*) They found him, Miss Maurrant!

ROSE (*her hand to her heart*): Oh! Is he hurt?

BUCHANAN: I don't know. He fired at the cops and they fired back at him. I was just passing the house, when it happened.

MRS. JONES (*leaning far out*): Here they come! (*She leaves the window. The low murmur of the approaching crowd can be heard, offstage left.*)

ROSE: Where? (*She comes down the stoop and looks off, at the left.*) Oh! (*She covers her eyes and turns away.*)

MRS. FIORENTINO: You better come inside.

SHIRLEY: Come up, Rose.

BUCHANAN: Yes, you better. (*He takes her by the arm.*)

ROSE (*resisting*): No. No. Please let me alone. I want to see him. (*She leans against the railing. Meanwhile, the murmur and tramp of the approaching crowd has grown nearer and nearer.*)

MRS. FIORENTINO: Look at him, vill you! (MISS CUSHING *comes out of the house, and stands on the stoop, followed a moment later, by* MRS. JONES. MAURRANT *appears at the left, between two* POLICEMEN. *Behind him a third* POLICEMAN *holds back a swarming crowd, which includes* SAM *and* LIPPO. MAURRANT'S *clothes are torn, and his right arm is in a crude sling. Sweat, blood and grime have made him almost unrecognizable. The* POLICEMEN, *too, show evidences of a struggle.*)

ROSE (*running forward*): Pop! Are you hurt?

MAURRANT (*seeing her for the first time*): Rose!

ONE OF THE POLICEMEN (*to whom* MAURRANT *is manacled*):
Keep back, miss!

MAURRANT: It's me daughter! Fer Chris' sake, boys, lemme
talk to me daughter! Maybe I'll never be seein' her again!

FIRST POLICEMAN: Give 'im a woid wit' her. (*He is the Of-*
FICER *who was on duty in the Maurrant apartment.*)

SECOND POLICEMAN (*after a moment's hesitation*): Well, all
right. (*Savagely to* MAURRANT.) But don't try to pull
nothin', hear? (*There is a forward movement in the crowd.*)

FIRST POLICEMAN (*to the crowd*): Keep back, youse!

MAURRANT: Rose! You're wearin' a black dress, Rose!

ROSE: Oh, Pop, why did you do it? Why did you?

MAURRANT: I must o' been out o' me head, Rose. Did she say
anythin'?

ROSE: She never opened her eyes again.

MAURRANT: I'd been drinkin', Rose—see what I mean?—an' all
the talk that was goin' around. I just went clean off me nut,
that's all.

ROSE: What'll they do to you, Pop?

MAURRANT: It's the chair for me, I guess. But I don't care—let
'em give me the chair. I deserve it all right. But it's her,
I'm thinkin' of, Rose—the way she looked at me. I oughtn't
to done it, Rose.

ROSE: She was always so good and sweet.

MAURRANT: Don't I know it? I ain't no murderer—you ought
to be the one to know that, Rose. I just went out o' me
head, that's all it was.

SECOND POLICEMAN: All right, that's all now. Come on!

MAURRANT: Gimme a minute, can't you? She's me daughter.
Gimme a chance, can't you? What's gonna happen to you,
Rose?

ROSE: I'll be all right, Pop. You don't need to worry about me.

MAURRANT: I ain't been a very good father, have I?

ROSE: Don't worry about that, Pop.

MAURRANT: It ain't that I ain't meant to be. It's just the way
things happened to turn out, that's all. Keep your eye on

213

Willie, Rose. Don't let Willie grow up to be a murderer, like his pop.

ROSE: I'm going to do all I can for him, Pop.

MAURRANT: You're a good girl, Rose. You was always a good girl.

ROSE (*breaking down*): Oh, Pop! (*She throws her arms about his neck and buries her head against him.* MAURRANT *sobs hoarsely.*)

FIRST POLICEMAN (*gently*): Come on, now, miss. (*He and* SAM *take* ROSE *away from* MAURRANT.)

SECOND POLICEMAN: All right. Come on, Charlie. (*THEY go towards the right, the crowd swarming behind them. Straggling along at the very end of the crowd, is an unkempt* WOMAN, *wheeling a ramshackle baby carriage.* MRS. JONES *and* MISS CUSHING *fall in with the crowd.* ROSE *gradually recovers her self-control, and stands at the stoop, with* SAM *beside her. The others watch the receding crowd for a moment. Then* KAPLAN *and* MRS. FIORENTINO *leave their windows. The* FIRST POLICEMAN *enters the house, followed by* LIPPO. MRS. OLSEN *goes to the cellar.* SHIRLEY *looks down at* ROSE *and* SAM, *for a moment, then abruptly leaves the window.*)

SAM (*taking* ROSE *by the arm*): Rose, you better come inside.

ROSE: No, I'm all right again, Sam—honestly I am. (*Trying to regain her self-composure.*) What about Willie, Sam?

SAM: I told him an accident had happened.

ROSE: It's better to break it to him, that way. But I'll have to tell him, I guess. He'd only find it out himself, tomorrow, with the papers all full of it. I saw Mrs. Sankey, down at Police Headquarters. It's terrible for her, with two little children.

SHIRLEY (*appearing at the* MAURRANT *window, a covered pot in her hand*): Rose!

ROSE (*looking up*): Yes, Miss Kaplan?

SHIRLEY: There's a chicken here, that I found on the gas stove.

ROSE: A chicken?

SHIRLEY: Yes. The policeman says he smelt it cooking, this morning, so he turned out the gas.

ROSE: Oh, I remember, now. My mother said she was going to make some soup for poor Mrs. Buchanan, upstairs.

SHIRLEY: It won't keep long, in this weather.

ROSE: No. I really think Mrs. Buchanan ought to have the good of it.

SHIRLEY: All right. I'll take it up to her.

ROSE: Thanks ever so much, Miss Kaplan. (SHIRLEY *leaves the window.*) It's only a few hours ago that she was standing right here, telling me about the chicken. And then, she went upstairs, and the next I saw of her, they were carrying her out. (*Abruptly, as she starts to go up the steps.*) Well, I've got to go up and get my things.

SAM: I must talk to you! What are you going to do, Rose?

ROSE: Well, I haven't really had any time to do much thinking. But I really think the best thing I could do, would be to get out of New York. You know, like we were saying, this morning—how things might be different, if you only had a chance to breathe and spread out a little. Only when I said it, I never dreamt it would be this way.

SAM: If you go, I'll go with you.

ROSE: But, Sam dear—

SAM: I don't care anything about my career. It's you—you—I care about. Do you think I can stay here, stifling to death, in this slum, and never seeing you? Do you think my life means anything to me, without you?

ROSE: But, Sam, we've got to be practical about it. How would we manage?

SAM: I don't care what I do. I'll be a day laborer; I'll dig sewers—anything. (*Taking her passionately in his arms.*) Rose, don't leave me!

ROSE: I like you so much, Sam. I like you better than anybody I know.

SAM: I love you, Rose. Let me go with you!

ROSE: It would be so nice to be with you. You're different

from anybody I know. But I'm just wondering how it would work out.

SAM: If we have each other, that's the vital thing, isn't it? What else matters but that?

ROSE: Lots of things, Sam. There's lots of things to be considered. Supposing something was to happen—well, suppose I was to have a baby, say. That sometimes happens, even when you don't want it to. What would we do, then? We'd be tied down then, for life, just like all the other people around here. They all start out loving each other and thinking that everything is going to be fine—and before you know it, they find out they haven't got anything and they wish they could do it all over again—only it's too late.

SAM: It's to escape all that, that we must be together. It's only because we love each other and belong to each other, that we can find the strength to escape.

ROSE (*shaking her head*): No, Sam.

SAM: Why do you say no?

ROSE: It's what you said just now—about people belonging to each other. I don't think people ought to belong to anybody but themselves. I was thinking, that if my mother had really belonged to herself, and that if my father had really belonged to himself, it never would have happened. It was only because they were always depending on somebody else, for what they ought to have had inside themselves. Do you see what I mean, Sam? That's why I don't want to belong to anybody, and why I don't want anybody to belong to me.

SAM: You want to go through life alone?—never loving anyone, never having anyone love you?

ROSE: Why, of course not, Sam! I want love more than anything else in the world. But loving and belonging aren't the same thing. (*Putting her arms about him.*) Sam dear, listen. If we say good-bye, now, it doesn't mean that it has to be forever. Maybe some day, when we're older and wiser, things will be different. Don't look as if it was the end of the world, Sam!

SAM: It *is* the end of my world.

ROSE: It isn't, Sam! If you'd only believe in yourself, a little more, things wouldn't look nearly so bad. Because once you're sure of yourself, the things that happen to you, aren't so important. The way I look at it, it's not what you do that matters so much; it's what you are. (*Warmly.*) I'm so fond of you, Sam. And I've got such a lot of confidence in you. (*Impulsively.*) Give me a nice kiss! (SAM *takes her in his arms and kisses her, passionately. A gawky* GIRL *of seventeen—one of Lippo's pupils, appears at the left, and looks at them, scandalized. Then she goes into the vestibule and rings the bell. The door clicks and she enters the house, as* SHIRLEY *comes out, carrying a wicker suitcase.* SHIRLEY *looks at* SAM *and* ROSE.)

ROSE (*to* SHIRLEY): I was just telling Sam, that I think I'll soon be going away from New York. (SAM *looks at her, for a moment, in agony, then goes abruptly into the house.*)

SHIRLEY: I put your things in this suitcase. (*She comes down to the pavement. The* GIRL, *in the Fiorentino apartment, begins tuning her violin.*)

ROSE (*taking the suitcase*): You've been awfully nice to me. Don't worry about Sam, Miss Kaplan. Everything will be all right with him.

SHIRLEY: I hope so. (*From the* FIORENTINO *apartment, comes the strains of Dvořák's "Humoresque," jerkily played on a violin.*)

ROSE: Oh, I just know it will! (*Extending her hand.*) Good-bye, Miss Kaplan.

SHIRLEY: Good-bye, Rose. (*Impulsively.*) You're a sweet girl! (*She hugs and kisses her.*)

ROSE: I hope I'll see you, again.

SHIRLEY (*crying*): I hope so, Rose. (ROSE *takes up the suitcase and goes off at the left.* SHIRLEY *stands watching her.*)

KAPLAN (*reappearing at his window*): Shoiley, vot's de metter again vit Sem? He's crying on de bed.

SHIRLEY: Let him alone, Papa, can't you? (*She turns and enters the house.* KAPLAN *sighs and, seating himself at the*

217

window, opens a newspaper. A shabby, middle-aged COUPLE *appears at the right, and approaches the stoop.*)

MAN (*reading the To-Let sign*): Here's a place. Six rooms. Want to take a look at it? (*A* GROUP OF CHILDREN *offstage left, begin singing "The Farmer in the Dell." This continues until after the curtain is down.*)

WOMAN: All right. No harm lookin'. Ring for the janitor. (*The* MAN *goes up the stoop and rings the janitor's bell.*) Somebody must o' just died.

MAN: Yeah, maybe that's why they're movin' out. (*Wiping his face with a handkerchief.*) Phoo! Seems to be gettin' hotter every minute. (MRS. FIORENTINO *seats herself, at her window, a sewing basket in her lap.* MRS. JONES *and* MISS CUSHING *appear at the right, busily engaged in conversation.*)

MISS CUSHING: The poor little thing!

MRS. JONES (*as they go up the steps*): Well, you never can tell with them quiet ones. It wouldn't surprise me a bit, if she turned out the same way as her mother. She's got a gentleman friend, that I guess ain't hangin' around for nothin'. I seen him, late last night, and this afternoon, when I come home from the police— (*She is still talking, as they enter the house.* MRS. OLSEN *comes up the cellar steps. A* SAILOR *appears at the left, with two* GIRLS, *an arm about the waist of each. They stroll slowly across.*)

Introduction

The Time of Your Life, the second of William Saroyan's plays to be produced, opened in New York on October 25, 1939, to the almost unanimous applause of the critics. By the season's end, it was awarded both the Critics' Circle Award and the Pulitzer Prize (the latter of which Saroyan refused—in a protest against awards to artists in general,, and against the singling out of this one of his works). The play was revived at the New York City Center in 1955, and in 1948 was made into a motion picture starring James Cagney. At least five anthologies have included it.

Saroyan attracted critical attention in the early thirties with his short stories. Then, in the spring of 1939, his unusual play *My Heart's in the Highlands,* revealed a new and unusual dramatic talent. Later he was to achieve considerable success with his motion picture and novel *The Human Comedy.* During the early forties he was one of the most frequently discussed authors, a typical portrait appearing in Robert Van Gelder's *Writers and Writing.*[1]

When *The Time of Your Life* appeared, it was appreciated as a fresh and stirring drama, although it seemed to be lacking in the formal construction of a well-made play. Nevertheless, all critics agreed that the characters for the most part were original and possessed a vividness far superior to the many characters who lead their brief lives in the course of a Broadway season. It is Saroyan's characters and his dialogue that made that evening an unforgettable one in the theatre. When

Pp. 29–33.

one thinks of the actors who appeared that opening night, one is not surprised at the warm reception the play received.

Eddie Dowling played Joe and also directed the play in association with Saroyan. Julie Haydon was Kitty Duval. William Bendix, who was later to have such a great success in films and television, was Krupp, the policeman. Gene Kelly practically started his career as Harry, the dancer. Celeste Holm, who went on to achieve success in so many outstanding roles both on Broadway and in Hollywood, was Mary L. As one reads the play, one should try to imagine the vigorous portrayal that these distinguished actors gave to their roles.

What Saroyan was trying to do was aptly described by Walter Pritchard Eaton, when he reviewed the published version of the play:

> [Saroyan has] a genuine love for all underdogs, and a deep understanding of the essential dignity of each individual spirit, however lowly; and this understanding is not clouded with any materialistic propaganda.[2]

Thus, it is not surprising that the old Arab in this play rarely speaks yet has a dignity all his own.

The play can be read and enjoyed on several different levels One New York reviewer subtitled his review "Barroom Talk." Another, who was quite enthusiastic, called it "a goofy binge with Saroyan." A third called the play "charming." Perhaps "charming" is a good description if one thinks of the original meaning of the word, for audiences were certainly held as i by magic for the greater part of the 1939–1940 season.

Characters in organized action do not make plays, and on must discuss Saroyan as the writer of the plays, as well as th creator of characters. Perhaps his dramatized compositions ar not "plays" as are the works of Ibsen, Pinero or other ex ponents of the well-made play. *The Time of Your Life* ma not be considered a "well-made play," but it most certainl is a beautifully and earnestly made literary compositio

---

[2] *New York Herald Tribune*, January 14, 1940.

which is capable of evoking emotions of pity, sadness and love. The great and wise George Pierce Baker, teacher of many outstanding American dramatists, states clearly and unmistakably, "A play exists to create emotional response in the audience." [3] That no sensitive playgoer can escape being moved emotionally by Saroyan's plays is undeniable.

How Saroyan learned to create such effective characters is one of those mysteries of genius that critics have been trying unsuccessfully to fathom since Aristotle wrote his *Poetics*. We have no record of Saroyan's having attended any classes in the writing of plays, and certainly his works break every rule laid down in the various textbooks on the subject. Perhaps Saroyan moves his audience by the sheer magic of his words —spoken poetry, as in the scene between Joe and the Unknown Lady who reminds him of his sweetheart. It is futile to try to put into words the beauty of this scene as played in the New York production by Eddie Dowling and Celeste Holm. And how difficult it is for the reader of the play to perceive the poignancy of this scene!

We respond to Saroyan not only because of his power over words, a gift that he exhibited early in his writing career. Words alone cannot sustain the attention of audiences or maintain a state of emotional stimulation. Saroyan appeals by *what* he says as much as by *how* he says it. He says many things. They seem so simple yet they are among the eternal verities. Nature has been extravagant in supplying the world with beautiful colors, sounds, textures, designs, but man has been slow to make this beauty a part of his life. Still, most of us yearn for some beauty and some freedom from the tyranny of ugliness and cruelty that enslaves so many millions today.

Saroyan knows from his family and later associations how little beauty exists for the great masses of peoples in the world; so there are in his works many sad characters of different nationalities. In *The Time of Your Life*, Nick, the saloonkeeper, is an Armenian; Kitty Duval is of Slavic origin; Wesley is a starving Negro piano player. Each is trying to forget

---

[3] *Dramatic Technique*, p. 43.

the ugliness that oppresses him. The Arab sits and dreams of his boyhood; Wesley plays wonderful music; Nick cannot understand why people want to hurt other people. And it is because we are trying to become aware of and to be refreshed by some of the beauty in life that a sympathetic chord is struck in us.

Saroyan presents such simple solutions to life's problems. Perhaps his lack of formal training in the humanities and social studies permits him to see relatively easy solutions to the troubles besetting us today. If Love reigned, if we let the other man live, if we stopped now and then to enjoy some of the endless glories of Nature, life would not be so difficult, says Saroyan. How simple, how true and how hard to realize!

To attempt a synopsis of Saroyan's plays would be a colorless procedure. His dramas are meant to be presented on the stage, not to be summarized. That they are good theatre is demonstrated by the interest in two of them by such a sensitive showman as Eddie Dowling, who was coproducer, codirector and star of *The Time of Your Life* and coproducer and codirector of *Love's Old Sweet Song*.

Herewith a brief attempt to convey the flavor of a few of his most important plays. *My Heart's in the Highlands* is "a fantasy about man's eternal hunger for beauty which was more of a melody than a play."[4] An old Shakespearean actor comes into the life of a starving poet and his son, and after enriching the entire neighborhood with the strange music of his horn, passes to his reward. He yearns for the beauty of his Highlands, as so many characters in Saroyan's works yearn for some other type of beauty.

In *The Time of Your Life,* Joe sits in a waterfront café and philosophizes about life. A dozen incidents begin and end. A starving pianist is given a job. A talented dancer at last gets his break. A young man falls in love and marries a young lady who has temporarily fallen from grace and is wanted by the Vice Squad. A society couple comes in to see how the "other half" lives. A philosophical policeman vents his anger against

---

[4] John Mason Brown, *Broadway in Review,* p. 189.

a system that compels him to do things he feels are ugly and inhuman. A boy plays a pinball machine until he rings the bell. The audience truly can have the time of its life!

In *Love's Old Sweet Song*, Saroyan's fertile imagination has produced another small army of characters doing a great many things. A traveling salesman comes into the sheltered life of a lady, and after many comings and goings, marries her. It seems like the boy-meets-girl formula over again, but how lavishly Saroyan has surrounded the simple story.

Other Saroyan plays produced on Broadway are: *The Beautiful People* (1941), *Across the Board on Tomorrow Morning* (1947), *Talking to You* (1942) and *Get Away, Old Man* (1944). His movie *The Human Comedy* is one of the most sensitive portrayals of an American family during the war years. Other plays include: *A Decent Birth, a Happy Funeral* (1949), *Don't Go Away Mad* (1949), *Hello Out There* (1949) and *Sam Ego's House* (1949).

FURTHER READING

Brown, John Mason. *Broadway in Review.* New York: W. W. Norton, 1940, pp. 189–194.

Clurman, Harold. *The Fervent Years.* New York: Knopf, 1945.

Gassner, John (ed.), *Best Plays of the Modern American Theatre, Second Series.* New York: Crown, 1947, p. xxv.

Hewitt, Barnard W. *Theatre U.S.A.: 1868–1957.* New York: McGraw-Hill, 1959, pp. 418–419.

Kunitz, Stanley J. *Twentieth Century Authors: First Supplement.* New York: H. W. Wilson, 1955, pp. 731–732.

———, and Haycraft, Howard. *Twentieth Century Authors.* New York: H. W. Wilson, 1942, pp. 1233–1234.

Morehouse, Ward. *Matinee Tomorrow.* New York: McGraw-Hill, 1949, pp. 261–262.

Saroyan, William. "How to See," *Theatre Arts Anthology.* New York: Theatre Arts, 1950, pp. 25–29.

Van Gelder, Robert. *Writers and Writing.* New York: Scribner's, 1946, pp. 29–33.

THE TIME OF
YOUR LIFE

WILLIAM SAROYAN

ACT I

*The Act takes place on the afternoon of a day in October,
1939.*
SCENE: *Nick's Pacific Street Saloon, Restaurant, and Entertainment Palace at the foot of Embarcadero, in San Francisco. There are double swinging doors to the street at the
front of the stage, with steps leading down to barroom; a
bar at right; a door center leading to kitchen; a piano on
platform at rear left center; a stage with steps leading up,
diagonally in upper left corner.*
*A marble game at the front of the stage; tables and chairs
right, center and left center; a wall telephone at rear left*

center; a phonograph front left; a chair right of door center; table and chairs in back room behind left end of bar.

At a table left center JOE; *always calm, always quiet, always thinking, always eager, always bored, always superior. His expensive clothes are casually and youthfully worn and give him an almost boyish appearance. At the moment he is in a sort of Debussy reverie.*

Behind the bar, NICK; *a big redheaded Italian with an enormous naked woman tattooed in red on the inside of his right arm. He is studying* The Racing Form.

The ARAB, *in his place sitting on chair at the end of the bar. He is a lean old man with a rather ferocious old-country black moustache, with the ends twisted up. Between the thumb and forefinger of his left hand is the Mohammedan tattoo indicating that he has been to Mecca. He is sipping a glass of beer.*

WILLIE, *the marble-game maniac, explodes through the swinging doors right, and lifts the forefinger of his right hand comically, indicating one beer. He is a very young man, scarcely more than twenty. He is wearing heavy shoes, a pair of old and dirty corduroys, a light green turtle-neck jersey with a large letter "F" on the chest, an oversize two-button tweed coat, and a green hat, with the brim up.* NICK *sets out a glass of beer for him, he drinks it, straightens up vigorously, saying, "Aaah," makes a solemn face, gives* NICK *a one-finger salute of adieu, and begins to leave, refreshed and restored in spirit. He walks by the marble game, halts suddenly, turns, studies the contraption, gestures as if to say, "Oh, no." Turns to go, stops, returns to the machine, studies it, takes a handful of small coins out of his pants pocket, lifts a nickel, indicates with a gesture, one game, no more. Puts the nickel in the slot, pushes in the slide, making an interesting noise.*

The marbles *fall, roll, and take their places. He pushes down the lever, placing one marble in position. Takes a very deep breath, walks in a small circle, excited at the beginning of great drama. Stands straight and pious before the contest.*

*Himself vs. the machine. Willie vs. Destiny. His skill and
daring vs. the cunning and trickery of the novelty industry
of America, and the whole challenging world. He is the last
of the American pioneers, with nothing more to fight but the
machine, with no other reward than lights going on and off,
and six nickels for one. Before him is the last champion, the
machine. He is the last challenger, the young man with
nothing to do in the world.* WILLIE *grips the knob delicately, studies the situation carefully, draws the knob back,
holds it a moment, and then releases it. The first marble rolls
out among the hazards, and the contest is on. At the very
beginning of the play "The Missouri Waltz" is coming from
the phonograph. The music ends here.*
This is the signal for the beginning of the play.

NEWSBOY (*enters cheerfully*): Good morning everybody. (*No
answer, to* NICK.) Paper, Mister? (NICK *shakes his head, no.
The* NEWSBOY *goes to* JOE.) Paper, Mister? (JOE *shakes his
head, no. The* NEWSBOY *walks away, counting papers.*)
JOE (*noticing him*): How many you got?
NEWSBOY: Five. (JOE *gives him a bill, takes all the papers,
throws them over his head;* NEWSBOY *takes money, exits.*)
ARAB (*picks up papers*): No foundation. All the way down
the line. (*The* DRUNK *enters right, crosses to the telephone.*
NICK *takes the* DRUNK *out. The* DRUNK *returns right.*)
DRUNK (*champion of the Bill of Rights*): This is a free coun-
try, ain't it?
NICK: You can't beat that machine.
WILLIE: Oh, yeah?
JOE (*calling*): Tom. (*To himself.*) Where the hell is he, every
time I need him? (*He looks around calmly: the nickel-in-
the-slot phonograph in the corner; the open public tele-
phone; the stage; the marble game; the bar; and so on. He
whistles again, this time a little louder.*) Hey, Tom. (*He
waits a moment, then whistles again, very loudly.*)
NICK (*with irritation*): What do you want?
JOE: I want the boy to get me a watermelon, that's what *I*

want. What do *you* want? Money, or love, or fame, or what? You won't get them studying *The Racing Form*.

NICK: I like to keep abreast of the times. (TOM *comes hurrying in right. He is a great big man of about thirty or so who appears to be much younger because of the childlike expression of his face: handsome, dumb, innocent, troubled, and a little bewildered by everything. He is obviously adult in years, but it seems as if by all rights he should still be a boy. He is defensive as clumsy, self-conscious, overgrown boys are. He is wearing a flashy cheap suit, a Woolworth watch-chain across his vest, and on the little finger of his right hand, a dice ring: number six. On the middle finger of his left hand a large skull-and-crossbones ring.* JOE *leans back and studies him with casual disapproval.* TOM *slackens his pace and becomes clumsy and embarrassed, waiting for the bawling-out he's afraid he's going to get.*)

JOE (*objectively, severely, but warmly*): Who saved your life?

TOM (*sincerely*): You did, Joe. Thanks.

JOE: How'd I do it?

TOM (*confused*): What?

JOE: *How'd I do it?*

TOM: Joe, you know how you did it.

JOE (*softly*): I want you to answer me. How'd I save your life? I've forgotten.

TOM (*remembering, with a big goofy smile*): You made me eat all that chicken soup three years ago when I was sick and hungry.

JOE (*fascinated*): *Chicken* soup?

TOM (*eagerly*): Yeah.

JOE: Three years? Is it that long?

TOM: Yeah, sure. 1937. 1938. 1939. This is 1939, Joe.

JOE: Never mind what year it is. Tell me the whole story.

TOM: You took me to the doctor. You gave me money for food and clothes, and paid my room rent. Aw, Joe, you know all the different things you did.

JOE (*nods*): You in good health now?

TOM: Yeah, Joe.

JOE: You got clothes?

TOM: Yeah, Joe.

JOE (*nods*): You eat three times a day. Sometimes four?

TOM: Yeah, Joe. Sometimes five.

JOE: You got a place to sleep?

TOM: Yeah, Joe.

JOE (*nods; pauses; studies* TOM *carefully; terrible irritation*): Then, where the hell have you been?

TOM (*humbly*): Joe, I was out in the street listening to the boys. They're talking about the trouble down here on the waterfront.

JOE (*very sharply*): I want you to be around when I need you.

TOM (*pleased that the bawling-out is over*): I won't do it again. Joe, one guy out there says there's got to be a revolution before anything will ever be all right.

JOE (*impatient*): I know all about it. Now, here. Take this money. Go up to the Emporium. You know where the Emporium is?

TOM: Yeah, sure, Joe.

JOE: All right. Take the elevator and go up to the fourth floor. Walk around to the back, to the toy department. Buy me a couple of dollars' worth of toys and bring them here.

TOM (*amazed*): Toys? What *kind* of toys, Joe?

JOE: Any kind of toys. Little ones that I can put on this table.

TOM: What do you want toys for, Joe?

JOE (*mildly angry*): What?

TOM: All right, all right. You don't have to get sore at *everything*. What'll people think, a big guy like me buying toys?

JOE: *What people?*

TOM: Aw, Joe, you're always making me do crazy things for you, and *I'm* the guy that gets embarrassed. You just sit in this place and make me do all the dirty work.

JOE (*looking away*): Do what I tell you.

TOM: O.K., but I wish I knew *why*.

JOE: Wait a minute. Here's a nickel. Put it in the phonograph. Number seven. I want to hear that waltz again.

TOM (*crossing below to phonograph*): Boy, I'm glad *I* don't

231

have to stay and listen to it. Joe, what do you hear in that
song anyway? We listen to that song ten times a day. Why
can't we hear number six, or two, or nine? There are a lot
of other numbers.

JOE (*emphatically*): Put the nickel in the phonograph.
(*Pause.*) Sit down and wait till the music's over. Then go
get me some toys.

TOM: O.K. O.K.

JOE (*loudly*): Never mind being a martyr about it either. The
cause isn't worth it.

(TOM *puts the nickel into the machine, with a ritual of impatient and efficient movement which plainly shows his lack
of sympathy or enthusiasm. His manner also reveals, however, that his lack of sympathy is spurious and exaggerated.
Actually, he is fascinated by the music, but he is so confused by it that he tries to pretend he dislikes it.*

(*The music begins.* TOM *turns chair left of left center table
and sits at the rear. It is another variation of "The Missouri
Waltz," played dreamily and softly, with perfect orchestral
form, and with a theme of weeping in the horns repeated
a number of times.*

(*At first* TOM *listens with something close to irritation, since
he cannot understand what is so attractive in the music
to* JOE, *and so painful and confusing to himself. Very soon,
however, he is carried away helplessly by the melancholy
story of grief and nostalgia in the stubborn, flowing
rhythm. He stands quarreling with the grief and confusion
in himself.*

(JOE, *on the other hand, listens as if he were* not *listening,
indifferent and unmoved. What he's interested in is* TOM.
He turns and glances at TOM.

(KITTY DUVAL, *who lives in a room in The New York Hotel,
around the corner, comes beyond the swinging doors
quietly, and walks slowly to the bar, her reality and
rhythm a perfect accompaniment to the sorrowful American
music, which is her music, as it is* TOM's. *Which the world*

drove out of her, putting in its place brokenness and all manner of spiritually crippled forms. She seems to understand this, and is angry. Angry with herself, full of hate for the poor world, and full of pity and contempt for its tragic, unbelievable, confounded people. She is a small, powerful girl, with that kind of delicate and rugged beauty which no circumstance of evil or ugly reality can destroy. This beauty is that element of the immortal which is in the seed of good and common people, and which is kept alive in some of the female of our kind, no matter how accidentally or pointlessly they may have entered the world. KITTY DUVAL *is somebody. There is an angry purity, and a fierce pride, in her. In her stance, and way of walking, there is grace and arrogance.)*

KITTY (*goes to bar*): Beer. (NICK *places a glass of beer before her. She swallows half and listens to the music again.* TOM *sees her and becomes dead to everything but her. He stands like a lump, fascinated and undone by his almost religious adoration for her.* JOE *notices him.*)

JOE (*gently*): Tom. (TOM *begins to move toward the bar, where* KITTY *is standing. Loudly.*) Tom. (TOM *halts, then turns, and* JOE *motions to him to come over to the table.* Have you got everything straight?

TOM (*out of the world, crossing to left of* JOE): What?

JOE: What do you mean, what? I just gave you some instructions.

TOM (*pathetically*): What do you want, Joe?

JOE: I want you to come to your senses. (*He stands up quietly and knocks* TOM'S *hat off.*)

TOM (*picks up his hat quickly*): I got it, Joe. I got it. The Emporium. Fourth floor. In the back. The toy department. Two dollars' worth of toys. That you can put on a table.

KITTY (*to herself*): Who the hell is he to push a big man like that around?

JOE: I'll expect you back in a half hour. Don't get sidetracked anywhere. Just do what I tell you.

TOM (*pleading*): Joe? Can't I bet four bits on a horse race? There's a long shot—Precious Time—that's going to win by ten lengths. I got to have money. (JOE *points to the street.* TOM *goes out right.* NICK *is combing his hair, looking in the mirror.*)

NICK: I thought you wanted him to get you a watermelon.

JOE: I forgot. (*To* KITTY, *clearly, slowly, with great compassion.*) What's the dream?

KITTY (*moving to* JOE): What?

JOE (*holding the dream for her*): What's the dream, *now?*

KITTY (*coming still closer*): What dream?

JOE: What dream! The dream you're dreaming.

NICK: Suppose he did bring you a watermelon? What the hell would you do with it?

JOE (*irritated*): I'd put it on this table. I'd look at it. Then I'd eat it. What do you *think* I'd do with it, sell it for a profit?

NICK: How should I know what *you'd* do with *anything?* What I'd like to know is, where do you get your money from? What work do you do?

JOE (*looking at* KITTY): Bring us a bottle of champagne.

KITTY (*at right of* JOE's *table*): Champagne?

JOE (*simply*): Would you rather have something else?

KITTY: What's the big idea?

JOE: I thought you might like some champagne. I myself am very fond of it.

KITTY: Yeah, but what's the big idea? You can't push me around.

JOE (*gently but severely*): It's not in my nature to be unkind to another human being. I have only contempt for wit. Otherwise I might say something obvious, therefore cruel, and perhaps untrue.

KITTY: You be careful what you think about me.

JOE (*slowly, not looking at her*): I have only the noblest thoughts for both your person, and your spirit.

NICK (*having listened carefully and not being able to make it out*): What are you talking about?

KITTY: You shut up. You—

JOE: He owns this place. He's an important man. All kinds of people come to him looking for work. Comedians. Singers. Dancers.

KITTY: I don't care. He can't call me names.

NICK: All right, sister. I know how it is with a two-dollar whore in the morning.

KITTY: Don't you dare call me names. I used to be in burlesque.

NICK (*profoundly, as it were*): If you were ever in burlesque, I used to be Charlie Chaplin.

KITTY (*swallowing beer*): I *was* in burlesque. I played the burlesque circuit from coast to coast. I've had flowers sent to me by European royalty. I've had dinner with young men of wealth and social position.

NICK: You're dreaming.

KITTY (*to* JOE): *I was in burlesque.* Kitty Duval. That was my name. Life-size photographs of me in costume in front of burlesque theaters all over the country.

JOE (*gently, coaxingly*): I believe you. Have some champagne.

NICK (*going behind her to left of* JOE's *table, with champagne*): There he goes again.

JOE: Miss Duval?

KITTY (*sincerely; going over to chair left of* JOE's *table; sits*): That's not my *real* name. That's my *stage* name.

JOE: I'll call you by your stage name.

NICK (*pouring*): All right, sister, make up your mind. Are you going to have champagne with him, or not?

JOE: Pour the lady some wine.

NICK: O.K., professor. Why you come to this joint instead of one of the high-class dumps uptown is more than I can understand. Why don't you have champagne at the St. Francis? Why don't you drink with a lady?

KITTY (*furiously*): Don't you call me names—you dentist.

JOE: Dentist?

NICK (*amazed, loudly*): What kind of cussing is that? (*Pause.*

Looking at KITTY, *then at* JOE, *bewildered.*) This guy doesn't belong here. The only reason I've got champagne is because *he* keeps ordering it all the time. (*To* KITTY.) Don't think you're the only one he drinks champagne with. He drinks with *all* of them. (*Pause.*) He's crazy. Or something.

JOE (*confidentially*): Nick, I think you're going to be all right in a couple of centuries.

NICK: I'm sorry, I don't understand your English. (*Takes* JOE's *hat and hangs it on hook at left.* JOE *lifts his glass.* KITTY *slowly lifts hers.*)

JOE (*putting everything he's got into it*): To the spirit, Kitty Duval.

KITTY (*beginning to understand, and very grateful, looking at him*): Thank you. (*They drink.*)

JOE (*calling*): Nick.

NICK: Yeah?

JOE: Would you mind putting a nickel in the machine again? Number—

NICK: Seven. I know. I know. I don't mind at all, Your Highness, although, personally, I'm not a lover of music. (*Going to the phonograph.*) As a matter of fact I think Tchaikovsky was a dope.

JOE: Tchaikovsky? Where'd you ever hear of Tchaikovsky?

NICK: He was a dope.

JOE: Yeah. Why?

NICK: They talked about him on the radio one Sunday morning. He was a sucker. He let a woman drive him crazy.

JOE: I see.

NICK: I stood behind that bar listening to the Goddamn stuff and cried like a baby. *None but the lonely heart!* He was a dope.

JOE: What made you cry?

NICK: What?

JOE (*sternly*): What made you cry, Nick?

NICK (*angry with himself*): I don't know.

JOE: I've been underestimating you, Nick. Play number seven.

NICK: They get everybody worked up. They give everybody stuff they shouldn't have. (NICK *puts the nickel into the machine and the Waltz begins again. He listens to the music. Then studies* The Racing Form.)

KITTY (*to herself, dreaming*): I like champagne, and everything that goes with it. Big houses with big porches, and big rooms with big windows, and big lawns, and big trees, and flowers growing everywhere, and big shepherd dogs sleeping in the shade.

NICK (*crossing toward stairs right*): I'm going next door to Frankie's to make a bet. I'll be right back.

JOE: Make one for me.

NICK (*stopping right of* JOE): Who do you like?

JOE (*giving him money*): Precious Time.

NICK: *Ten dollars?* Across the board?

JOE: No. On the nose.

NICK: O.K. (*He goes out.*)

(DUDLEY R. BOSTWICK, *as he calls himself, breaks through the swinging doors and practically flings himself upon the open telephone.*

(DUDLEY *is a young man of about twenty-four or twenty-five, ordinary and yet extraordinary. He is smallish, as the saying is, neatly dressed in bargain clothes, overworked and irritated by the routine and dullness and monotony of his life, apparently nobody and nothing, but in reality a great personality. The swindled young man. Educated, but without the least real understanding. A brave, dumb, salmon-spirit struggling for life in weary, stupefied flesh, dueling ferociously with a banal mind which has been only irritated by what it has been taught. He is a great personality because, against all these handicaps, what he wants is simple and basic: a woman. This urgent and violent need, common yet miraculous enough in itself, considering the unhappy environment of the animal, is the*

*force which elevates him from nothingness to greatness.
A ridiculous greatness, but in the nature of things beautiful to behold. All that he has been taught, and everything
he believes, is phony, and yet he himself is real, almost
super-real, because of this indestructible force in himself.
His face is ridiculous. His personal rhythm is tense and
jittery. His speech is shrill and violent. His gestures are
wild. His ego is disjointed and epileptic. And yet deeply
he possesses the same wholeness of spirit, and directness of
energy, that is in all species of animals. There is little innate
or cultivated spirit in him, but there is no absence of innocent animal force. He is a young man who has been
taught that he has a chance, as a person, and believes
it. As a matter of fact, he hasn't a chance in the world,
and should have been told by somebody, or should not
have had his natural and valuable ignorance spoiled by
education, ruining an otherwise perfectly good and
charming member of the human race.*

*(At the telephone he immediately begins to dial furiously,
hangs up furiously, and furiously begins to turn the pages
of the telephone book, looking for the right number.*

*(Not more than half a minute after the firecracker arrival
of DUDLEY R. BOSTWICK, occurs the polka-and-waltz arrival of HARRY, right.*

*(HARRY is another story. He comes in timidly, turning about
uncertainly, awkward, out of place everywhere, embarrassed and encumbered by the contemporary costume,
sick at heart, but determined to fit in somewhere. His
arrival constitutes a dance.*

*(His clothes don't fit. The pants are a little too large. The
coat, which doesn't match, is also a little too large, and
loose.*

*(He is a dumb young fellow, but he has ideas. A philosophy,
in fact. His philosophy is simple and beautiful. The world
is sorrowful. The world needs laughter. HARRY is funny.
The world needs HARRY. HARRY will make the world laugh.*

(He has probably had a year or two of high school. He has

also listened to the boys at the poolroom. He's looking for NICK.

HARRY (*goes to* ARAB): Are you Nick? (ARAB *shakes his head.* HARRY *stands at the bar, waiting. He waits very busily. As* NICK *returns.*) You Nick?

NICK (*very loudly*): I am *Nick*.

HARRY (*acting*): Can you use a great comedian?

NICK (*behind the bar*): Who, for instance?

HARRY (*almost angry*): Me.

NICK: You? What's funny about you? (DUDLEY *at the telephone, is dialing. Because of some defect in the apparatus the dialing is very loud.*)

DUDLEY: Hello. Sunset 7349? May I speak to Miss Elsie Mandelspiegel? (*Pause.*)

HARRY (*with spirit and noise, dancing*): I dance and do gags and stuff.

NICK: In costume? Or are you wearing your costume?

DUDLEY: All I need is a cigar.

KITTY: I'd walk out of the house, and stand on the porch, and look at the trees, and smell the flowers, and run across the lawn, and lie down under a tree, and read a book. A book of poems, maybe.

DUDLEY (*very, very clearly*): Elsie Mandelspiegel. (*Impatiently.*) She has a room on the fourth floor. She's a nurse at the Southern Pacific Hospital. Elsie Mandelspiegel. She works at night. Elsie. Yes. (*He begins waiting again.* WESLEY, *a colored boy, comes from right to the bar and stands near* HARRY, *waiting.*)

NICK: Beer?

WESLEY: No, sir. I'd like to talk to you.

NICK (*to* HARRY): All right. Get funny.

HARRY (*getting funny, an altogether different person, an actor with great energy, both in power of voice, and in force and speed of physical gesture*): Now, I'm standing on the corner of Third and Market. I'm looking around. I'm figuring it out. There it is. Right in front of me. The whole city. The whole world. People going by. They're going somewhere. I don't know where, but they're going. I ain't going *anywhere*. Where the hell can you go? I'm figuring it out. All right, I'm a citizen. A fat guy bumps his stomach into the face of an old lady. They were in a *hurry. Fat* and old. *They bumped.* Boom. I don't know. It may mean war. *War.* Germany. England. Russia. I don't know for sure. (*Loudly, dramatically, he salutes, about faces, presents arms, aims and fires.*) WAAAAAR. (*He blows a call to arms.* NICK *gets sick of this, indicates with a gesture that* HARRY *should hold it, and goes to* WESLEY.)

NICK: What's on *your* mind?

WESLEY (*confused*): Well—

NICK: Come on. Speak up. Are you hungry, or what?

WESLEY: Honest to God, I ain't hungry. All I want is a job. I don't want no charity.

NICK: Well, what can you do, and how good are you?

WESLEY: I can run errands, clean up, wash dishes, anything.

DUDLEY (*on the telephone, very eagerly*): Elsie? Elsie, this is Dudley. Elsie, I'll jump in the bay if you don't marry me. Life isn't worth living without you. I can't sleep. I can't think of anything but you. All the time. Day and night and night and day. Elsie, I love you. I love you. What? (*Burning up.*) Is this Sunset 7-3-4-9? 7943? (*Calmly, while* WILLIE *begins making a small racket.*) Well, what's *your* name? *Lorene? Lorene Smith?* I thought you were Elsie Mandelspiegel. What? Dudley. Yeah. Dudley R. Bostwick. Yeah. R. It stands for Raoul, but I never spell it out. I'm pleased to meet *you*, too. What? There's a lot of noise around here. (WILLIE *stops hitting the marble game.*) Where am I? At Nick's, on Pacific Street. I work at the S. P. I told them I was sick and they gave me the afternoon off. Wait a minute. I'll ask them. I'd like to meet *you*, too. Sure. I'll ask them. (*Turns around to* NICK.) What's this address?

NICK: Number Three Pacific Street, you cad.

HARRY (*stopping*): That's my own idea. I'm a natural-born dancer and comedian. (WESLEY *begins slowly, one note, one chord at a time, to play the piano.*)

NICK (*going to back of bar*): You're no good. Why don't you try some other kind of work? Why don't you get a job in a store, selling something? What do you want to be a comedian for?

HARRY (*to upper end of bar*): I've got something for the world and they haven't got sense enough to let me give it to them. Nobody knows me.

DUDLEY: Elsie. Now I'm waiting for some dame I've never seen before. Lorene Smith. Never saw her in my life. Just happened to get the wrong number. She turns on the personality, and I'm a cooked Indian. Give me a beer, please.

HARRY: Nick, you've got to see my act. It's the greatest thing of its kind in America. (NICK *comes to* DUDLEY *with beer.* HARRY *follows him.*) All I want is a chance. No salary to begin. Let me try it out tonight. If I don't wow 'em, O.K., I'll go home. If vaudeville wasn't dead, a guy like me would have a chance.

NICK (*crosses up behind bar;* HARRY *follows him*): You're not funny. You're a sad young punk. What the hell do you want to try to be funny for? You'll break everybody's heart. What's there for you to be funny about? You've been poor all your life, haven't you?

HARRY: I've been poor all right, but don't forget that some things count more than some other things.

NICK: What counts more, for instance, than what else, for instance?

HARRY: Talent, for instance, counts more than money, for instance, that's what, and I've got talent. I get new ideas night and day. Everything comes natural to me. I've got style, but it'll take me a little time to round it out. That's all. (*By now* WESLEY *is playing something of his own which is very good and out of the world. He plays about half a minute, after which* HARRY *begins to dance.*)

NICK (*watching*): I run the lousiest dive in Frisco, and a guy arrives and makes me stock up with champagne. The whores come in and holler at me that they're ladies. Talent comes in and begs me for a chance to show itself. Even society people come here once in a while. I don't know what for. Maybe it's liquor. Maybe it's the location. Maybe it's my personality. Maybe it's the crazy personality of the joint. The old honky-tonk. (*Pause.*) Maybe they can't feel at home anywhere else. (*By now* WESLEY *is really playing, and* HARRY *is going through a new routine.* DUDLEY *grows sadder and sadder.*)

KITTY: Please dance with me.

JOE (*loudly*): I never learned to dance.

KITTY: Anybody can dance. Just hold me in your arms.

JOE: I'm very fond of you. I'm *sorry*. I *can't* dance. I wish to God I could.

KITTY: Oh, please.

JOE: Forgive me. I'd like to very much. (KITTY *dances alone.* TOM *comes in right with a package. He sees* KITTY *and goes ga-ga again. He comes out of the trance and puts the bundle on the left center table in front of* JOE. NICK *comes to behind* JOE's *table, gets bottle and glasses and returns to back of bar.*)

JOE (*taking the package*): What'd you get?

TOM: Two dollars' worth of toys. That's what you sent me for. The girl asked me what I wanted with toys. I didn't know what to tell her. (*He turns and looks at* KITTY.) Joe? I've got to have some money. After all you've done for me, I'll do anything in the world for you, but, Joe, you got to give me some money once in a while.

JOE: What do you want it for?

(TOM *turns and stares at* KITTY *dancing.*)

JOE (*noticing*): Sure. Here. Here's five. (*Shouting.*) Can you dance?

TOM (*proudly*): I got second prize at the Palomar in Sacramento five years ago.

JOE (*loudly, opening package*): O.K., dance with her.

TOM: You mean *her?*

JOE (*loudly*): I mean Kitty Duval, the burlesque queen. I mean the queen of the world burlesque. Dance with her. She wants to dance.

TOM (*helplessly*): Joe, can I tell you something?

JOE (*he brings out a toy and winds it*): You don't have to. I know. You love her. You *really* love her. I'm not blind. I know. But take care of yourself. Don't get sick that way again.

NICK (*looking at and listening to* WESLEY *with amazement*): Comes in here and wants to be a dishwasher. Faints from hunger. And then sits down and plays better than Heifetz.

JOE: Heifetz plays the violin.

NICK: All right, don't get careful. He's good, ain't he?

TOM (*to* KITTY): Kitty.

JOE (*he lets the toy go, loudly*): Don't *talk*. Just *dance*. (TOM *and* KITTY *dance.* NICK *is at the bar, watching everything.* HARRY *is dancing.* DUDLEY *is grieving into his beer.* LORENE SMITH, *about thirty-seven, very overbearing and funny-looking, comes to the bar from right.*)

NICK: What'll it be, lady?

LORENE (*looking about and scaring all the young men*): I'm looking for the young man I talked to on the telephone. Dudley R. Bostwick.

DUDLEY (*jumping, running to her, stopping, shocked*): Dudley R. (*slowly*) Bostwick? Oh, yeah. He left here ten minutes ago. You mean Dudley Bostwick, that poor man on crutches?

LORENE: Crutches?

DUDLEY: Yeah. Dudley Bostwick. That's what he *said* his name was. He said to tell you not to wait.

LORENE: Well. (*She begins to go, turns around.*) Are you sure *you're* not Dudley R. Bostwick?

DUDLEY: Who—me? (*Grandly.*) My name is Roger Tene-francia. I'm a French-Canadian. I never saw the poor fellow before.

LORENE: It seems to me your voice is like the voice I heard over the telephone.

DUDLEY: A coincidence. An accident. A quirk of fate. One of those things. Dismiss the thought. That poor cripple hobbled out of here ten minutes ago.

LORENE (*crossing to door right*): He said he was going to commit suicide. I only wanted to be of help. (*She goes out right.*)

DUDLEY: Be of help? What kind of help could she be, of? (DUDLEY *runs to the telephone in the corner.*) Gee whiz, Elsie. Gee whiz. I'll never leave you again. (*He turns the pages of a little address book.*) Why do I always forget the number? I've tried to get her on the phone a hundred times this week and I still forget the number. She won't come to the phone, but I keep trying anyway. She's out. She's not in. She's working. I get the wrong number. Everything goes haywire. I can't sleep. (*Defiantly.*) She'll come to the phone one of these days. If there's anything to true love at all, she'll come to the phone. Sunset 7349. (*He dials the number, as* JOE *goes on studying the toys. They are one big mechanical toy, whistles and a music box.* JOE *blows into the whistles, quickly, by way of getting casually acquainted with them.* TOM *and* KITTY *stop dancing.* TOM *stares at her.*)

DUDLEY: Hello. Is this Sunset 7349? May I speak to Elsie? Yes. (*Emphatically, and bitterly.*) No, this is *not* Dudley Bostwick. This is Roger Tenefrancia of Montreal, Canada. I'm a childhood friend of Miss Mandelspiegel. We went to kindergarten together. (*Hand over phone.*) Goddamn it. (*Into phone.*) Yes. I'll wait, thank you.

TOM: I love you. (*Leading* KITTY *to in front of door right.*)

KITTY: You want to go to my room? (TOM *can't answer.*) Have you got two dollars?

TOM (*shaking his head with confusion*): I've got *five* dollars, but I *love* you.

KITTY (*looking at him*): You want to spend *all* that money?

(TOM *embraces her. They go out right.* JOE *watches, goes back to the toy.*)

JOE: Where's that longshoreman, McCarthy?

NICK: He'll be around.

JOE: What do you think he'll have to say today?

NICK (*coming around bar*): Plenty, as usual. I'm going next door to see who won that third race at Laurel.

JOE: Precious Time won it.

NICK: That's what you think. (*He goes out right.*)

JOE (*to himself*): A horse named McCarthy is running in the sixth race today.

DUDLEY (*on the phone*): Hello. Hello, Elsie? Elsie? (*His voice weakens; also his limbs.*) My God. She's come to the phone. Elsie, I'm at Nick's on Pacific Street. You've got to come here and talk to me. Hello. Hello, Elsie? (*Amazed.*) Did she hang up? Or was I disconnected? (*He hangs up and goes to bar.* WESLEY *is still playing the piano.* HARRY *is still dancing.* JOE *has wound up the big mechanical toy and is watching it work.*)

NICK (*returns from right; goes to right of* JOE, *watching the toy*): Say. That's some gadget.

JOE: How much did I win?

NICK: How do you know you *won?*

JOE: Don't be silly. He said Precious Time was going to win by ten lengths, didn't he? He's in love, isn't he?

NICK (*handing* JOE *money*): O.K. I don't know why, but Precious Time won. You got eighty for ten. How do you do it?

JOE (*roaring*): Faith. Faith. How'd he win?

NICK: By a nose. Look him up in *The Racing Form.* The slowest, the cheapest, the worst horse in the race, and the worst jockey. What's the matter with my luck?

JOE: How much did you lose?

NICK: Fifty cents.

JOE: You should never gamble.

NICK: Why not?

JOE: You always bet fifty cents. You've got no more faith than a flea, that's why.

HARRY (*shouting*): How do you like this, Nick? (*He is really busy now, all legs and arms.*)

NICK (*turning and watching, crossing to piano*): Not bad. Hang around. You can wait table. (*To* WESLEY.) Hey. Wesley. Can you play that again tonight?

WESLEY (*turning, but still playing the piano*): I don't know for sure, Mr. Nick. I can play *something.*

NICK: Good. *You* hang around, too. (*He goes behind the bar.*)

(*The atmosphere is now one of warm, natural, American ease; every man innocent and good; each doing what he believes he should do, or what he must do. There is deep American naïveté and faith in the behavior of each person. No one is competing with anyone else. No ones hates anyone else. Every man is living, and letting live. Each man is following his destiny as he feels it should be followed; or is abandoning it as he feels it must, by now, be abandoned; or is forgetting it for the moment as he feels he should forget it. Although everyone is dead serious, there is unmistakable smiling and humor in the scene; a sense of the human body and spirit emerging from the world-imposed state of stress and fretfulness, fear and awkwardness, to the more natural state of casualness and grace. Each person belongs to the environment, in his own person, as himself:* WESLEY *is playing better than ever.* HARRY *is hoofing better than ever.* NICK *is behind the bar shining glasses.* JOE *is smiling at the toy and studying it.* DUDLEY, *although still troubled, is at least calm now and full of melancholy poise.* WILLIE, *at the marble game, is happy. The* ARAB *is deep in his memories, where he wants to be.*

(*Into this scene and atmosphere comes* BLICK *from right.*

(BLICK *is the sort of human being you dislike at sight. He is no different from anybody else physically. His face is an ordinary face. There is nothing obviously wrong with him, and yet you know that it is impossible, even by the*

most generous expansion of understanding, to accept him
as a human being. He is the strong man without strength—
strong only among the weak—the weakling who uses force
on the weaker.
(BLICK *enters casually, as if he were a customer, and immediately* HARRY *begins slowing down.*)

BLICK (*oily, and with mock friendliness*): Hello, Nick.

NICK (*stopping his work and leaning across the bar*): What
do you want to come here for? You're too big a man for a
little honky-tonk.

BLICK (*flattered*): Now, Nick.

NICK: Important people never come here. *Here.* Have a drink.
(*Puts out whisky bottle and glass.*)

BLICK: Thanks, I don't drink.

NICK (*drinking the whisky himself*): Well, why don't you?

BLICK: I have responsibilities.

NICK: You're head of the lousy Vice Squad. There's no vice
here.

BLICK (*sharply*): Streetwalkers are working out of this place.

NICK (*angry*): What do you want?

BLICK (*loudly*): I just want you to know that it's got to *stop.*
(*The music stops. The mechanical toy runs down. There is
absolute silence, and a strange fearfulness and disharmony
in the atmosphere now.* HARRY *doesn't know what to do
with his hands or feet.* WESLEY'S *arms hang at his sides.*
JOE *quietly pushes the toy to one side of the table eager to
study what is happening.* WILLIE *stops playing the marble
game, turns around and begins to wait.* DUDLEY *straightens
up very, very vigorously, as if to say:* "Nothing can scare
me. I know love is the only thing." *The* ARAB *is the same as
ever, but watchful.* NICK *is arrogantly aloof. There is a moment of this silence and tension, as though* BLICK *were waiting for everybody to acknowledge his presence. He is obviously flattered by the acknowledgment of* HARRY, DUDLEY,
WESLEY *and* WILLIE, *but a little irritated by* NICK'S *aloof-
ness and unfriendliness.*)

NICK: Don't look at me. I can't tell a streetwalker from a lady. You married?

BLICK: You're not asking *me* questions. *I'm* telling *you.*

NICK (*interrupting*): You're a man of about forty-five or so. You *ought* to know better.

BLICK (*angry*): Streetwalkers are working out of this place.

NICK (*beginning to shout*): Now, don't start any trouble with me. People come here to drink and loaf around. I don't care who they are.

BLICK: Well, I do.

NICK: The only way to find out if a lady is a streetwalker is to walk the streets with her, go to bed, and make sure. You wouldn't want to do that. You'd *like* to, of course.

BLICK: Any more of it, and I'll have your joint closed.

NICK (*very casually, without ill will*): Listen. I've got no use for you, or anybody like you. You're out to change the world from something bad to something worse. Something like yourself.

BLICK (*furious pause, and contempt*): I'll be back tonight. (*He begins to go right.*)

NICK (*very angry but very calm*): Do yourself a big favor and don't come back tonight. Send somebody else. I don't like your personality.

BLICK: Don't break any laws. I don't like yours, either. (*He looks the place over, and goes out right. There is a moment of silence. Then* WILLIE *turns and puts a new nickel in the slot and starts a new game.* WESLEY *turns to the piano and rather falteringly begins to play. His heart really isn't in it.* HARRY *walks about, unable to dance.* DUDLEY *lapses into his customary melancholy, at a table.* NICK *whistles a little: suddenly stops.* JOE *winds the toy.*)

JOE (*comically*): Nick. You going to kill that man?

NICK: I'm disgusted.

JOE: Yeah? Why?

NICK: Why should I get worked up over a guy like that? Why should I hate *him?* He's nothing. He's nobody. He's a mouse. But every time he comes into this place I get burned up. He doesn't want to drink. He doesn't want to sit down. He doesn't want to take things easy. Tell me one thing?

JOE: Do my best.

NICK: What's a punk like *that* want to go out and try to change the world for?

JOE (*amazed*): Does *he* want to change the world, too?

NICK (*irritated*): You know what I mean. What's he want to bother people for? He's *sick*.

JOE (*almost to himself, reflecting on the fact that* BLICK *too wants to change the world*): I guess he wants to change the world at that.

NICK: So I go to work and hate him.

JOE: It's not him, Nick. It's everything.

NICK: Yeah, *I know*. But I've still got no use for him. He's *no good*. You know what I mean? He hurts little people. (*Confused.*) One of the girls tried to commit suicide on account of him. (*Furiously.*) I'll break his head if he hurts anybody around here. This is *my* joint. (*Afterthought.*) Or anybody's *feelings*, either.

JOE: He may not be so bad, deep down underneath.

NICK: I know all about him. He's no good. (*During this talk* WESLEY *has really begun to play the piano, the toy is rattling again, and little by little* HARRY *has begun to dance.* NICK *has come around the bar, and now, very much like a child—forgetting all his anger—is watching the toy work. He begins to smile at everything: turns and listens to* WESLEY: *watches* HARRY: *nods at the* ARAB: *shakes his head at* DUDLEY *and gestures amiably about* WILLIE. *It's his joint all right. It's a good, low-down, honky-tonk American place that lets people alone.*)

NICK (*crossing to chair left of center table*): I've got a good joint. There's nothing wrong here. Hey. Comedian. Stick to the dancing tonight. I think you're O.K. (HARRY *goes to telephone and dials.*) Wesley? Do some more of that tonight. That's fine!

HARRY: Thanks, Nick. Gosh, I'm on my way at last. (*On tele-*

phone.) Hello, Ma? Is that you, Ma? Harry. I got the job. (*He hangs up and walks around, smiling.*)

NICK (*watching the toy all this time*): Say, that really is something. What is that, anyway? (MARY L. *comes in right.*)

JOE (*holding it toward* NICK, *and* MARY L.): Nick, this is a toy. A contraption devised by the cunning of man to drive boredom, or grief, or anger out of children. A noble gadget. A gadget, I might say, infinitely nobler than any other I can think of at the moment. (*Everybody gathers around* JOE's *table to look at the toy. The toy stops working.* JOE *winds the music box. Lifts a whistle: blows it, making a very strange, funny and sorrowful sound.*) Delightful. Tragic, but delightful. (WESLEY *plays the music-box theme on the piano.* MARY L. *takes a table center.*)

NICK: Joe. That girl, Kitty. What's she mean, calling me a dentist? I wouldn't hurt anybody, let alone a tooth. (NICK *goes to* MARY L.'s *table.* HARRY *imitates the toy. Dances. The piano music comes up, and the light dims slowly, while the piano solo continues.*)

Act ii

SCENE: *Nick's, an hour later. All the people who were there when the curtain came down are still there.* DUDLEY *at table right,* ARAB *seated in the rear at right.* HARRY *and* WESLEY *at piano.* JOE *at his table, quietly shuffling and turning a deck of cards, and at the same time watching the face of the* WOMAN, *and looking at the initials on her handbag as though they were the symbols of the lost glory of the world. At center table,* WOMAN, *in turn, very casually regards* JOE, *occasionally—or rather senses him; has sensed him in fact the whole hour. She is mildly tight on beer, and* JOE *himself is tight, but as always, completely under control; simply sharper. The others are about, at tables, and so on.*

JOE: Is it Madge—Laubowitz?

MARY: Is what *what?*

JOE: Is the name Mabel Lepescu?

MARY: What name?

JOE: The name the initials M. L. stand for. The initials on your bag.

MARY: No.

JOE (*after a long pause, thinking deeply what the name might be, turning a card, looking into the beautiful face of the* WOMAN): Margie Longworthy?

MARY (*all this is very natural and sincere, no comedy on the part of the people involved: they are both solemn, being drunk*): No.

JOE (*his voice higher-pitched, as though he were growing a*

253

little alarmed): Midge Laurie? (MARY *shakes her head.*)
My initials are J. T.

MARY (*pause*): John?

JOE: No. (*Pause.*) Martha Lancaster?

MARY: No. (*Slight pause.*) Joseph?

JOE: Well, not exactly. That's my first name, but everybody
calls me Joe. The last name is the tough one. I'll help you a
little. I'm Irish. Is it just plain Mary?

MARY: Yes, it is. I'm Irish, too. At least on my father's side.
English on my mother's side.

JOE: I'm Irish on both sides. Mary's one of my favorite names.
I guess that's why I didn't think of it. I met a girl in Mexico
City named Mary once. She was an American from Phila-
delphia. She got married there. In Mexico City, I mean.
While I was *there*. We were in love, too. At least *I* was. You
never know about anyone else. They were engaged, you see,
and her mother was with her, so they went through with it.
Must have been six or seven years ago. She's probably got
three or four children by this time.

MARY: Are you still in love with her?

JOE: Well—no. To tell you the truth, I'm not sure. I guess I
am. I didn't even know she was engaged until a couple of
days before they got married. I thought *I* was going to
marry her. I kept thinking all the time about the kind of
kids we would be likely to have. My favorite was the third
one. The first two were fine. Handsome and fine and intelligent, but that third one was different. Dumb and goofy-
looking. I liked *him* a lot. When she told me she was going
to be married, I didn't feel so bad about the first two, it was
that dumb one.

MARY (*after a pause of some few seconds*): What do you do?

JOE: Do? To tell you the truth, nothing.

MARY: Do you always drink a great deal?

JOE (*scientifically*): Not *always*. Only when I'm awake. I sleep
seven or eight hours every night, you know.

MARY: How nice. I mean to drink when you're awake.

JOE (*thoughtfully*): It's a privilege.

MARY: Do you really *like* to drink?

JOE (*positively*): As much as I like to *breathe*.

MARY (*beautifully*): Why?

JOE (*dramatically*): Why do I like to drink? Because I don't like to be gypped. Because I don't like to be dead most of the time and just a little alive every once in a long while. (*Pause.*) If I don't drink, I become fascinated by unimportant things—like everybody else. I get busy. Do things. All kinds of little stupid things, for all kinds of little stupid reasons. Proud, selfish, *ordinary* things. I've done them. Now I don't do anything. *I live all the time.* Then I go to sleep.

MARY: Do you sleep well?

JOE (*taking it for granted*): Of course.

MARY (*quietly, almost with tenderness*): What are your plans?

JOE (*loudly, but also tenderly*): Plans? I haven't *got* any. *I just get up.*

MARY (*beginning to understand everything*): Oh, yes. Yes, of course. (DUDLEY *puts a nickel in the phonograph.*)

JOE (*thoughtfully*): Why do I drink? (*Pause, while he thinks about it. The thinking appears to be profound and complex, and has the effect of giving his face a very comical and naïve expression.*) That question calls for a pretty complicated answer. (*He smiles abstractly.*)

MARY: Oh, I didn't mean—

JOE (*swiftly, gallantly*): No. No. I *insist.* I *know* why. It's just a matter of finding words. Little ones.

MARY: It really doesn't matter.

JOE (*seriously*): Oh, yes, it does. (*Clinically.*) Now, why do I drink? (*Scientifically.*) No. Why does *anybody* drink? (*Working it out.*) Every day has twenty-four hours.

MARY (*sadly, but brightly*): Yes, that's true.

JOE: Twenty-four hours. Out of the twenty-four hours at *least* twenty-three and a half are—my God, I don't know why—dull, dead, boring, empty, and murderous. Minutes on the clock, *not time of living.* It doesn't make any difference who you are or what you do, twenty-three and a half hours of the twenty-four are spent *waiting.*

MARY: Waiting?

JOE (*gesturing, loudly*): And the more you wait, the less there is to wait *for*.

MARY (*attentively, beautifully his student*): Oh?

JOE (*continuing*): That goes on for days and days, and weeks and months and years, and years, and the first thing you know *all* the years are dead. All the minutes are dead. You yourself are dead. There's nothing to wait for any more. Nothing except *minutes* on the *clock*. No time of life. Nothing but minutes, and idiocy. Beautiful, bright, intelligent idiocy. (*Pause.*) Does that answer your question?

MARY (*earnestly*): I'm afraid it does. Thank you. You shouldn't have gone to all the trouble.

JOE: No trouble at all. (*Pause.*) You have children?

MARY: Yes. Two. A son and a daughter.

JOE (*delighted*): How swell. Do they look like you?

MARY: Yes.

JOE: Then why are you sad?

MARY: I was always sad. It's just that after I was married I was allowed to drink.

JOE (*eagerly*): Who are you waiting for?

MARY: No one.

JOE (*smiling*): I'm not waiting for anybody, either.

MARY: My husband, of course.

JOE: Oh, sure.

MARY: He's a lawyer.

JOE (*standing, leaning on the table*): He's a great guy. I like him. I'm very fond of him.

MARY (*listening*): You have responsibilities?

JOE (*loudly; rises*): One, and *thousands*. As a matter of fact, I feel responsible to everybody. At least to everybody I meet. I've been trying for three years to find out if it's possible to live what I think is a civilized life. I mean a life that can't hurt any other life.

MARY: You're famous?

JOE: Very. Utterly unknown, but very famous. Would you like to dance?

MARY: All right.

JOE (*loudly*): I'm *sorry*. I don't dance. I didn't think *you'd* like to.

MARY: To tell you the truth, I don't like to dance at all.

JOE (*proudly; commentator*): I can hardly walk.

MARY: You mean you're tight?

JOE (*smiling*): No. I mean *all* the time.

MARY (*sitting forward*): Were you ever in Paris?

JOE: In 1929, and again in 1934.

MARY: What month of 1934?

JOE: Most of April, all of May and a little of June.

MARY: I was there in November and December that year.

JOE: We were there almost at the same time. You were married?

MARY: Engaged. (*They are silent a moment, looking at one another. Quietly and with great charm.*) Are you *really* in love with me?

JOE: Yes.

MARY: Is it the champagne?

JOE: Yes. Partly, at least. (*He sits down.*)

MARY: If you don't see me again, will you be very unhappy?

JOE: Very.

MARY (*getting up*): I'm so pleased. (*JOE is deeply grieved that she is going. In fact, he is almost panic-stricken about it, getting up in a way that is full of furious sorrow and regret.*) I must go now. Please don't get up. (*JOE is up, staring at her with amazement.*) Good-by.

JOE (*simply*): Good-by. (*Music ends. The WOMAN stands looking at him a moment, then turns and goes slowly out right. JOE stands staring after her for a long time. Just as he is slowly sitting down again, the NEWSBOY enters right, and goes to JOE's table.*)

NEWSBOY: Paper, Mister?

JOE: How many you got this time?

NEWSBOY: Eleven. (*JOE buys them all, looks at all, throws them away. ARAB crosses, picks up one and returns to his seat at rear right. The* NEWSBOY *looks at* JOE, *shakes head, goes to bar, troubled.*) Hey, Mister, do you own this place?

NICK: I own this place.

NEWSBOY: Can you use a great lyric tenor?

NICK (*almost to himself*): Great lyric tenor? (*Loudly.*) Who?

NEWSBOY: Me. I'm getting too big to sell papers. I don't want to holler headlines all the time. I want to *sing.* You can use a great lyric tenor, can't you?

NICK: What's lyric about you?

NEWSBOY (*voice high-pitched, confused*): My voice.

NICK: Oh. (*Slight pause, giving in.*) All right, then—sing!
(*The* NEWSBOY *breaks into swift and beautiful song: "When Irish Eyes Are Smiling."* NICK *and* JOE *listen carefully:* NICK *with wonder,* JOE *with amazement and delight.*)

NEWSBOY (*singing*):

> When Irish eyes are smiling,
> Sure 'tis like a morn in spring.
> In the lilt of Irish laughter,
> You can hear the angels sing.
> When Irish hearts are happy,
> All the world seems bright and gay.
> But when Irish eyes are smiling—

NICK (*loudly, swiftly*): Are you Irish?

NEWSBOY (*speaking swiftly, loudly, a little impatient with the irrelevant question*): No. I'm Greek. (*He finishes the song, singing louder than ever.*) "Sure they steal your heart away." (*He turns to* NICK *dramatically, like a vaudeville singer begging his audience for applause.* NICK *studies the boy eagerly.* JOE *gets to his feet and leans toward the* BOY *and* NICK.)

NICK: Not bad. Let me hear you again about a year from now.

NEWSBOY (*thrilled*): Honest?

NICK: Yeah. Along about November 7th, 1940.

NEWSBOY (*happier than ever before in his life, running over to* JOE): Did you hear it too, Mister?

JOE: Yes, and it's great. What part of Greece?

NEWSBOY: Salonica. Gosh, Mister. Thanks.

JOE: Don't wait a year. Come back with some papers a little later. You're a great singer.

NEWSBOY (*thrilled and excited*): Aw, thanks, Mister. So long. (*Running, to* NICK.) Thanks, Mister. (*He runs out right.* JOE *and* NICK *look at the swinging doors.* JOE *sits down.* NICK *laughs.*)

NICK: Joe, people are so wonderful. Look at that kid.

JOE: Of course they're wonderful. Every one of them is wonderful.

(McCARTHY *and* KRUPP *come in right, talking.* McCARTHY *is a big man in work clothes, which make him seem very young. He is wearing black jeans, and a blue workman's shirt. No tie. No hat. He has broad shoulders, a lean intelligent face, thick black hair. In his right back pocket is the longshoreman's hook. His arms are long and hairy. His sleeves are rolled up to just below his elbows. He is a casual man, easygoing in movement, sharp in perception, swift in appreciation of charm or innocence or comedy, and gentle in spirit. His speech is clear and full of warmth. His voice is powerful, but modulated. He enjoys the world, in spite of the mess it is, and he is fond of people, in spite of the mess they are.*

(KRUPP *is not quite as tall or broad-shouldered as* McCARTHY. *He is physically encumbered by his uniform, club, pistol, belt and cap. And he is plainly not at home in the role of policeman. His movement is stiff and unintentionally pompous. He is a naïve man, essentially good. His understanding is less than* McCARTHY'S, *but he is honest and he doesn't try to bluff.*)

KRUPP: You don't understand what I mean. Hiya, Joe. (*Crossing to center of bar.*)

JOE: Hello, Krupp.

McCARTHY (*crossing to behind* KRUPP): Hiya, Joe.

JOE: Hello, McCarthy.

KRUPP: Two beers, Nick. (*To* McCARTHY.) All I do is carry

out orders, carry out orders. I don't know what the idea is behind the order. Who it's for, or who it's against, or why. All I do is carry it out. (NICK *gives them beer*.)

MCCARTHY: You don't read enough.

KRUPP: I do read. I read *The Examiner* every morning. *The Call-Bulletin* every night.

MCCARTHY: And carry out orders. What are the orders now?

KRUPP: To keep the peace down here on the waterfront.

MCCARTHY: Keep it for who? (*To* JOE.) Right?

JOE (*sorrowfully*): Right.

KRUPP: How do I know for who? The peace. Just keep it.

MCCARTHY: It's got to be kept for somebody. Who would you suspect it's kept for?

KRUPP (*thinking*): For citizens!

MCCARTHY: I'm a citizen.

KRUPP: All right, I'm keeping it for you.

MCCARTHY: By hitting me over the head with a club? (*To* JOE.) Right?

JOE (*melancholy, with remembrance*): I don't know.

KRUPP: Mac, you know I never hit you over the head with a club.

MCCARTHY: But you will if you're on duty at the time and happen to stand on the opposite side of myself, on duty.

KRUPP: We went to Mission High together. We were always good friends. The only time we ever fought was that time over Alma Haggerty. Did *you* marry Alma Haggerty? Right?

JOE: Everything's right.

MCCARTHY: No. Did you? (*To* JOE.) Joe, are you with me or against me?

JOE: I'm with everybody. One at a time.

KRUPP: No. And that's just what I mean.

MCCARTHY: You mean neither one of us is going to marry the thing we're fighting for?

KRUPP: *I don't even know what it is.*

MCCARTHY: You don't read enough, I tell you.

KRUPP: Mac, you don't know what you're fighting for, either.

MCCARTHY: It's so simple, it's fantastic.

KRUPP: All right, what are you fighting for?

McCARTHY: For the rights of the inferior. Right?

JOE: Something like that.

KRUPP: The who?

McCARTHY: The inferior. The world full of Mahoneys who haven't got what it takes to make monkeys out of everybody else, near by. The men who were created equal. Remember?

KRUPP: Mac, you're not inferior.

McCARTHY: I'm a longshoreman. And an idealist. I'm a man with too much brawn to be an intellectual, exclusively. (*Crossing to right of* JOE.) I married a small, sensitive, cultured woman so that my kids would be sissies instead of suckers. A strong man with any sensibility has no choice in this world but to be a heel, or a *worker*. I haven't the heart to be a heel, so I'm a worker. I've got a son in high school who's already thinking of being a writer.

KRUPP: I wanted to be a writer once.

JOE: Wonderful. (*He puts down the paper, looks at* KRUPP *and* McCARTHY.)

McCARTHY: They *all* wanted to be writers. Every maniac in the world that ever brought about the murder of people through war started out in an attic or a basement writing poetry. It stank. So they got even by becoming important heels. And it's still going on.

KRUPP: Is it really, Joe?

JOE: Look at today's paper.

McCARTHY: Right now on Telegraph Hill is some punk who is trying to be Shakespeare. Ten years from now he'll be a senator. Or a Communist.

KRUPP: Somebody ought to do something about it.

McCARTHY (*mischievously, with laughter in his voice*): The thing to do is to have more magazines. Hundreds of *them*. *Thousands*. Print everything they write, so they'll believe they're immortal. That way keep them from going haywire.

KRUPP: Mac, you ought to be a writer yourself.

McCARTHY: I hate the tribe. They're mischief-makers. Right?

JOE (*swiftly*): Everything's right. Right and wrong.

KRUPP: Then why do you read?

MCCARTHY (*laughing*): It's relaxing. It's soothing. (*Pause.*)
The lousiest people born into the world are writers. Language is all right. It's the people who use language that are
lousy. (*The* ARAB *has moved a little closer, and is listening
carefully. To the* ARAB.) What do you think, Brother?

ARAB (*at first step forward to the right; after making many
faces, thinking very deeply*): No foundation. All the way
down the line. What. What-not. Nothing. I go walk and
look at sky. (*He goes out right.*)

KRUPP (*follows to in front of bar*): What? What-not? (*To*
JOE.) What's that mean?

JOE (*slowly, thinking, remembering*): What? What-not? That
means this side, that side. Inhale, exhale. What: birth.
What-not: death. The inevitable, the astounding, the magnificent seed of growth and decay in all things. Beginning,
and end. That man, in his own way, is a prophet. He is one
who, with the help of *beer*, is able to reach that state of
deep understanding in which what and what-not, the rea-
sonable and the unreasonable, are *one*.

MCCARTHY: Right.

KRUPP: If you can understand that kind of talk, how can you
be a longshoreman?

MCCARTHY: I come from a long line of McCarthys who never
married or slept with anything but the most powerful and
quarrelsome flesh. (*He drinks beer.*)

KRUPP: I could listen to you two guys for hours, but I'll be
damned if I know what the hell you're talking about.

MCCARTHY: The consequence is that all the McCarthys are
too great and too strong to be heroes. Only the weak and
unsure perform the heroic. They've *got* to. The more heroes
you have, the worse the history of the world becomes.
Right?

JOE: Go outside and look at it.

KRUPP: You sure can philos—philosoph— Boy, you can talk.

MCCARTHY: I wouldn't talk this way to anyone but a man in
uniform, and a man who couldn't understand a word of

what I was saying. The party I'm speaking of, my friend, is
YOU. (*The phone rings.* HARRY *gets up from his table suddenly and begins a new dance.*)

KRUPP (*noticing him, with great authority*): Here. Here.
What do you think you're doing?

HARRY (*stopping*): I just got an idea for a new dance. I'm
trying it out. Nick. Nick, the phone's ringing. (NICK *goes
to phone.*)

KRUPP (*to* MCCARTHY): Has he got a right to do that?

MCCARTHY: The living have danced from the beginning of
time. I might even say, the dance and the life have moved
along together, until now we have— (*To* HARRY.) Go into
your dance, son, and show us what we have.

HARRY: I haven't got it worked out *completely* yet, but it starts
out like this. (*He dances.*)

NICK (*on phone*): Nick's Pacific Street Restaurant, Saloon,
and Entertainment Palace. Good Afternoon. Nick speaking.
(*Listens.*) Who? (*Turns around.*) Is there a Dudley Bostwick in the joint? (DUDLEY *jumps to his feet and goes to
phone.* NICK *goes to behind bar.*)

DUDLEY (*on phone*): Hello. Elsie? (*Listens.*) You're coming
down? (*Elated. To the saloon.*) She's coming down. (*Pause.*)
No. I won't drink. Aw, gosh, Elsie. (*He hangs up, looks
about him strangely, as if he were just born, walks around
touching things, putting chairs in place, and so on.*)

MCCARTHY (*to* HARRY): Splendid. Splendid.

HARRY: Then I go into this little routine. (*He demonstrates.*)

KRUPP: Is that good, Mac?

MCCARTHY: It's awful, but it's honest and ambitious, like
everything else in this great country.

HARRY: Then I work along into this. (*He demonstrates.*) And
this is where I *really* get going. (*He finishes the dance.*)

MCCARTHY: Excellent. A most satisfying demonstration of the
present state of the American body and soul. (*Crossing to
HARRY and shaking his hand.*) Son, you're a genius.

HARRY (*delighted*): I go on in front of an audience for the
first time in my life tonight.

McCARTHY: They'll be delighted. Where'd you learn to dance?

HARRY: Never took a lesson in my life. I'm a natural-born dancer. And *comedian,* too.

McCARTHY (*astounded*): You can make people *laugh?*

HARRY (*dumbly*): I can be funny, but they won't laugh.

McCARTHY: That's odd. Why not?

HARRY: I don't know. They just won't laugh.

McCARTHY: Would you care to be funny now?

HARRY: I'd like to try out a new monologue I've been thinking about.

McCARTHY: Please do. I promise you if it's funny I shall *roar* with laughter.

HARRY: This is it. (*Goes into the act, with much energy.*) I'm up at Sharkey's on Turk Street. It's a quarter to nine, daylight saving. Wednesday, the eleventh. What I've got is a headache and a 1918 nickel. What I *want* is a cup of coffee. If I buy a cup of coffee with the nickel, I've got to walk home. I've got an eight-ball problem. George the Greek is shooting a game of snooker with Pedro the Filipino. *I'm in rags.* They're wearing thirty-five-dollar suits, made to order. I haven't got a cigarette. They're smoking Bobby Burns panatelas. I'm thinking it over, like I always do. George the Greek is in a tough spot. If I buy a cup of coffee, I'll want another cup. What happens? My *ear* aches! My ear. George the Greek takes the cue. Chalks it. Studies the table. Touches the cue ball delicately. Tick. What happens? He makes the three ball! What do I do? I get confused. *I go out and buy a morning paper.* What the hell do I want with a morning paper? What I *want* is a cup of coffee, and a good used car. I go out and buy a morning paper. Thursday, the twelfth. Maybe the headline's about *me.* I take a quick look. *No. The headline is not about me.* It's about Hitler. Seven thousand miles away. I'm here. Who the hell is Hitler? Who's behind the eight ball? I turn around. *Everybody's behind the eight ball!* (*Pause.* KRUPP *moves toward* HARRY *as if to make an important arrest.* HARRY *moves to the swinging doors.* McCARTHY *stops* KRUPP.)

MCCARTHY: It's the funniest thing I've ever heard. Or *seen,* for that matter.

HARRY: Then, why don't you laugh?

MCCARTHY: I don't know, *yet.*

HARRY: I'm always getting funny ideas that nobody will laugh at.

MCCARTHY: It may be that you've stumbled headlong into a new kind of comedy.

HARRY: Well, what good is it if it doesn't make anybody laugh?

MCCARTHY: There are *kinds* of laughter, son. I must say, in all truth, that I *am* laughing, although not *out loud.*

HARRY: I want to *hear* people laugh. *Out loud.* That's why I keep thinking of funny things to say.

MCCARTHY (*crossing to front right*): Well. They may catch on in time. Let's go, Krupp. So long, Joe. (MCCARTHY *and* KRUPP *go out right.*)

JOE: So long. (*After a moment's pause.*) Hey, Nick.

NICK: Yeah. (HARRY *exits rear center.* DUDLEY *goes to bar and gets beer.*)

JOE: Bet McCarthy in the last race.

NICK: You're crazy. That horse is a double-crossing, no-good—

JOE: Bet everything you've got on McCarthy.

NICK: I'm not betting a nickel on him. *You* bet everything you've got on McCarthy.

JOE: I don't need money.

NICK: What makes you think McCarthy's going to win?

JOE: McCarthy's name's McCarthy, isn't it?

NICK: Yeah, so what?

JOE: The *horse* named McCarthy is going to win, *that's all.* Today.

NICK: Why?

JOE: You do what I tell you, and everything will be all right.

NICK: McCarthy likes to talk, that's all. Where's Tom?

JOE: He'll be around. He'll be miserable, but he'll be around. Five or ten minutes more.

NICK: You don't believe that Kitty, do you? About being in burlesque?

JOE (*very clearly*): I believe dreams sooner than statistics.

NICK (*remembering*): She sure is somebody. Called me a dentist. (TOM, *turning about, confused, troubled, comes in, right, and hurries to Joe's table.*)

JOE: What's the matter?

TOM (*giving* JOE *money*): Here's your five, Joe. I'm in trouble again.

JOE: If it's not organic, it'll cure itself. If it *is* organic, science will cure it. What is it, organic or non-organic?

TOM: Joe, I don't know— (*He sits at right of table, buries his head on his arms and seems to be completely broken-down.*)

JOE: What's eating you? I want you to go on an errand for me.

TOM: It's Kitty.

JOE: What about her?

TOM: She's up in her room, crying.

JOE: Crying?

TOM: Yeah, she's been crying for over an hour. I been talking to her all this time, but she won't stop.

JOE: What's she crying about?

TOM: I don't know. I couldn't understand anything. She kept crying and telling me about a big house and collie dogs all around and flowers and one of her brother's dead and the other one lost somewhere. Joe, I can't stand Kitty crying.

JOE: You want to marry the girl?

TOM (*nodding*): Yeah.

JOE (*curious and sincere*): Why?

TOM: I don't know why, exactly, Joe. (*Pause.*) Joe, I don't like to think of Kitty out in the streets. I guess I love her, that's all.

JOE: She's a nice girl.

TOM: She's like an angel. She's not like those other street-walkers.

JOE (*swiftly*): Here. Take all this money and run next door to Frankie's and bet it on the nose of McCarthy.

TOM (*swiftly*): All this money, Joe? McCarthy?

JOE: Yeah. Hurry.

TOM (*going*): Ah, Joe. If McCarthy wins we'll be rich.

JOE: Get going, will you? (TOM *runs out right and nearly knocks over the* ARAB *coming back in.* NICK *fills him a beer without a word.*)

ARAB: No foundation, anywhere. Whole world. No foundation. All the way down the line.

NICK (*angry*): McCarthy! Just because you got a little lucky this morning, you have to go to work and throw away eighty bucks.

JOE: He wants to marry her.

NICK: Suppose she doesn't want to marry *him?*

JOE (*amazed*): Oh, yeah. (*Thinking.*) Now, why wouldn't she want to marry a nice guy like Tom?

NICK: She's been in burlesque. She's had flowers sent to her by European royalty. She's dined with young men of quality and social position. She's above Tom.

TOM (*comes running in, crossing to* JOE; *disgusted*): They were running when I got there. Frankie wouldn't take the bet. McCarthy didn't get a call till the stretch. I thought we were going to save all this money. Then McCarthy won by *two* lengths.

JOE: What'd he pay, fifteen to one?

TOM: Better, but Frankie wouldn't take the bet.

NICK (*throwing a dish towel across the room*): Well, for the love of Mike.

JOE: Give me the money.

TOM (*giving back the money*): We would have had about a thousand five hundred dollars.

JOE (*pause; bored, displeased*): Go up to Schwabacher-Frey and get me the biggest Rand-McNally map of the nations of Europe they've got. On your way back stop at one of the pawn shops on Third Street, and buy me a good revolver and some cartridges.

TOM: She's up in her room crying, Joe.

JOE: Go get me those things.

NICK (*crossing to center table; gets glasses*): What are you going to do, study the map, and then go out and shoot somebody?

JOE: I want to read the names of some European towns and rivers and valleys and mountains.

NICK: What do you want with the revolver? (*Goes to back of bar. Dries glasses.*)

JOE: I want to study it. I'm interested in things. Here's twenty dollars, Tom. Now go get them things.

TOM: A big map of Europe. And a revolver.

JOE: Get a good one. Tell the man you don't know anything about firearms and you're trusting him not to fool you. Don't pay more than ten dollars.

TOM: Joe, you got something on your mind. Don't go fool with a revolver.

JOE: Be sure it's a good one.

TOM: Joe.

JOE: What, Tom?

TOM: Joe, what do you send me out for crazy things for all the time?

JOE: They're not crazy, Tom. Now, get going.

TOM: What about Kitty, Joe?

JOE: Let her cry. It'll do her good.

TOM: If she comes in here while I'm gone, talk to her, will you, Joe? Tell her about me.

JOE: O.K. Get going. Don't load that gun. Just buy it and bring it here.

TOM (*going to stair landing, right*): You won't catch me loading any gun.

JOE: Wait a minute. Take these toys away.

TOM (*crossing to right of* JOE): Where'll I take them?

JOE: Give them to some kid. No. Take them up to Kitty. Toys stopped me from crying once. That's the reason I had you buy them. I wanted to see if I could find out *why* they stopped me from crying. I remember they seemed awfully stupid at the time.

Tom: Shall I, Joe? Take them up to Kitty? Do you think they'd stop *her* from crying?

Joe: They might. You get curious about the way they work and you forget whatever it is you're remembering that's making you cry. That's what they're for.

Tom: Yeah. Sure. The girl at the store asked me what I wanted with toys. I'll take them up to Kitty. (*Tragically.*) She's like a little girl. (*He goes out right.*)

Wesley: Mr. Nick, can I play the piano again?

Nick: Sure. Practice all you like—until I tell you to stop.

Wesley: You going to pay me for playing the piano?

Nick: Sure. I'll give you enough to get by on.

Wesley (*amazed and delighted*): Get money for playing the piano? (*He goes to the piano and begins to play quietly. Harry goes up on the little stage and listens to the music. After a while he begins a soft-shoe dance which is very quiet and relaxing.*)

Nick: What were you crying about?

Joe: My mother.

Nick: What about her?

Joe: She was dead. I stopped crying when they gave me the toys. (Nick's Mother, *a little old woman of sixty or so, dressed plainly in black, her face shining, comes in briskly, chattering loudly in Italian, gesturing.* Nick *is delighted to see her.*)

Nick's Mother (*in Italian*): Everything all right, Nickie?

Nick (*in Italian*): Sure, Mamma. (Nick's Mother *leaves as gaily and as noisily as she came.*)

Joe: Who was that?

Nick (*to* Joe, *proudly and a little sadly*): My mother. (*Still looking at the swinging doors.*)

Joe: What'd she say?

Nick: Nothing. Just wanted to see me. What do you want with that gun?

JOE: I study things, Nick. (*An old man who looks like* KIT CARSON *staggers in right, looks around; edges to bar; reaction to* NICK; *goes to left and moves about aimlessly and finally goes to chair left of center table.*)

KIT CARSON: Murphy's the name. Just an old trapper. Mind if I sit down?

JOE: Be delighted. What'll you drink?

KIT CARSON (*sitting down*): Beer. Same as I've been drinking. And thanks.

JOE (*to* NICK): Glass of beer, Nick. (NICK *brings the beer to the table, and goes back of bar.* KIT CARSON *swallows it in one swig, wipes his big white mustache with the back of his right hand.*)

KIT CARSON (*moving in*): I don't suppose you ever fell in love with a midget weighing thirty-nine pounds?

JOE: Can't say I have, but have another beer.

KIT CARSON (*intimately*): Thanks, thanks. Down in Gallup, twenty years ago. Fellow by the name of Rufus Jenkins came to town with six white horses and two black ones. Said he wanted a man to break the horses for him because his left leg was wood and he couldn't do it. Had a meeting at Parker's Mercantile Store and finally came to blows, me and Henry Walpal. Bashed his head with a brass cuspidor and ran away to Mexico, but he didn't die. (SAILOR *enters right and goes to bar.*) Couldn't speak a word. Took up with a cattle-breeder named Diego, educated in California. Spoke the language better than you and me. Said, "Your job, Murph, is to feed them prize bulls." I said, "Fine, what'll I feed them?" He said, "Hay, lettuce, salt, beer and aspirin." Came to blows two days later over an accordion he claimed I stole. I had *borrowed* it. During the fight I busted it over his head; ruined one of the finest accordions I ever saw. Grabbed a horse and rode back across the border. Texas. Got to talking with a fellow who looked honest. Turned out to be a Ranger who was looking for me. (KILLER *enters right. Sits in front of bar.*)

JOE: Yeah. You were saying, a thirty-nine-pound midget.

KIT CARSON: Will I ever forget that lady? Will I ever get over that amazon of small proportions?

JOE: Will you?

KIT CARSON: If I live to be sixty.

JOE: Sixty? You look more than sixty now.

KIT CARSON: That's trouble showing in my face. Trouble and complications. I was fifty-eight three months ago.

JOE: That accounts for it, then. Go ahead, tell me more.

KIT CARSON: Told the Texas Ranger my name was Rothstein, mining engineer from Pennsylvania, looking for something worth while. Mentioned two places in Houston. Nearly lost an eye early one morning, going down the stairs. (*Rises.*) Ran into a six-footer with an iron claw where his right hand was supposed to be. Said, "You broke up my home." Told him I was a stranger in Houston. The girls gathered at the top of the stairs to see a fight. Seven of them. Six feet and an iron claw. That's bad on the nerves. Kicked him in the mouth when he swung for my head with the claw. Would have lost an eye except for quick thinking. He rolled into the gutter and pulled a gun. Fired seven times. I was back upstairs. Left the place an hour later, dressed in silk and feathers, with a hat swung around over my face. Saw him standing on the corner, waiting. (*Crossing left.*) Said, "Care for a wiggle?" Said he didn't. I went on down the street and left town. I don't suppose you ever had to put a dress on to save your skin, did you? (*Crosses to left of center table and sits.*)

JOE (*signals* NICK *for beer*): No, and I never fell in love with a midget weighing thirty-nine pounds. Have another beer?

KIT CARSON: Thanks. Ever try to herd cattle on a bicycle? (NICK *crosses to left of center table with beer which* KIT *takes.* NICK *goes back to bar.*)

JOE: No. I never got around to that.

KIT CARSON: Left Houston with sixty cents in my pocket, gift of a girl named Lucinda. Walked fourteen miles in fourteen hours. Big house with barbwire all around, and big dogs. One thing I never could get around. Walked past the gate, anyway, from hunger and thirst. Dogs jumped up and came for me. Walked right into them, growing older every second. Went up to the door and knocked. Big Negress opened the door, closed it quick. Said, "On your way, white trash." Knocked again. Said, "On your way." Again. "On your way." Again. This time the old man himself opened the door, ninety, if he was a day. Sawed-off shotgun, too. Said, "I ain't looking for trouble, Father. I'm hungry and thirsty, name's Cavanaugh." Took me in and made mint juleps for the two of us. Said, "Living here alone, Father?" Said, "Drink and ask no questions. Maybe I am and maybe I ain't. You saw the lady. Draw your own conclusions." I'd heard of that, but didn't wink out of tact. If I told you that old Southern gentleman was my grandfather, you wouldn't believe me, would you?

JOE: I might.

KIT CARSON: Well, it so happens he wasn't. Would have been romantic if he had been, though.

JOE: Where did you herd cattle on a bicycle?

KIT CARSON: Toledo, Ohio, 1918.

JOE: Toledo, Ohio? They don't herd cattle in Toledo.

KIT CARSON: They don't anymore. They did in 1918. One fellow did, least-a-ways. Bookkeeper named Sam Gold. Straight from the East Side, New York. Sombrero, lariats, Bull Durham, two head of cattle and two bicycles. Called his place The Gold Bar Ranch, two acres, just outside the city limits. That was the year of the War, you'll remember.

JOE: Yeah, I remember, but how about herding them two cows on a bicycle? How'd you do it?

KIT CARSON: Easiest thing in the world. Rode no hands. Had to, otherwise couldn't lasso the cows. Worked for Sam Gold till the cows ran away. Bicycles scared them. They went into Toledo. Never saw hide nor hair of them again. Advertised in every paper, but never got them back.

Broke his heart. Sold both bikes and returned to New York. Took four aces from a deck of red cards and walked to town. Poker. Fellow in the game named Chuck Collins, liked to gamble. Told him with a smile I didn't suppose he'd care to bet a hundred dollars I wouldn't hold four aces the next hand. Called it. My cards were red on the blank side. The other cards were blue. Plumb forgot all about it. Showed him four aces. Ace of spades, ace of clubs, ace of diamonds, ace of hearts. I'll remember them four cards if I live to be sixty. Would have been killed on the spot except for the hurricane that year.

JOE: Hurricane?

KIT CARSON: You haven't forgotten the Toledo hurricane of 1918, have you?

JOE: No. There was no hurricane in Toledo in 1918, or any other year.

KIT CARSON: For the love of God, then what do you suppose that commotion was? And how come I came to in Chicago dream-walking down State Street?

JOE: I guess they scared you.

KIT CARSON: No, that wasn't it. You go back to the papers of November, 1918, and I think you'll find there was a hurricane in Toledo. I remember sitting on the roof of a two-story house, floating northwest.

JOE (*seriously*): Northwest?

KIT CARSON: Now, son, don't tell me *you* don't believe me, either?

JOE (*very seriously, energetically and sharply*): Of course I believe you. Living is an art. It's not bookkeeping. It takes a lot of rehearsing for a man to get to be himself.

KIT CARSON (*thoughtfully, smiling*): You're the first man I've ever met who believes me.

JOE (*seriously*): Have another beer. (TOM *comes in right with the Rand-McNally book, the revolver and the box of cartridges.*)

JOE (*to* TOM): Did you give her the toys?

TOM: Yeah, I gave them to her.

JOE: Did she stop crying?

TOM: No. She started crying harder than ever.

JOE: That's funny. I wonder why.

TOM: Joe, if I was a minute earlier, Frankie would have taken the bet and now we'd have about a thousand five hundred dollars. How much of it would you have given me, Joe?

JOE: If she'd marry you—*all* of it.

TOM: Would you, Joe?

JOE (*opening packages, examining book first, and revolver next*): Sure. In this realm there's only one subject, and you're it. It's my duty to see that my subject is happy.

TOM: Joe, do you think we'll ever have eighty dollars for a race sometime again when there's a fifteen-to-one shot that we like, weather good, track fast, they get off to a good start, our horse doesn't get a call till the stretch, we think we're going to lose all that money, and then it wins, by a nose?

JOE: I didn't quite get that.

TOM: You know what I mean.

JOE: You mean the impossible. No, Tom, we won't. We were just a little late, that's all.

TOM: We might, Joe.

JOE: It's not likely.

TOM: Then how am I ever going to make enough money to marry her?

JOE: I don't know, Tom. Maybe you aren't.

TOM: Joe, I got to marry Kitty. (*Shaking his head.*) You ought to see the crazy room she lives in.

JOE: What kind of a room is it?

TOM: It's little. It crowds you in. It's bad, Joe. Kitty don't belong in a place like that.

JOE: You want to take her away from there?

TOM: Yeah. I want her to live in a house where there's room enough to live. Kitty ought to have a garden, or something.

JOE: You want to take care of her?

Tom: Yeah, sure, Joe. I ought to take care of somebody good that makes me feel like *I'm* somebody.

Joe: That means you'll have to get a job. What can you do?

Tom: I finished high school, but I don't know what I can do.

Joe: Sometimes when you think about it, what do you think you'd like to do?

Tom: Just sit around like you, Joe, and have somebody run errands for me and drink champagne and take things easy and never be broke and never worry about money.

Joe: That's a noble ambition.

Nick: How do you do it?

Joe: I really don't know, but I think you've got to have the full co-operation of the Good Lord.

Nick: I can't understand the way you talk.

Tom: Joe, shall I go back and see if I can get her to stop crying?

Joe: Give me a hand and I'll go with you.

Tom (*amazed*): What! You're going to get up already?

Joe: She's crying, isn't she?

Tom: She's crying. Worse than ever now.

Joe: I thought the toys would stop her.

Tom: I've seen you sit in one place from four in the morning till two the next morning.

Joe: At my best, Tom, I don't travel by foot. That's all. Come on. Give me a hand. I'll find some way to stop her from crying.

Tom: Joe, I never did tell you. You're a different kind of a guy.

Joe: Don't be silly. I don't understand things. I'm trying to understand them. (Tom *helps* Joe *up. He is a little drunk. They go out right together. The telephone rings.* Dudley *jumps to his feet and runs to it.*)

Act III

SCENE: *Room Twenty-one of The New York Hotel, around the corner from Nick's. This is set inside the main set. There is a bed right; a screen above bed; a door back of screen; a window in back of bed. A dresser is painted on the screen. A small table above right of bed.* KITTY DUVAL, *in a dress she has carried around with her from the early days in Ohio, is seated on the bed, tying a ribbon in her hair. She looks at herself in the mirror. She is deeply grieved at the change she sees in herself. She stares at the bare, desolate walls of the room. Looks into the mirror again. Takes off the ribbon, angry and hurt. She lifts a book from the bed and tries to read. She begins to sob again. Takes an old picture of herself from foot of bed and looks at it. And sobs harder than ever, falling on the bed and burying her face. She turns over on the other side, as if even with her eyes closed she cannot escape her sorrow. From one of the other rooms of the hotel is coming the voice of a young man singing "My Gal Sal." There is a knock at the door.*

KITTY (*sobbing*): Who is it?

TOM'S VOICE: Kitty, it's me. Tom. Me and Joe. (KITTY *looks around the room, smiles at the remembrance of* TOM, *looks around the desolate room and falls back sobbing.* JOE, *followed by* TOM, *comes in quietly.* JOE *is holding a rather large toy carousel. He takes the room in swiftly. Amazed. He sets the toy carousel on the floor, at the foot of* KITTY'S *bed.*)

276

Tom (*standing over* Kitty *and bending down close to her*):
Don't cry any more, Kitty.

Kitty (*not looking up, sobbing*): I don't like this life. (Joe *starts the carousel which makes a strange, sorrowful, tinkling music. The music begins slowly, becomes swift, gradually slows down, and ends.* Joe *himself is interested in the toy, watches and listens to it carefully.*)

Tom: Kitty. Joe got up from his chair at Nick's just to get you a toy and come here. This one makes music. We rode all over town in a cab to get it. Listen. (Kitty *sits up slowly, listening, while* Tom *watches her and* Joe. *Everything happens slowly and somberly.* Kitty *notices the photograph of herself when she was a little girl. Lifts it, and looks at it again.*)

Tom (*looking*): Who's that little girl, Kitty?

Kitty: That's me. When I was seven. (*Hands the photo to* Tom.)

Tom: Gee, you're pretty, Kitty. (Joe *reaches up for the photograph, which* Tom *hands to him.* Tom *returns to* Kitty *whom he finds as pretty now as she was at seven.* Joe *studies the photograph.* Kitty *looks up at* Tom. *There is no doubt that they really love one another.* Joe *looks up at them.*)

Kitty: Tom?

Tom (*eagerly*): Yeah, Kitty.

Kitty: Tom, when you were a little boy what did you want to be?

Tom (*a little bewildered, but eager to please her*): What, Kitty?

Kitty: Do you remember when you were a little boy?

Tom (*thoughtfully*): Yeah, I remember sometimes, Kitty.

Kitty: What did you want to be?

Tom (*looks at* Joe. Joe *holds* Tom's *eyes a moment; then* Tom *is able to speak*): Sometimes I wanted to be a locomotive engineer. Sometimes I wanted to be a policeman.

KITTY: I wanted to be a great actress. (*She looks up into* TOM's *face*.) Tom, didn't you ever want to be a doctor?

TOM (*looks at* JOE; JOE *holds* TOM's *eyes again, encouraging* TOM *by his serious expression to go on talking*): Yeah, now I remember. Sure, Kitty. I wanted to be a doctor—*once*.

KITTY (*smiling sadly*): I'm so glad. Because I wanted to be an actress and have a young doctor come to the theater and see me and fall in love with me and send me flowers. (JOE *pantomimes to* TOM, *demanding that he go on talking*.)

TOM: I would do that, Kitty.

KITTY: I wouldn't know who it was, and then one day I'd see him in the street and fall in love with him. I wouldn't know *he* was the one who was in love with me. I'd think about him all the time. I'd dream about him. I'd dream of being near him the rest of my life. I'd dream of having children that looked like him. I wouldn't be an actress all the time. Only until I found him and fell in love with him. After that we'd take a train and go to beautiful cities and see the wonderful people everywhere and give money to the poor and whenever people were sick he'd go to them and make them well again. (TOM *looks at* JOE, *bewildered, confused, and full of sorrow.* KITTY *is deep in memory, almost in a trance.*)

JOE (*gently*): Talk to her, Tom. Be the wonderful young doctor she dreamed about and never found. Go ahead. Correct the errors of the world.

TOM: Joe. (*Pathetically.*) I don't know what to say. (*There is rowdy singing in the hall. A loud young* VOICE *sings:* "*Sailing, sailing, over the bounding main.*")

VOICE: Kitty. Oh, Kitty! (KITTY *stirs, shocked, coming out of the trance.*) Where the hell are you? Oh, Kitty. (TOM *jumps up, furiously.*)

WOMAN'S VOICE (*in the hall*): Who you looking for, Sailor Boy?

VOICE: The most beautiful lay in the world.

WOMAN'S VOICE: Don't go any further.

VOICE (*with impersonal contempt*): You? No. Not you. Kitty. You stink.

WOMAN'S VOICE (*rasping, angry*): Don't you dare talk to me that way. You pickpocket.

VOICE (*still impersonal, but louder*): Oh, I see. Want to get tough, hey? Close the door. Go hide.

WOMAN'S VOICE: You pickpocket. All of you. (*The door slams.*)

VOICE (*roaring with laughter which is very sad*): Oh—Kitty. Room Twenty-one. Where the hell is that room?

TOM (*to* JOE): Joe, I'll kill him.

KITTY (*fully herself again, terribly frightened*): Who is it? (*She looks long and steadily at* TOM *and* JOE. TOM *is standing, excited and angry.* JOE *is completely at ease, his expression full of pity.*)

JOE (*gently*): Tom. Just take him away.

VOICE: Here it is. Number Twenty-one. Three naturals. Heaven. My blue heaven. The west, a nest, and you. Just Molly and me. (*Tragically.*) Ah, to hell with everything. (*There is a loud knock at the door.* KITTY *turns away, as if seeking some place to be safe and protected.* JOE *doesn't even look toward the door.* TOM *opens the door.* JOE *turns and looks. In the doorway stands a young* SAILOR *—a good-looking boy of no more than twenty or so who is only drunk and lonely.*)

SAILOR: Hiya, Kitty. (*Pause.*) Oh. Visitors. Sorry. A thousand apologies. I'll come back later.

TOM (*taking him by the shoulders, furiously*): If you do, I'll kill you. (*He pushes the frightened* SAILOR *away and closes the door.*)

JOE: Tom, you stay with Kitty. I'm going down to Union Square to hire an automobile. I'll be back in a few minutes. We'll ride out to the ocean and watch the sun go down. Then we'll ride down the Great Highway to Half Moon Bay. We'll have supper down there, and you and Kitty can dance.

Tom (*stupefied, unable to express his amazement and grati-tude*): Joe, you mean you're going to go on an errand for *me?* You mean you're not going to send me?

Joe: That's right. (*He gestures toward* Kitty, *indicating that* Tom *shall talk to her, protect the innocence in her which is in so much danger when* Tom *isn't near, which* Tom *loves so deeply.*)

ACT IV

SCENE: Nick's again, *a little later. We are back to the time when* TOM *is helping* JOE *out of the place, on their way to* KITTY'S. *They are almost offstage when the lights are on.*

WESLEY, *the colored boy, is at the piano, playing the same song—at the same place.* HARRY *is on the little stage dancing.* WILLIE *is at marble game.* NICK *is behind the bar.* DUDLEY *is at table right. The* ARAB *is in his place.* KIT CARSON *is asleep on his folded arms.*

DRUNK *comes in right, goes to the telephone for nickel that might be in the return chute.* NICK *goes to him.* DRUNK *shows money. Both cross to bar.* NICK *to back of bar, hands* DRUNK *a shot glass and bottle.*

DRUNK: To the old, God bless them. (*Another.*) To the new, God love them. (*Another.*) To—children and small animals, like little dogs that don't bite. (*Another. Loudly.*) To reforestation. (*Searches for money. Finds some.*) To—President Taft. (*He goes out right. The telephone rings.* KIT CARSON *jumps up and starts to shadow box.* DUDLEY *runs to phone.*)

KIT CARSON: Come on, *all* of you, if you're looking for trouble. I never asked for quarter and I always gave it.

NICK (*reproachfully*): Hey, Kit Carson.

DUDLEY (*on the phone*): Hello. Who? Nick? Yes. He's here. (*To* NICK.) It's for you. I think it's important.

NICK (*crossing to the phone*): Important! *What's* important?

DUDLEY: He sounded like big shot.

NICK: Big *what?* (*To* WESLEY *and* HARRY.) Hey, you. Quiet.
I want to hear this important stuff. (WESLEY *stops playing
the piano.* HARRY *stops dancing.* KIT CARSON *comes close to
right of* NICK.)

KIT CARSON: If there's anything I can do, name it. I'll do it for
you. I'm fifty-eight years old; been through three wars;
married four times; the father of countless children whose
names I don't even know. I've got no money. I live from
hand to mouth. But if there's anything I can do, name it. I'll
do it.

NICK: Listen, Pop. For a moment, please sit down and go
back to sleep—*for me.*

KIT CARSON (*crossing to left of center table*): I can do that,
too. (*He sits down, folds his arms, and puts his head into
them. But not for long. As* NICK *begins to talk, he listens
carefully, gets to his feet, and then begins to express in
pantomime the moods of each of* NICK's *remarks.*)

NICK (*on phone*): Yeah? (*Pause.*) Who? Oh, I see. (*Listens.*)
Why don't you leave them alone? (*Listens.*) The church
people? Well, to hell with the church people. I'm a Catholic
myself. (*Listens.*) All right. I'll send them away. I'll tell
them to lay low for a couple of days. Yeah, I know how it is.
(*Is about to hang up.* NICK's *daughter* ANNA *comes in right
shyly, looking at her father, and stands unnoticed by the
piano.*) What? (*very angry*): Listen. I don't like that Blick.
He was here this morning, and I told him not to come back.
I'll keep the girls out of here. You keep Blick out of here.
(*Listens.*) I know his brother-in-law is important, but I
don't want him to come down here. He looks for trouble
everywhere, and he always finds it. I don't break any laws.
I've got a dive in the lousiest part of town. Five years nobody's been robbed, murdered or gypped. I leave people
alone. Your swanky joints uptown make trouble for you
every night. (NICK *gestures to* WESLEY—*keeps listening on
the phone—puts his hand over the mouthpiece. To* WESLEY
and HARRY.) Start playing again. My ears have got a headache. Go into your dance, son. (WESLEY *begins to play*

again. HARRY *begins to dance.* NICK, *into mouthpiece.*)
Yeah. I'll keep them out. Just see that Blick doesn't come
around and start something. O.K. (*He hangs up, crosses to
rear center.*)

KIT CARSON (*following to left of* NICK): Trouble coming?

NICK: That lousy Vice Squad again. It's that gorilla Blick.

KIT CARSON: Anybody at all. You can count on me. What kind
of a gorilla is this gorilla Blick?

NICK: Very dignified. Toenails on his fingers.

ANNA (*to* KIT CARSON, *with great, warm, beautiful pride,
pointing at* NICK): That's my father.

KIT CARSON (*leaping with amazement at the beautiful voice,
the wondrous face, the magnificent event*): Well, bless your
heart, child. Bless your lovely heart. I had a little daughter
point me out in a crowd once.

NICK (*surprised*): Anna. What the hell are you doing here?
Get back home where you belong and help Grandma cook
me some supper. (ANNA *smiles at her father, understanding
him, knowing that his words are words of love. She turns
and goes right, looking at him all the way out, as much as
to say that she would cook for him the rest of her life.* NICK
stares at the swinging doors. KIT CARSON *moves toward
them, two or three steps.* ANNA *pushes open one of the
doors and peeks in, to look at her father again. She waves
to him. Turns and runs.* NICK *is very sad. He doesn't know
what to do. He gets a glass and a bottle. Pours himself a
drink. Swallows some. It isn't enough, so he pours more and
swallows the whole drink. To himself.*) My beautiful, beautiful baby. Anna, she is you again. (*He brings out a handkerchief, touches his eyes, and blows his nose.* KIT CARSON
moves close to NICK, *watching* NICK's *face.* NICK *looks at
him. Loudly, almost making* KIT *jump.*) You're broke,
aren't you?

KIT CARSON: Always. *Always.*

NICK: All right. Go into the kitchen and give Sam a hand. Eat
some food and when you come back you can have a couple
of beers.

KIT CARSON (*studying* NICK): Anything at all. I know a good man when I see one. (*He goes out back center.* ELSIE MANDELSPIEGEL *comes in right. She is a beautiful, dark girl, with a sorrowful, wise, dreaming face, almost on the verge of tears, and full of pity. There is an aura of dream about her. She moves softly and gently, as if everything around her were unreal and pathetic.* DUDLEY *doesn't notice her for a moment or two. When he does finally see her, he is so amazed, he can barely move or speak. Her presence has the effect of changing him completely. He gets up from his chair, as if in a trance, and walks toward her, smiling sadly.*)

ELSIE (*crossing to chair right of center table*): Hello, Dudley.

DUDLEY: Elsie.

ELSIE (*sits*): I'm sorry. So many people are sick. Last night a little boy died. I love you, but—

DUDLEY (*crossing to chair left of center table*): Elsie. You'll never know how glad I am to see you. (*Sits.*) Just to *see* you. I was afraid I'd never see you again. It was driving me crazy. I didn't want to live. Honest. (*The* KILLER *and her* SIDEKICK *come in right and go to bar.*) I know. You told me before, but I can't help it, Elsie. I love you.

ELSIE: I know you love me, and I love you, but don't you see love is impossible in this world?

DUDLEY: Maybe it isn't, Elsie.

ELSIE: Love is for birds. They have wings to fly away on when it's time for flying. For tigers in the jungle because they don't know their end. We know *our* end. Every night I watch over poor, dying men. I hear them breathing, crying, talking in their sleep. Crying for air and water and love, for mother and field and sunlight. *We* can never know love or greatness. We *should* know both.

DUDLEY: Elsie, I love you.

ELSIE: You want to live. *I* want to live, too, but where? Where can we escape our poor world?

DUDLEY: Elsie, we'll find a place.

ELSIE: All right. We'll try again. We'll go together to a room in a cheap hotel, and dream that the world is beautiful, and that living is full of love and greatness. But in the morning, can we forget debts, and duties, and the cost of ridiculous things?

DUDLEY: Sure, we can, Elsie.

ELSIE: All right, Dudley. Of course. (*Rises.*) Come on. The time for the new pathetic war has come. Let's hurry, before they dress you, stand you in line, hand you a gun, and have you kill and be killed. (*She leads him out right.*)

KILLER: Nick, what the hell kind of a joint are you running?

NICK: Well, it's not out of the world. It's on a street in a city, and people come and go. They bring whatever they've got with them and they say what they must say.

THE OTHER STREETWALKER: It's floozies like her that raise hell with our racket.

NICK: Oh, yeah. Finnegan telephoned.

KILLER: That mouse in elephant's body?

THE OTHER STREETWALKER: What the hell does *he* want?

NICK: Spend your time at the movies for the next couple of days.

KILLER: They're all lousy. (*Mincing and smoking.*) All about love.

NICK: Lousy or not lousy, for a couple of days the flatfoots are going to be romancing you, so stay out of here, and lay low.

KILLER: I always was a pushover for a man in uniform, with a badge, a club and a gun. (KRUPP *comes in right. The* GIRLS *put down their drinks.*)

NICK: O.K., get going. (*The* GIRLS *begin to leave and meet* KRUPP, *who pauses to look them over.*)

THE OTHER STREETWALKER: We was just going.

KILLER: We was formerly models at Magnin's. (*They go out right.*)

KRUPP (*at the bar*): The strike isn't enough, so they've got to put us on the tails of the girls, too. I don't know. I wish to God I was back in the Sunset holding the hands of kids going home from school, where I belong. I don't like trouble. Give me a beer. (NICK *gives him a beer. He drinks some.*) Right now, McCarthy, my best friend, is with sixty strikers who want to stop the finks who are going to try to unload the *Mary Luckenbach* tonight. Why the hell McCarthy ever became a longshoreman instead of a professor of some kind is something I'll never know.

NICK: Cowboys and Indians, cops and robbers, longshoremen and finks.

KRUPP: They're all guys who are trying to be happy; trying to make a living; support a family; bring up children; enjoy sleep. Go to a movie; take a drive on Sunday. They're all good guys, so out of nowhere, comes trouble. All they want is a chance to get out of debt and relax in front of a radio while Amos and Andy go through their act. What the hell do they always want to make trouble for? I been thinking everything over, Nick, and you know what I think?

NICK: No. What?

KRUPP: I think we're all crazy. It came to me while I was on my way to Pier Twenty-seven. All of a sudden it hit me like a ton of bricks. A thing like that never happened to me before. Here we are in this wonderful world, full of all the wonderful things—here we are—all of us, and look at us. Just look at us. We're crazy. We're nuts. We've got everything, but we always feel lousy and dissatisfied just the same.

NICK: Of course we're crazy. Even so, we've got to go on living together.

KRUPP: There's no hope. I don't suppose it's right for an officer of the law to feel the way I feel, but, by God, right or not right, that's how I feel. Why are we all so lousy? This is a good world. It's wonderful to get up in the morning and go out for a little walk and smell the trees and see the streets and the kids going to school and the clouds in the sky. It's wonderful just to be able to move around and whistle a song if you feel like it, or maybe try to sing one. This is a nice world. So why do they make all the trouble?

NICK: I don't know. Why?

KRUPP: We're crazy, that's why. We're no good any more. All the corruption everywhere. The poor kids selling themselves. A couple of years ago they were in grammar school. Everybody trying to get a lot of money in a hurry. Everybody betting the horses. Nobody going quietly for a little walk to the ocean. Nobody taking things easy and not wanting to make some kind of a killing. Nick, I'm going to quit being a cop. Let somebody else keep law and order. The stuff I hear about at headquarters. I'm thirty-seven years old, and I still can't get used to it. The only trouble is, the wife'll raise hell.

NICK: Ah, the wife.

KRUPP: She's a wonderful woman, Nick. We've got two of the swellest boys in the world. Twelve and seven years old.

NICK: I didn't know that. (ARAB, WESLEY *and* WILLIE *listen to* KRUPP.)

KRUPP: Sure. But what'll I do? I've wanted to quit for seven years. I wanted to quit the day they began putting me through the school. I didn't quit. What'll I do if I quit? Where's money going to be coming in from?

NICK: That's one of the reasons we're all crazy. We don't know where it's going to be coming in from, except from wherever it happens to be coming in from at the time, which we don't usually like. (ARAB, WESLEY *and* WILLIE *go back to former interests.*)

KRUPP: Every once in a while I catch myself being mean, hating people just because they're down and out, broke and hungry, sick or drunk. And then when I'm with the stuffed shirts at headquarters, all of a sudden I'm nice to them, trying to make an impression. On who? People I don't like. And I feel disgusted. (*With finality.*) I'm going to quit. That's all. Quit. Out. I'm going to give them back the uniform and the gadgets that go with it. I don't want any part of it. (*Takes off badge and slams it on bar.*) This is a good world. What do they want to make all the trouble for all the time?

ARAB: No foundation. All the way down the line.

KRUPP: What?

ARAB: No foundation. No foundation.

KRUPP: I'll say there's no foundation.

ARAB: All the way down the line.

KRUPP (*to* NICK): Is that all he ever says?

NICK: That's all he's been saying *this* week.

KRUPP: What is he, anyway?

NICK: He's an Arab, or something like that.

KRUPP: No, I mean what's he do for a living?

NICK (*to* ARAB): What do you do for a living, brother?

ARAB: Work. Work all my life. All my life, work. From small boy to old man, work. In old country, work. In new country, work. In New York. Pittsburgh. Detroit. Chicago. Imperial Valley. San Francisco. Work. No beg. Work. For what? Nothing. Three boys in old country. Twenty years, not see. Lost. Dead. Who knows? What. What-not. No foundation. All the way down the line.

KRUPP: What'd he say last week?

NICK: Didn't say anything. Played the harmonica.

ARAB: Old country song, I play. (*He brings a harmonica from his back pocket and begins to play an old country song.*)

KRUPP: Seems like a nice guy.

NICK: Nicest guy in the world.

KRUPP (*bitterly*): But crazy. Just like all the rest of us. Stark raving mad. (WESLEY *and* HARRY *long ago stopped playing and dancing. They sat at left center table together and talked for a while; then began playing casino or rummy. When the* ARAB *begins his solo on the harmonica, they stop their game to listen.*)

WESLEY: You hear that?

HARRY: That's *something.*

WESLEY: That's crying. That's crying.

HARRY: I want to make people laugh.

WESLEY: That's deep, deep crying. That's crying a long time ago. That's crying a thousand years ago. Some place five thousand miles away.

HARRY: Do you think you can play to that?

WESLEY: I want to *sing* to that, but I can't *sing.*

HARRY: You try and play to that. I'll try to dance. (WESLEY

goes to the piano, and after closer listening, he begins to accompany the harmonica solo. HARRY goes to the little stage and after a few efforts begins to dance to the song. This keeps up quietly for some time. KRUPP and NICK have been silent, KRUPP drinking a beer; NICK fooling around behind the bar.)

KRUPP: Well, anyhow, Nick. (*Picks up badge and puts it on.*)

NICK: Hmmmmmmm?

KRUPP: What I said. Forget it.

NICK: Sure.

KRUPP: It gets me down once in a while.

NICK: No harm in talking.

KRUPP: Keep the girls out of here. (*Starts for door right. HARRY starts double time whirl.*)

NICK: Take it easy.

ACT V

SCENE: *Nick's, that evening. Foghorns are heard throughout
this scene. A* GENTLEMAN *in evening clothes and a top hat,
and his* LADY, *also in evening clothes, are entering right.*

WILLIE, *the marble-game maniac, is still at the marble game.*
NICK *is behind the bar.* JOE *is at center table, looking at the
book of maps of the countries of Europe. The box containing the revolver and the box containing cartridges are on
the table, beside his glass. He is at peace, his hat tilted back
on his head, a calm expression on his face.* TOM *is leaning
against the bar, dreaming of love and* KITTY. *The* ARAB *is
gone.* WESLEY *and* HARRY, *the comedian, are gone for the
moment.* KIT CARSON *is watching the boy play the marble
game.*

The MAN *and* LADY *take left center table. She sits right of it,
he left.* NICK *gives them a menu.*

*Outside, in the street, the Salvation Army people are playing
a song. Big drum, cornet, big horn, and tambourine. They
are singing too. "The Blood of the Lamb." The music and
words come into the place faintly and comically. This is followed by an old sinner testifying; it's the* DRUNK. *All his
words are not intelligible, but his message is unmistakable.
He is saved. He wants to sin no more. And so on.*

LADY: Oh, come on, please. (*The* GENTLEMAN *follows miser-
ably.*)

DRUNK (*testifying, unmistakably drunk*): Brothers and sisters.
I was a sinner. I chewed tobacco and chased women. Oh, I

290

sinned, brothers and sisters. And then I was saved. Saved by the Salvation Army, God forgive me.

JOE: Let's see now. Here's a city. Pribor. Czechoslovakia. Little, lovely, lonely Czechoslovakia. I wonder what kind of a place Pribor was? (*Calling.*) Pribor! *Pribor!* (TOM *leaps.*)

LADY: What's the matter with him?

MAN: Drunk.

TOM: Who you calling, Joe?

JOE: Pribor.

TOM: Who's Pribor?

JOE: He's a Czech. And a Slav. A Czechoslovakian.

LADY: How interesting.

MAN: He's drunk.

JOE: Tom, Pribor's a city in Czechoslovakia.

TOM: Oh. (*Pause.*) You sure were nice to her, Joe.

JOE: Kitty Duval? She's one of the finest people in the world.

TOM: It sure was nice of you to hire an automobile and take us for a drive along the ocean-front and down to Half Moon Bay.

JOE: Those three hours were the most delightful, the most somber, and the most beautiful I have ever known.

TOM: Why, Joe?

JOE: Why? I'm a student. (*Lifting his voice.*) Tom. (TOM *crosses and sits left of center table; quietly.*) I'm a student. I study all things. All. All. And when my study reveals something of beauty in a place or in a person where by all rights only ugliness or death should be revealed, then I know how full of goodness this life is. And that's a good thing to know. That's a truth I shall always seek to verify.

LADY: Are you *sure* he's drunk?

MAN: He's either drunk, or just naturally crazy.

TOM: Joe?

JOE: Yeah.

TOM: You won't get sore or anything?

JOE: What is it, Tom?

TOM: Joe, where do you get all that money? You paid for the automobile. You paid for supper and the two bottles of

champagne at the Half Moon Bay Restaurant. You moved
Kitty out of The New York Hotel around the corner to the
St. Francis Hotel on Powell Street. I saw you pay her rent.
I saw you give her money for new clothes. Where do you
get all that money, Joe? Three years now and I've never
asked.

JOE (*gestures the question aside impatiently. He smiles with
some inner thought and suddenly lifts the box containing
the gun, and the other with the cartridges. Looking at* TOM
sorrowfully, a little irritated, not so much with TOM *as with
the world and himself, his own superiority. He speaks clearly, slowly, and solemnly*): Now don't be a fool, Tom. Listen
carefully. If anybody's got any money—to hoard or to throw
away—you can be sure he stole it from other people. Not
from rich people who can spare it, but from poor people
who can't. From their lives and from their dreams. I'm no
exception. I *earned* the money I throw away. I stole it like
everybody else does. I hurt people to get it. Loafing around
this way, I *still* earn money. The money itself earns *more*. I
still hurt people. I don't know who they are, or where they
are. If I did, I'd feel worse than I do. I've got a Christian
conscience in a world that's got no conscience at all. The
world's trying to get some sort of a *social* conscience, but
it's having a devil of a time trying to do *that*. I've got
money. I'll always have money, as long as this world stays
the way it is. I don't work. I don't make anything. (*He
sips*.) I drink. I worked when I was a kid. I worked *hard*.
I mean hard, Tom. People are supposed to enjoy living. I
got tired. (*He lifts the gun and looks at it while he talks*.)
I decided to get even on the world. Well, you can't enjoy
living unless you work. Unless you do something. I don't
do anything. I don't *want* to do anything any more. There
isn't anything I can do that won't make me feel embarrassed. Because I can't do simple, good things. I haven't the
patience. And I'm too smart. Money is the guiltiest thing
in the world. It stinks. Now, don't ever bother me about it
again.

TOM: I didn't mean to make you feel bad, Joe.

JOE (*slowly*): Here. Take this gun out in the street and give it to some worthy holdup man.

LADY: What's he saying?

MAN (*uncrosses legs*): You wanted to visit a honky-tonk. Well, *this* is a honky-tonk. (*To the world.*) Married twenty-eight years and she's still looking for adventure.

TOM: How should I know who's a holdup man?

JOE: Take it away. Give it to somebody.

TOM (*bewildered*): Do I *have* to *give* it to somebody?

JOE: Of course.

TOM: Can't I take it back and get some of our money?

JOE: Don't talk like a business man. Look around and find somebody who appears to be in need of a gun and give it to him. It's a good gun, isn't it?

TOM: The man said it was, but how can I tell who needs a gun?

JOE: Tom, you've seen good people who needed guns, haven't you?

TOM: I don't remember. Joe, I might give it to the wrong kind of guy. He might do something crazy.

JOE: All right. I'll find somebody myself. (TOM *rises*.) Here's some money. Go get me this week's *Life, Liberty, Time,* and six or seven packages of chewing gum.

TOM (*swiftly, in order to remember each item*): *Life, Liberty, Time,* and six or seven packages of chewing gum?

JOE: That's right.

TOM: All that chewing gum? What kind?

JOE: Any kind. Mix 'em up. All kinds.

TOM: Licorice, too?

JOE: Licorice, by all means.

TOM: Juicy Fruit?

JOE: Juicy Fruit.

TOM: Tutti-frutti?

JOE: Is there such a gum?

TOM: I think so.

JOE: All right. Tutti-frutti, too. Get *all* the kinds. Get as many kinds as they're selling.

TOM: *Life, Liberty, Time,* and all the different kinds of gum. (*He begins to go right.*)

JOE (*calling after him loudly*): Get some jelly beans too. All the different colors.

TOM: All right, Joe.

JOE: And the longest panatela cigar you can find. Six of them.

TOM: Panatela. I got it.

JOE: Give a news-kid a dollar.

TOM: O.K., Joe.

JOE: Give some old man a dollar.

TOM: O.K., Joe.

JOE: Give them Salvation Army people in the street a couple of dollars and ask them to sing that song that goes— (*He sings loudly.*) "Let the lower lights be burning, send a gleam across the wave."

TOM (*swiftly*): "Let the lower lights be burning, send a gleam across the wave."

JOE: That's it. (*He goes on with the song, very loudly and religiously.*) "Some poor, dying, struggling seaman, you may rescue, you may save." (*Halts.*)

TOM: O.K., Joe. I got it. *Life, Liberty, Time,* all the kinds of gum they're selling, jelly beans, six panatela cigars, a dollar for a news-kid, a dollar for an old man, two dollars for the Salvation Army. "Let the lower lights be burning, send a gleam across the wave."

JOE: That's it. (TOM *goes out right.*)

LADY: He's absolutely insane.

MAN (*wearily*): You asked me to take you to a honky-tonk, instead of to the Mark Hopkins. You're *here* in a honky-tonk. I can't help it if he's crazy. Do you want to go back to where people *aren't* crazy?

LADY: No, not just yet.

MAN: Well, all right then. Don't be telling me every minute that he's crazy.

LADY: You needn't be huffy about it. (MAN *refuses to answer.*

When JOE *began to sing,* KIT CARSON *turned away from the marble game and listened. While the* MAN *and* LADY *are arguing he comes over to* JOE's *table.*)

KIT CARSON: Presbyterian?

JOE: I attended a Presbyterian Sunday school.

KIT CARSON: Fond of singing?

JOE: On occasion. Have a drink?

KIT CARSON: Thanks.

JOE: Get a glass and sit down. (KIT CARSON *gets a glass from* NICK, *returns to the table, sits down,* JOE *pours him a drink, they touch glasses just as the Salvation Army people begin to fulfill the request. They sip some champagne, and at the proper moment begin to sing the song together, sipping champagne, raising hell with the tune, swinging it, and so on.*) Always was fond of that song. Used to sing it at the top of my voice. Never saved a seaman in my life.

KIT CARSON: I saved a seaman once. Well, he wasn't exactly a seaman. He was a darky named Wellington. Heavy-set sort of a fellow. Nice personality, but no friends to speak of. Not until I came along, at any rate. In New Orleans. In the summer of the year 1899. No, '98. I was a lot younger of course, and had no mustache, but was regarded by many people as a man of means.

JOE: Know anything about guns?

KIT CARSON: All there is to know. Didn't fight the Ojibways for nothing. Up there in the Lake Takalooca Country, in Michigan. (*Remembering.*) Along about in 1881 or two. Fought 'em right up to the shore of the Lake. Made 'em swim for Canada. One fellow in particular, an Indian named Harry Daisy.

JOE (*opening the box containing the revolver*): What sort of a gun would you say this is? Any good?

KIT CARSON (*at sight of gun, he is scared to death*): Yep. That looks like a pretty nice hunk of shooting iron. That's a six-shooter. Shot a man with a six-shooter once. Got him through the palm of his right hand. Lifted his arm to wave to a friend. Thought it was a bird. Fellow named, I believe, Carroway. Larrimore Carroway.

JOE: Know how to work one of these things? (*He offers* KIT CARSON *the revolver, which is old and enormous.*)

KIT CARSON (*laughing at the absurd question*): Know how to work it? Hand me that little gun, son, and I'll show you all about it. (JOE *hands* KIT *the revolver. Obviously bluffing.*) Let's see now. This is probably a new kind of six-shooter. After my time. Haven't nicked an Indian in years. I believe this here place is supposed to move out. (*He fools around and gets the barrel out for loading.*) That's it. There it is.

JOE: Look all right?

KIT CARSON: It's a good gun. You've got a good gun there, son. I'll explain it to you. You see these holes? Well, that's where you put the cartridges.

JOE (*taking some cartridges out of the box*): Here. Show me how it's done.

KIT CARSON (*scared to death but bluffing beautifully*): Well, son, you take 'em one by one and put 'em in the holes, like this. There's one. Two. Three. Four. Five. Six. Then you get the barrel back in place. Then cock it. Then all you got to do is aim and fire. (*He points the gun at the* LADY. *The gun is loaded, but uncocked.*)

JOE: It's all set?

KIT CARSON: Ready to kill.

JOE: Let me hold it. (KIT *hands* JOE *the gun. The* LADY *and* MAN *are scared to death.* LADY *rises.*)

KIT CARSON: Careful, now, son. Don't cock it. Many a man's lost an eye fooling with a loaded gun. Fellow I used to know named Danny Donovan lost a nose. Ruined his whole life (LADY *sits.*) Hold it firm. Squeeze the trigger. Don't snap it. Spoils your aim.

JOE: Thanks. Let's see if I can unload it. (*He begins to unload it.*)

KIT CARSON: Of course you can. (JOE *unloads the revolver, looks at it very closely, puts the cartridges back into the box and puts them away in his overcoat pocket.*)

JOE (*looking at gun*): I'm mighty grateful to you. Always wanted to see one of those things close up. Is it really a good one?

KIT CARSON: It's a beaut, son.

JOE (*aims the empty gun at a bottle on the bar*): Bang! (*Grinding of marble game.*)

WILLIE (*at the marble game*): Oh, boy! (*Loudly, triumphantly.*) There you are, Nick. Thought I couldn't do it, hey? *Now*, watch. (*The machine begins to make a special kind of noise. Lights go on and off. Some red, some green. A bell rings loudly six times.*) One. Two. Three. Four. Five. Six. (*An American flag jumps up. WILLIE comes to attention. Salutes.*) Oh, boy, what a beautiful country. (*A music-box version of the song* "America." *Singing.*) "My country, 'tis of thee, sweet land of liberty, of thee I sing." (*Everything quiets down. The flag goes back into the machine. WILLIE is thrilled, amazed, delighted. Everybody has watched the performance of the defeated machine from wherever he happened to be when the performance began. WILLIE, looking around at everybody, as if they had all been on the side of the machine.*) O.K. How's that? I knew I could do it. (*To NICK.*) Six nickels. (*NICK hands him six nickels. WILLIE goes over to JOE and KIT. Exuberantly, pointing a finger, gesturing wildly.*) Took me a little while, but I finally did it. It's scientific, really. With a little skill a man can make a modest living beating the marble games. Not that that's what I want to do. I just don't like the idea of anything getting the best of me. A machine or anything else. (*Doubling his fist.*) Myself, I'm the kind of guy who makes up his mind to do something, and then goes to work and does it. There's no other way a man can be a success at anything. (*Indicating the letter* "F" *on his sweater.*) See that letter? That don't stand for some little-bitty high school somewhere. That stands for *me*. Faroughli. Willie Faroughli. I'm an Assyrian. We've got a civilization six or seven centuries old, I think. Somewhere along in there. Ever hear of Osman? Harold Osman? He's an Assyrian, too. He's got an orchestra down in Fresno. (*He goes to the* LADY *and* MAN.) I've never seen you before in my life, but I can tell from the clothes you wear and the company you keep (*graciously indicating the* LADY) that you're a man who looks every problem straight in the eye, and then goes to work and *solves* it. (*He bangs his fist into his left palm violently.*) I'm that way myself. (*Three swift, ferocious bangs.*) Well. (*He smiles beautifully.*) It's been wonderful talking to a nicer type of people for a change. Well. I'll be seeing you. So long. (*He turns, takes two steps, returns to the table. Very politely and seriously.*) Good-by, lady. You've got a good man there. Take good care of him. (WILLIE *exits right, saluting* JOE *and the world.* NICK *goes into the kitchen, rear center.*)

KIT CARSON (*to* JOE): By God, for a while there I didn't think that young Assyrian was going to do it. That fellow's got something. (TOM *comes back right with the magazines and other stuff.*)

JOE: Get it all?

TOM: Yeah. I had a little trouble finding the jelly beans.

JOE: Let's take a look at them.

TOM: These are the jelly beans. (JOE *puts his hand into the cellophane bag and takes out a handful of the jelly beans, looks at them, smiles and tosses a couple into his mouth.*)

JOE: Same as ever. Have some. (*He offers the bag to* KIT.)

KIT CARSON (*flirting*): Thanks! I remember the first time I ever ate jelly beans. I was six, or at the most seven. Must have been in (*slowly*) 1877. Seven or eight. Baltimore.

JOE: Have some, Tom.

TOM (*takes some*): Thanks, Joe.

JOE: Let's have some of that chewing gum. (*He dumps all the packages of gum out of the bag onto the table.*)

KIT CARSON (*flirting*): Me and a boy named Clark. Quinton Clark. Became a Senator.

JOE: Yeah. Tutti-frutti, all right. (*He opens a package and folds all five pieces into his mouth.*) Always wanted to see how many I could chew at one time. Tell you what, Tom. I'll bet I can chew more at one time than you can.

Tom (*delighted*): All right. (*They both begin to fold gum into their mouths.*)

Kit Carson: I'll referee. Now, one at a time. How many you got?

Joe: Six.

Kit Carson: All right. Let Tom catch up with you.

Joe (*while* Tom's *catching up*): Did you give a dollar to a news-kid?

Tom: Yeah, sure.

Joe: What'd he say?

Tom: Thanks.

Joe: What sort of a kid was he?

Tom: Little, dark kid. I guess he's Italian.

Joe: Did he seem pleased?

Tom: Yeah.

Joe: That's good. Did you give a dollar to an old man?

Tom: Yeah.

Joe: Was he pleased?

Tom: Yeah.

Joe: Good. How many you got in your mouth?

Tom: Six.

Joe: All right. I got six, too. (*Folds one more in his mouth.* Tom *folds one too.*)

Kit Carson: Seven. Seven each. (*They each fold one more into their mouths, very solemnly, chewing them into the main hunk of gum.*) Eight. Nine. Ten.

Joe (*delighted*): Always wanted to do this. (*He picks up one of the magazines.*) Let's see what's going on in the world. (*He turns the pages and keeps folding gum into his mouth and chewing.*)

Kit Carson: Eleven. Twelve. (Kit *continues to count while* Joe *and* Tom *continue the contest. In spite of what they are doing, each is very serious.*)

Tom: Joe, what'd you want to move Kitty into the St. Francis Hotel for?

Joe: She's a better woman than any of them tramp society dames that hang around that lobby.

TOM: Yeah, but do you think she'll feel at home up there?

JOE: Maybe not at first, but after a couple of days she'll be all right. A nice big room. A bed for sleeping in. Good clothes. Good food. She'll be all right, Tom.

TOM: I hope so. Don't you think she'll get lonely up there with nobody to talk to?

JOE (*looking at* TOM *sharply, almost with admiration, pleased but severe*): There's nobody *anywhere* for *her* to talk to— except *you*.

TOM (*amazed and delighted*): *Me*, Joe?

JOE (*while* TOM *and* KIT CARSON *listen carefully,* KIT *with great appreciation*): Yes, you. By the grace of God, you're the other half of that girl. Not the angry woman that swaggers into this waterfront dive and shouts because the world has kicked her around. *Anybody* can have *her*. You belong to the little kid in Ohio who once dreamed of living. Not with her carcass, for *money*, so she can have food and clothes, and pay rent. With *all* of her. I put her in that hotel, so she can have a chance to gather herself together again. She can't do that in The New York Hotel. You saw what happens there. There's nobody anywhere for her to talk to, except you. They all make her talk like a whore. After a while, she'll *believe* them. Then she won't be able to remember. She'll get lonely. Sure. People can get lonely for *misery*, even. I want her to go on being lonely for *you*, so she can come together again the way she was meant to be from the beginning. Loneliness is good for people. Right now it's the only thing for Kitty. Any more licorice?

TOM (*dazed*): What? Licorice? (*Looking around busily.*) I guess we've chewed all the licorice in. We still got Clove, Peppermint, Doublemint, Beechnut, Teaberry, and Juicy Fruit.

JOE: Licorice used to be my favorite. Don't worry about her, Tom, she'll be all right. You really want to marry her, don't you?

TOM (*nodding*): Honest to God, Joe. (*Pathetically.*) Only, I haven't got any money.

JOE: Couldn't you be a prize fighter or something like that?

TOM: Naaaah. I couldn't hit a man if I wasn't sore at him. He'd have to do something that made me hate him.

JOE: You've got to figure out something to do that you won't mind doing very much.

TOM: I wish I could, Joe.

JOE (*thinking deeply, suddenly*): Tom, would you be embarrassed driving a truck?

TOM (*hit by a thunderbolt*): Joe, I never thought of that. I'd like that. Travel. Highways. Little towns. Coffee and hot cakes. Beautiful valleys and mountains and streams and trees and daybreak and sunset.

JOE: There *is* poetry in it, at that.

TOM: Joe, that's just the kind of work I *should* do. Just sit there and travel, and look, and smile, and bust out laughing. Could Kitty go with me, sometimes?

JOE: I don't know. Get me the phone book. Can you drive a truck?

TOM (*crossing to phone*): Joe, you know I can drive a truck, or any kind of thing with a motor and wheels. (TOM *takes* JOE *the phone book.* JOE *turns the pages.*)

JOE (*looking*): Here! Here it is. Tuxedo 7900. Here's a nickel. Get me that number. (TOM *goes to telephone, dials the number.*)

TOM: Hello.

JOE: Ask for Mr. Keith.

TOM: I'd like to talk to Mr. Keith. (*Pause.*) Mr. Keith.

JOE: Take that gum out of your mouth for a minute.

TOM (*removes the gum*): Mr. Keith. Yeah. That's right. Hello, Mr. Keith?

JOE: Tell him to hold the line.

TOM: Hold the line, please.

JOE: Give me a hand, Tom. (TOM *helps* JOE *to the telephone. At phone, wad of gum in fingers delicately.*) Keith? Joe. Yeah. Fine. Forget it. (*Pause.*) Have you got a place for a good driver? (*Pause.*) I don't think so. (*To* TOM.) You haven't got a driver's license, have you?

TOM (*worried*): No. But I can get one, Joe.

JOE (*at phone*): No, but he can get one easy enough. To hell with the union. He'll join later. All right, call him a vice-president and say he drives for relaxation. Sure. What do you mean? Tonight? I don't know why not. San Diego? All right, let him start driving without a license. What the hell's the difference? Yeah. Sure. Look him over. Yeah. I'll send him right over. Right. (*He hangs up.*) Thanks. (*To telephone.*)

TOM (*helping* JOE *back to his seat*): Am I going to get the job?

JOE (*sits*): He wants to take a look at you.

TOM (*breaks to right*): Do I look all right, Joe?

JOE (*looking at him carefully*): Hold up your head. Stick out your chest. How do you feel?

TOM (*does these things*): Fine.

JOE: You *look* fine, too. (KIT CARSON *has now reached twenty-seven sticks each.* JOE *takes his wad of gum out of his mouth and wraps* Liberty *magazine around it.*)

JOE: You win, Tom. Now, look. (*He bites off the tip of a very long panatela cigar, lights it, and hands one to* TOM, *and another to* KIT.) Have yourselves a pleasant smoke. Here. (*He hands two more to* TOM.) Give those slummers one each. (*He indicates the* LADY *and* MAN. TOM *goes over and without a word gives a cigar each to the* MAN *and the* LADY *then crosses to right of* JOE. *At first they are a little offended; then the* MAN *lights his cigar. The* LADY *looks at the cigar a moment, then bites off the tip the way* JOE *did.*)

MAN: What do you think you're doing?

LADY: Really, dear. I'd like to.

MAN: Oh, this is too much.

LADY: I'd *really*, really like to, dear. (*Turns to* KIT, *who rises and crosses to right of* LADY.)

MAN (*loudly*): The mother of five grown men, and she's still looking for *romance*. (*The* LADY *timidly scratches a match, puts the cigar in her mouth;* KIT *lights it for her, and she begins to smoke, feeling wonderful.*) No. I forbid it.

JOE (*shouting*): What's the matter with you? Why don't you leave her alone? What are you always pushing your women around for? (*Almost without a pause.*) Now, look, Tom. Here's ten bucks.

TOM: Ten bucks?

JOE: He may want you to get into a truck and begin driving to San Diego tonight.

TOM: Joe, I got to tell Kitty.

JOE: I'll tell her.

TOM: Joe, take care of her.

JOE: She'll be all right. Stop worrying about her. She's at the St. Francis Hotel. Now, look. Take a cab to Townsend and Fourth. You'll see the big sign. Keith Motor Transport Company. He'll be waiting for you.

TOM: O.K., Joe. (*Trying hard.*) Thanks, Joe.

JOE: Don't be silly. Get going. (TOM *goes out right.* LADY *starts puffing on cigar. As* TOM *goes,* WESLEY *and* HARRY *come in together, right, and cross to piano.*)

NICK (*enters from rear center and goes behind bar*): Where the hell have you been? We've got to have some entertainment around here. Can't you see them fine people from uptown? (*He points at the* LADY *and* MAN.)

WESLEY: You said to come back at ten for the second show.

NICK: Did I say that?

WESLEY: Yes, sir, Mr. Nick, that's exactly what you said.

HARRY: Was the first show all right?

NICK: That wasn't a show. There was no one here to see it. How can it be a show when no one sees it? People are afraid to come down to the waterfront.

HARRY: Yeah. We were just down to Pier Twenty-seven. One of the longshoremen and a cop had a fight and the cop hit him over the head with a blackjack. We saw it happen, didn't we?

WESLEY: Yes, sir, we was standing there looking when it happened.

NICK (*crossing from behind bar to center*): Anything else happen?

WESLEY: They was all talking.

HARRY: A man in a big car came up and said there was going to be a meeting right away and they hoped to satisfy everybody and stop the strike.

WESLEY: Right away. *Tonight.*

NICK: Well, it's about time. Them poor cops are liable to get nervous and—shoot somebody. (*To* HARRY.) Come back here. I want you to tend bar for a while. I'm going to take a walk over to the pier.

HARRY: Yes, sir. (*Crossing to back of bar.*)

NICK (*to the* LADY *and* MAN): You society people made up your minds yet?

LADY: Have you champagne?

NICK (*indicating* JOE): What do you think he's pouring out of that bottle, water or something?

LADY: Have you a chill bottle?

NICK: I've got a dozen of them chilled. He's been drinking champagne here all day and all night for a month now.

LADY: May we have a bottle?

NICK: It's six dollars.

LADY: I think we can manage.

MAN: I don't know. I *know* I don't know. (NICK *takes off his coat and helps* HARRY *into it.* HARRY *takes a bottle of champagne and two glasses to the* LADY *and the* MAN, *collects six dollars and goes back behind the bar.* NICK *gets his coat and hat.*)

NICK (*to* WESLEY): Rattle the keys a little, son. Rattle the keys.

WESLEY: Yes, sir, Mr. Nick. (*Starts piano.* NICK *is on his way out right. The* ARAB *enters and goes to his chair.*)

NICK: Hiya, *Mahmed.*

ARAB: No foundation.

NICK: All the way down the line. (*He goes out.* WESLEY *is at the piano, playing quietly. The* ARAB *swallows a glass of beer, takes out his harmonica, and begins to play.* WESLEY *fits his playing to the* ARAB's. KITTY DUVAL, *strangely beautiful, in new clothes, comes in right. She walks shyly, as if she were embarrassed by the fine clothes, as if she had no right to wear them. The* LADY *and* MAN *are very impressed.* HARRY *looks at her with amazement.* JOE *is reading* Time *magazine.* KITTY *goes to his table.* JOE *looks up from the magazine, without the least amazement.*)

JOE: Hello, Kitty.

KITTY: Hello, Joe.

JOE: It's nice seeing you again.

KITTY: I came in a cab.

JOE: You been crying again? (KITTY *can't answer. To* HARRY.) Bring a glass. (HARRY *comes over with a glass and returns to bar.* JOE *pours* KITTY *a drink.*)

KITTY: I've got to talk to you.

JOE: Have a drink.

KITTY: I've never been in burlesque. We were just poor.

JOE: Sit down, Kitty.

KITTY (*sits down left of center table*): I tried other things.

JOE: Here's to you, Katerina Koranovsky. Here's to you. And Tom.

KITTY (*sorrowfully*): Where *is* Tom?

JOE: He's getting a job tonight driving a truck. He'll be back in a couple of days.

KITTY (*sadly*): I told him I'd marry him.

JOE: He wanted to see you and say good-by.

KITTY: He's too good for me. He's like a little boy. (*Wearily.*) I'm— Too many things have happened to me.

JOE: Kitty Duval, you're one of the few truly innocent people I have ever known. He'll be back in a couple of days. Go back to the hotel and wait for him.

KITTY: That's what I mean. I can't stand being alone. I'm no good. I tried very hard. I don't know what it is. I miss— (*She gestures.*)

JOE (*gently*): Do you really want to come back here, Kitty?

KITTY: I don't know. I'm not sure. Everything *smells* different. I don't know how to feel, or what to think. (*Gesturing pathetically.*) I know I don't belong there. It's what I've wanted all my life, but it's too *late*. I try to be happy about it, but all I can do is remember everything and cry.

JOE: I don't know what to tell you, Kitty. I didn't mean to hurt you.

KITTY: You haven't hurt me. You're the only person who's ever been good to me. I've never known anybody like you. I'm not sure about love any more, but I know I love you, and I know I love Tom.

JOE: I love you too, Kitty Duval.

KITTY: He'll want babies. I know he will. I know *I* will, too. Of course I will. I can't— (*She shakes her head.*)

JOE: Tom's a baby himself. You'll be very happy together. He wants you to ride with him in the truck. Tom's good for you. You're good for Tom.

KITTY: Do you want me to go back and wait for him?

JOE: I can't *tell* you what to do. I think it would be a good idea, though.

KITTY: I wish I could tell you how it makes me feel to be alone. It's almost worse.

JOE: It might take a whole week, Kitty. (*He looks at her sharply, at the arrival of an idea.*) Didn't you speak of reading a book? A book of poems?

KITTY: I didn't know what I was saying.

JOE (*trying to get up*): Of course you knew. I think you'll like poetry. Wait here a minute, Kitty. I'll go see if I can find some books.

KITTY: All right, Joe. (*He walks out of the place right, trying very hard not to wobble.* KITTY *looks at* LADY *and they exchange smiles. Foghorn. Music. The* NEWSBOY *comes in right. Looks for* JOE.)

NEWSBOY: Paper?

MAN: No.

NEWSBOY (*goes to the* ARAB): Paper, Mister?

ARAB: No foundation.

NEWSBOY: What?

ARAB (*very angry*): No foundation.

NEWSBOY (*starts out, turns, looks at the* ARAB, *shakes head*):

No foundation? How do you figure? (*Goes out right as* BLICK *and* Two COPS *enter. The* COPS *go to bar.*)

NEWSBOY (*to* BLICK): Paper, Mister? (BLICK *pushes him aside. The* NEWSBOY *goes out right.*)

BLICK: Where's Nick?

HARRY: He went for a walk.

BLICK: Who are you?

HARRY: Harry.

BLICK (*to the* ARAB *who is playing harmonica*): Hey, you. Shut up. (*The* ARAB *stops playing and exits right.* WESLEY *looks around, stops playing;* BLICK *studies* KITTY, *crosses to right of her*): What's your name, sister?

KITTY (*looking at him*): Kitty Duval. What's it to you? (KITTY's *voice is now like it was at the beginning of the play: tough, independent, bitter and hard.*)

BLICK (*angry*): Don't give me any of your gutter lip. Just answer my questions.

KITTY: You go to hell, you.

BLICK (*coming over, enraged*): Where do you live?

KITTY: The New York Hotel. Room Twenty-one.

BLICK: Where do you work?

KITTY: I'm not working just now. I'm looking for work. (*Lights cigarette.*)

BLICK: What kind of work? (KITTY *can't answer.*) What kind of work? (KITTY *can't answer. Furiously.*) WHAT KIND OF WORK?

KIT CARSON (*comes over to right of center table*): You can't talk to a lady that way in *my* presence. (BLICK *turns and stares at* KIT. *The* COPS *begin to move from the bar to back of* KIT CARSON.)

BLICK (*to the* COPS): It's all right, boys. I'll take care of this. (*To* KIT.) *What'd you say?*

KIT CARSON: You got no right to hurt people. Who are *you?* (BLICK, *without a word, takes* KIT *out right to the street. Sounds of a blow and a groan.* BLICK *returns with his face flushed.*)

BLICK (*to the* COPS): O.K., boys. You can go now. Take care

of him. Put him on his feet and tell him to behave himself
from now on. (*To* KITTY *again*.) Now answer my question.
What kind of work?

KITTY (*quietly*): I'm a whore, you son of a bitch. You know
what kind of work I do. And I know what kind you do.

MAN (*rises; shocked and really hurt*): Excuse me, officer, but
it seems to me that your attitude—

BLICK: Shut up.

MAN (*quietly*): —is making the poor child say things that are
not true.

BLICK: Shut up, I said.

LADY: Well. (*To the* MAN.) Are you going to stand for such
insolence?

BLICK (*crosses to right of* LADY; *to* MAN, *who is standing*):
Are you?

MAN: I'll get a divorce. I'll start life all over again. Come on.
Get the hell out of here! (*The* MAN *hurries his* LADY *out of
the place,* BLICK *watching them go. To left of* KITTY.)

BLICK (*to* KITTY): Now. Let's begin again, and see that you
tell the truth. What's your name?

KITTY: Kitty Duval.

BLICK: Where do you live?

KITTY: Until this evening I lived at The New York Hotel.
Room Twenty-one. This evening I moved to the St. Francis
Hotel.

BLICK: Oh. To the St. Francis Hotel. Nice place. Where do
you work?

KITTY: I'm looking for work.

BLICK: What kind of work do you do?

KITTY: I'm an actress.

BLICK: I see. What movies have I seen you in?

KITTY: I've worked in burlesque.

BLICK: You're a liar.

KITTY (*pathetically, as at the beginning of the play*): It's the
truth.

BLICK: What are you doing here?

KITTY: I came to see if I could get a job here.

BLICK: Doing what?

KITTY: Singing—and—dancing.

BLICK: You can't sing or dance. What are you lying for?

KITTY: I can. I sang and danced in burlesque all over the country.

BLICK: You're a liar.

KITTY: I said lines, too.

BLICK: So you danced in burlesque?

KITTY: Yes.

BLICK: All right. Let's see what you did.

KITTY: I can't. There's no music, and I haven't got the right clothes.

BLICK: There's music. (*To* WESLEY.) Put a nickel in that phonograph. Come on. Put a nickel in that phonograph. (WESLEY *does so. To* KITTY.) All right. Get up on that stage and do a hot little burlesque number. Get going, now. Let's see you dance the way you did in burlesque, all over the country. (KITTY *goes up on stage sings a few lines and then tries to do a burlesque dance. It is beautiful in a tragic way, tragic and incredible.*) All right, start taking them off! (KITTY *removes her hat and starts to remove her jacket.* JOE *enters right, crosses to center.*)

JOE (*hurrying to* KITTY): Get down from there. (*He takes* KITTY *into his arms. She is crying. To* BLICK.) What the hell do you think you're doing!

WESLEY: It's that man, Blick. *He* made her take off her clothes. He beat up the old man, too. (BLICK *pushes* WESLEY *off stage center and begins beating him.*)

TOM (*enters right*): What's the matter, Joe? What's happened?

JOE: Is the truck out there?

TOM: Yeah, but what's happened? Kitty's crying again!

JOE: You driving to San Diego?

TOM: Yeah, Joe. But what's he doing to that poor colored boy?

JoE: Get going. Here's some money. Everything's O.K. (*To* KITTY.) Dress in the truck. Take these books.

WESLEY'S VOICE: You can't hurt me. You'll get yours. You wait and see.

TOM: Joe, he's hurting that boy. I'll kill him!

JoE: Get out of here! Get married in San Diego. I'll see you when you get back. (TOM *and* KITTY *exit right.* NICK *enters and stands at the lower end of bar.* JoE *takes the revolver out of his pocket. Looks at it.*) I've always wanted to kill somebody, but I never knew who it should be. (*He cocks the revolver, stands real straight, holds it in front of him firmly and walks to the center door.* NICK *exits right. He stands a moment watching* BLICK, *aims very carefully, and pulls trigger. There is no shot. He cocks the pistol again and again presses the trigger. Again there is no shot.* NICK *and* McCARTHY *come in right.* JoE *is cocking the pistol again.* NICK *runs over and grabs the gun, and takes* JoE *aside.*)

NICK: What the hell do you think you're doing?

JoE (*casually, as if it were nothing*): That dumb Tom. Buys a six-shooter that won't even shoot once. (NICK *hides the gun in a hurry.* BLICK *comes in center, panting for breath.*)

NICK (*looks at* BLICK, *infuriated*): Blick! I told you to stay out of here! Now get out of here. (*Starts to push* BLICK *off right.*) If you come back again, I'm going to take you in that room where you've been beating up that colored boy, and I'm going to murder you—slowly—with my hands. Beat it! (*He pushes* BLICK *out right. To* HARRY.) Go take care of the colored boy. (HARRY *runs out center.* WILLIE *returns and doesn't sense that anything is changed.* WILLIE *puts another nickel into the machine, but he does so very violently. The consequence of this violence is that the flag comes up again.* WILLIE, *amazed, stands at attention and salutes. The flag goes down. He shakes his head.*)

WILLIE (*thoughtfully*): As far as I'm concerned, this is the *only* country in the world. If you ask me, *nuts* to Europe! (*He is about to push the slide in again when the flag comes up again. Furiously, to* NICK, *while he salutes and stands at attention, pleadingly.*) Hey, Nick. This machine is out of order.

NICK (*somberly*): Give it a whack on the side. (WILLIE *does so. A hell of a whack. The result is the flag comes up and down, and* WILLIE *keeps saluting.*)

WILLIE (*saluting*): Hey, Nick. Something's wrong. (*The machine quiets down abruptly.* WILLIE *very stealthily slides a new nickel in, and starts a new game. From a distance three shots are heard, each carefully timed.* NICK *runs out right followed by* McCARTHY. *The* NEWSBOY *enters right, crosses to* JOE's *table, senses something is wrong.*)

NEWSBOY (*softly*): Paper, Mister? (JOE *takes them all, hands him money, shoves them off the table to floor without glancing at them.* ARAB *enters right, picks up paper, throws it down, crosses to right, sits down.* DRUNK *enters right, goes to bar.* NEWSBOY *backs to center, wishes he could cheer* JOE *up. Notices phonograph, goes to it and puts coin in it hoping it will make* JOE *happier.* NEWSBOY *sits down, left, he watches* JOE. *Music begins—"The Missouri Waltz.")*

NICK (*enters, crosses to* JOE): Joe, Blick's dead! Somebody just shot him, and none of the cops are trying to find out who. (JOE *looks up slowly. Shouting.*) Joe.

JOE (*looking up*): What?

NICK: Blick's dead.

JOE: Blick? Dead? Good! That Goddamn gun wouldn't go off. I *told* Tom to get a good one.

NICK (*picking up gun and looking at it*): Joe, you wanted to kill that guy! (HARRY *returns.*) I'm going to buy you a bottle of champagne. (NICK *goes to bar.* JOE *rises, takes hat from rack, puts coat on. The* NEWSBOY *jumps up, helps* JOE *with coat.*) What's the matter, Joe?

JOE: Nothing. Nothing.

NICK: How about the champagne?

JOE: Thanks. (*Crosses to center.*)

NICK: It's not eleven yet. Where you going, Joe?

JOE: I don't know. Nowhere.

NICK: Will I see you tomorrow?

Joe: I don't know. I don't think so. (KIT CARSON *enters right,* *walks to* Joe.)

Joe: Somebody just shot a man. How are you feeling?

KIT: Never felt better in my life. (*Quietly.*) I shot a man once. In San Francisco. Shot him two times. In 1939, I think it was. In October. Fellow named Blick or Glick or something like that. Couldn't stand the way he talked to ladies. Went up to my room and got my old pearl-handled revolver and waited for him on Pacific Street. Saw him walking, and let him have it, two times. Had to throw the beautiful revolver into the Bay. (HARRY, NICK, *the* ARAB *and the* DRUNK *close in around him.* Joe *walks slowly to the stairs leading to the street, turns and waves. Exits.*)

Production Notes

This anthology is designed for your reading pleasure. In most instances a performance fee is required from any group desiring to produce a play. Usually the organization that handles such performance rights also publishes individual production copies of the plays. Any group interested in additional information concerning performance fees or production copies of the plays in this anthology should apply to the following companies:

Idiot's Delight

Harold Freedman
c/o Brandt & Brandt
Dramatic Department
101 Park Avenue
New York 17, N.Y.

Street Scene

Samuel French, Inc.
25 West 45th Street
New York 36, N.Y.

The Time of Your Life

PROFESSIONAL RIGHTS:
Harold Matson Company
30 Rockefeller Plaza
New York 20, N.Y.

AMATEUR RIGHTS:
Samuel French, Inc.
25 West 45th Street
New York 36, N.Y.